BERT HAD

A SON OF BIRMINGHAM

CW00548776

A TRIBUTE
COMPILED BY GEOFF ROE

Edited by Nigel Hancock

The Pre-War Austin Seven Club Ltd.

1962 2012

FIFTY YEARS OF PROGRESS

www.pwa7c.co.uk

To Absent Friends
R.I.P.

'H.L.Hadley (Bert to you) is one of the nicest chaps in British Motor Racing. He is 29 years of age, short, on the broad side and usually beaming with smiles. However he takes Motor Racing very seriously indeed, studies his rivals, watches their style, scrutinizes cornering methods and does everything in his power to get the utmost from his diminutive racing car without overstraining the tiny power unit. Even in the excitement of a duel, Hadley refuses to over-rev in the gears.

Hadley was apprenticed to the Austin Works after leaving school in Birmingham and takes an active part in preparing the car he races. He also takes part in as many reliability trials, speed trials and hill climbs as he can and would dearly love to race on the continent. He is a firm believer in the potency of his starting numbers, preferring "one" or "six". One of his greatest feats was running second to Mays at Shelsley Walsh and there are those who think that, one day, he will crack that hill climb record with the Austin.........'

'The Motor' August 29th 1939.

in association with

The Michael Sedgwick Trust

This work is published with the financial assistance of the Michael Sedgwick Memorial Trust. This Trust was founded in memory of the famous motoring researcher and author Michael Sedgwick, 1926-1983. The Trust is a registered charity (charity no. 290841) set up to encourage the publication of new motoring research and the recording of motoring history. Full details and contact address can be found on the Trust's web site www.michaelsedgwicktrust.co.uk. The Trust welcomes suggestions for new projects and financial donations to help with future work. Support by the Michael Sedgwick Memorial Trust does not infer any involvement in the editorial process which remains the sole responsibility of the author, editor and publisher.

2013 © G.C.Roe

All rights reserved. No part of this publication may be reproduced, stored in a retrieval system, or transmitted in any form or by any means, electronic, mechanical, photocopying or otherwise, without the prior permission of the publisher and copyright holder.

Geoff Roe has asserted the moral right to be identified as the author of this work.

ISBN: 978-0-9572426-2-3
Published by the Pre-War Austin Seven Club Ltd, in conjunction with Bali Books.
Font Tahoma 11 with lengthy quotations in Tahoma 10.
Printed by Adlard Print & Reprographics Ltd. Ruddington, Nottingham NG11 6HH.

Contents

Acknowledgements

Whilst largely a personal tribute to HLH, this could not have been achieved without the help of many friends, individuals and organisations, to whom my grateful thanks:-

Phil Baildon, the late Bill Boddy O.B.E., Brian and Douglas Butler, Anders Clausager, Ken Cooke, Ian Dussek, Hazel Gore, Chris Gould, Phil Groves, David Harvey, Peter Hornby, Julian Hunt, Tony Hutchings, Pauline Jamieson, Vince Leek, Hilary Lewis, Roger McDonald, Terry McGrath, Peter Mitchell O.B.E., the late David Murray Jamieson, Edmund Nankivell, Peter and May Penny, Ira Pritchard, Graham Robson, Michael Shearer, Mike Spencer, Brian Taylor, Michael E Ware, Barrie Williams.

Ashbourne Library, Brooklands Museum, Brooklands Society, Bugatti Trust, Midland Automobile Club, Upton-Upon-Severn Civic Society, Vintage Sports Car Club Library.

The various Editors of 'The Light Car', 'Brooklands Society Gazette', 'M.A.C. Gazette', 'Austin Seven Clubs' Association Magazine' and 'Sports Newsletter', Graham Bosworth G.M.A., Keith Woodcock G.M.A., G.Av.A.

Especial thanks to Neville Barr (Ashbourne/Fauld research), Keith Bostock, Chris Garner, the late Clive Hadley, Jean Hadley (access to family archives), Andy Lowe (Birmingham research), Brenda Roe (Hadley ancestry and other research) and Dee Roe (typing and patience!).

The late Dave Wilcox did the majority of the scanning of old images and offered much valuable advice on layout.

I am most grateful to Nigel Hancock for stepping into the breach at short notice and helping with the scanning, proofing and editing processes.

My apologies for any omissions to the above.

Recommended Reading

'Austin Racing History'	Roland C. Harrison
'Austin Seven Competition History 1922-1939'	Beatrice Canning Brown
'City to the Lickeys'	David Harvey
'Making cars at Longbridge'	Gillian Bardsley/Colin Corke
'Montlhéry'	William Boddy
'Peakland Air Crashes – The South'	Pat Cunningham
'The Austin Seven – The Motor for the Millions 1922 – 1939'	R. J. Wyatt
'The Best of Le Mans' (DVD)	Heritage Motoring Films
'The Man who Supercharged Bond'	Paul Kenny

Foreword

On the creation of British Leyland in 1968 and as something of an afterthought, an effort was made to bring all archive material and assorted vehicles inherited from companies absorbed into the conglomerate into some sort of order for public display. The late Tom Wheatcroft offered space in his then recently opened Grand Prix Collection at Donington Park and 'Leyland Historic Vehicles' (LHV) was established. Stored items were kept at Castle Road, Studley, Warwickshire and elsewhere.

Whilst the search for a permanent home for the collection continued, this was to take a number of years before the former V-Bomber base at Gaydon was eventually chosen and what became the British Motor Industry Heritage Trust would be established in a purpose-built museum complex.

In 1980, LHV moved en bloc to another site, namely Syon Park in Brentford, Middlesex. Re-branded 'The Heritage Collection', the exhibits were housed in various buildings amongst the ornamental gardens of Syon House. The official opening was to be performed by the founder of Jaguar Cars, Sir William Lyons. As the Collection did not have a car suitable as a centrepiece, the late Barrie Foster of Nottingham was asked to provide his 1938 SS Jaguar 100 sports car for the occasion. I had rebuilt 'SY6684' several years before and Barrie kindly invited me to accompany him for the opening ceremony. Many motoring celebrities were present and it was to prove an interesting day out!

Seeing someone I actually knew, I passed the time of day with Ken Cooke, a fellow Austin Seven enthusiast. Standing alongside Ken was a stocky silver haired gentleman of some seventy summers. *'Have you met Bert Hadley?'* Up to that moment I'd merely read of his exploits behind the wheel of Twin-cam single seaters, Grasshoppers and of course the post war drives at Le Mans. From his firm handshake, twinkling eyes and 'Brummie' accent I knew I was in the presence of one of my sporting heroes. As it turned out, that meeting was to have an effect on my life for years to come and subsequently I paid several visits to the Hadley home in Kenilworth where Bert and his wife Rose made me very welcome. Rose was a kindly Welsh lady and later on I met their only son, Clive. In addition we met up with the Hadleys at various venues, often when there were Austin Sevens competing.

Sometime later Bert was to become a surrogate 'Uncle' to me, offering wise counselling when I needed someone older to talk to. During his Civil Service career he'd interviewed hundreds, maybe thousands, of people and immediately spotted 'something' was amiss. For that simple act of kindness I remain forever grateful.

This then is my modest tribute to Herbert Lewis Hadley – a remarkable Englishman and a true Son of Birmingham. I hope you enjoy it.

Geoff Roe. Cropwell Bishop. 2013.

Introduction

H. L. (Bert) Hadley

This is the story of a Birmingham boy from a humble background who by a combination of ambition, application, self belief and sheer bloody mindedness, rose to the pinnacle of British Motor Sport whilst still an employee of the Austin Motor Company at Longbridge. Without doubt he would have reached even greater heights were it not for the outbreak of World War Two. He did resume racing at International level after the conflict but, by this time, Bert was well into his second career with the Ministry of Labour.

We shall see how his forefathers made the journey from rural Worcestershire to Victorian Birmingham 'The Workshop of the World', his parents' connections with Cadburys and the Trade Union Movement and not least his 'knack' of being in the right place at the right time and, conversely, the wrong place at the right time on more than one occasion!

Also included are fascinating details of those around him at various stages of his career not least of Tom Murray Jamieson, the young and gifted designer drafted in by Sir Herbert Austin to develop an MG-beating race car in the 1930s and who was to have such a lasting influence on the young Hadley's progress.

Particularly after his retirement in 1975, Bert Hadley wrote with great clarity about his apprenticeship days and subsequent racing experiences and his reminiscences form a major part of this tribute. He provided articles which appeared in The Magazine of The Austin Seven Clubs' Association, Light Car, Brooklands Gazette, The Automobile and elsewhere. He was also a prolific letter writer. Such was the quality of his writings that only light editing has been necessary, mainly to avoid repetition of certain facts. All images are from the Hadley Archives unless otherwise stated.

(David Harvey)

This scene is virtually identical to that which would have been familiar to young Bert during his formative years. Pershore Road is busy as usual with the No.36 tram taking on more passengers bound for the city centre. The undeveloped land behind the lofty advertising hoarding could have been the site of the Hadley 'lock-up'.

- 1 -

'HADLEY'

According to books on surnames, Hadley is likely to have originated from a settlement of that title. There are but two in England, one is in The Wrekin, west of Telford. However, there is another more probable option. Just west of Droitwich on today's A449 lies the present village of Hadley. Passing through the village is one way to Shelsley Walsh, some 10 miles distant and the venue of the UK's oldest speed hill climb, opened in 1905. We shall hear more of Shelsley in due course...

It is pretty certain however, that 'our' Hadleys did indeed have their roots in rural Worcestershire, with the early reference to a Charles Hadley, born in 1797 at Hartlebury, some 6 miles north of Hadley village. Although the Industrial Revolution was changing our whole way of life, most of the population still scratched a living of some sort from the land, usually working for the local 'Squire' or other major estate. Charles Hadley was no exception and was to spend his whole working life as an agricultural labourer.

By 1841 Charles and his wife Caroline had moved to nearby Charlton at Pooling Farm. Their eldest son Thomas was now 10 years old and there were three younger siblings. Ten years on and two more children, Joseph and Mary, arrived and Thomas himself was now a farm labourer. Charles moved back to Hartlebury at Inn Lane and at the age of 55 was now employed as a 'farm waggoner'. The 1861 Census also informs us that Thomas moved to the village of North Piddle, about 10 miles east of Worcester and was married to Sarah, a dress maker. However, they were soon on the move to the next village, Flyford Flavell. Sadly, Sarah did not enjoy the best of health and died during childbirth around 1867.

Perhaps as a result of this, wishing to start a new life and maybe attracted by the better wages on offer for factory work, Thomas was drawn to the expanding Township of Birmingham, just north of the county border. As old as the Staffordshire iron mines upon which the foundations of its later prosperity were laid, Birmingham has a long history. By the 16th Century, it was regarded as a *'good market town'* with a quarter mile single Main Street, inhabited by *'Smiths making knives and all manner of cutting tools. Also many lorimers that make bitts* [horse bits & spurs] *and a great many nailors* [nail makers]'. So wrote the historian John Leland. During the reign of Charles II, political acts drove wealthy industrial nonconformists into the town which was until then of little importance. As the Industrial Revolution really got going in the late 18th century, Birmingham was well on its way to becoming the 'City of 1000 Trades' particularly under the influence of the likes of Matthew Boulton.

Thomas Hadley eventually found lodgings at 19 Navigation Street, the home of John Lewis, a shoemaker and his family. This was adjacent to New Street Railway Station, opened in 1854 as a joint venture by The London & North Western and The Midland Railway companies. It just happened that the Lewis' had a daughter and so Thomas and Jane Lewis, some eleven years younger at 29, married on 29th September 1870 at Christ Church, Birmingham. The name Lewis will be celebrated in future generations.

Jane Hadley née Lewis.
'A handsome lady'.

After being surrounded by all the smoke and grime of 19th century industry, Thomas decided to take his new bride back to his native Worcestershire where the air was cleaner and employment available at Church Farm, Flyford Flavell. Despite the sad memories generated by the loss of Sarah and their unborn child, his new wife Jane produced the family he'd always longed for, Louisa (1872) and Edith (1874). Eventually, it was time for the Hadleys to move on. This entailed a short journey to the small village of Hanley Castle, just north of the historic town of Upton-Upon-Severn. The local land owners were the Lechmeres whose main residence was Rhydd Court. Sir Edmund Lechmere was in process of modernising the estate and it would appear to have been a good move for the Hadleys, Thomas being appointed as Head Woodsman, responsible for management and coppicing of all the estates trees and timber. With the job went a tied cottage. The adjacent manor house was known as 'The Cliffy' and it still stands today, being used as a special needs school. It was here that Jane gave birth on 8th April 1876 to Herbert Charles Hadley (HCH).

The 1870s was a time of mixed fortunes for English farming with crop prices at a record low and with increasing mechanisation coming, there was less need for armies of manual labour. These changes also affected many of the traditional rural crafts, so the drift to the industrial manufacturing centres continued at pace. It even became cheaper to import complete cartwheels from the United States, than have them produced locally.

By 1880 the Hadleys had moved again, Thomas finding another employer – Charles Pelham Lane, J.P. of Moundsley Hall, Kings Norton. Two more sons were added to the family, Lewis (1880) and Edward Charles (1883). The following decade was to be a period of stability for the Hadleys, but sadly ending in the death of Jane.

The 1891 Census return records Thomas living at Moundsley Lodge. He is now a widower and has a live-in housekeeper, Sarah Moles and her daughter. The three sons, Herbert, Lewis and Edward are also present. At 14 years old, Herbert was already earning his keep, being described as 'an engine driver at the Sawmill'. This would have been steam driven, a responsible job for one so young. Moundsley Hall was demolished in the 1950s but the Lodge survives as a Grade 2 listed building. At 59, Thomas was probably a senior employee of the estate staff, hence his residency at the Lodge.

(© Barry Pearson 2004)
Moundsley Hall Lodge (Grade 2 listed). Home of Thomas Hadley and his family including Herbert Charles Hadley during the 1880s.

H. L. Hadley ('Bert') always maintained that his father Herbert had been a toolmaker by trade. It is possible Herbert may have been apprenticed during this decade, but no evidence has come to light so far. However we do know that HCH had worked his way up to become manager of a small engineering firm, but the constant pressure put upon him had a detrimental effect on his health. Eventually he took on a lighter job at Bournville where he settled in and was able to put versatile engineering skills to good use.

In 1901 he is recorded as living at 23 Redland Road, Cotteridge, Kings Norton and working as an 'engine driver in factory'. He is lodging with George Brazewell, his wife Louisa and their three children. Louisa is in fact Herbert's eldest sister. He appears to have started his term with Cadbury Brothers around this time, finally retiring from the company 33 years later.

John and George Cadbury originally started as provision merchants in the Bull Ring, one of the oldest parts of Birmingham. Heavily blitzed during the 1940s, it was redeveloped two decades later only to be razed once again in the nineties. It is now part of the retail heart of the city. By 1879 they had re-established the business on a new site at Bournville, just south of the town. Being Quakers, the family had a paternalistic attitude to their employees and encouraged them to make use of the many facilities they provided. These included opportunities for advancement in education, sporting and spiritual matters. All intended to promote 'Fulfilment in Life, Work and Pleasure'. By 1895 there was even a 'Model Village', a major housing development laid out with gardens and open spaces, which still stands today. A far cry from the dismal and unhealthy conditions then prevailing in the many back-to-back Victorian terraces.

By the start of the new century, Cadbury cocoa-based products were known throughout the British Empire, with the company having some 3000 full time employees – the majority being young women. The girls, always dressed in white, were known as 'Cadbury Angels'. The Bournville site became virtually self contained, even the packaging was designed and printed 'in-house'. Raw materials came in by canal but also by rail, in the company wagons, shunted by their own steam locomotives and the finished products went out in similar fashion.

Before today's air conditioned environment, a prolonged warm spell would prevent chocolate products from setting. Those workers affected by this would be sent home or encouraged to spend time making use of the Company's cultural facilities on 85% of full pay until the weather cooled down. Little wonder, it was thought a privilege to work at Bournville.

This then was the bustling environment that the 24 year old Herbert Hadley found himself. His ten years experience of stationary steam engines would be invaluable to the company as virtually the whole factory would be steam powered, though this would change in later years. No doubt, his accumulated engineering skills would be put to good use throughout the Bournville Works. With all these 'Angels' about the place, it was perhaps not surprising that the minority male staff, particularly unmarried ones, were given 'the eye' and in no time at all, young Hadley was courting Lydia Luckman. A diminutive, feisty young woman with a short temper and somewhat sharp of tongue, but in whom Herbert saw potential. At 29 Lydia might have been considered to be 'on the shelf'. Five years older than Hadley, Lydia had been at Cadburys since she left school. She was a daughter of Isaac and Sarah Ann Luckman, born in Bleak Lane, Kings Norton, now part of Birmingham. Her father was a journeyman gun barrel roller, a common trade in the locality, small arms manufacture being a staple industry in Birmingham. A journeyman was an artisan who had received a recognised apprenticeship, but had no regular employer and thus took work on a day-to-day basis. A precarious existence – making today's 'short contracts' look cosy by comparison!

Lydia Luckman as a young girl and Herbert Charles Hadley aged about 21.

Although they were quite poor, Mrs Luckman had musical ambitions and in 1894 had obtained a 'Miont' Walnut Cottage Pianoforte from Crane & Sons, Scotland Road, Liverpool. The price was twenty eight guineas (£29.40) with ten shillings (50p) payable on the first of each month at 120 Sherlock Street, Birmingham. The family were then living at 71 Kings Road, Kings Heath.

At the time, Cadbury policy was to employ only unmarried women and so on 11th December 1901, Miss Luckman left the Bournville Works after 15 years 'Faithful Service'.

Two weeks later, actually on Christmas Day, Herbert and Lydia were married at All Saints Church, Kings Heath. They settled in nearby Stirchley, at 38 Charlotte Road, renting a terrace house from 'The Ten Acres and Stirchley Co-operative Society' who had their main premises nearby.

(Andy Lowe 2008)
38 Charlotte Road, Stirchley B30. Birthplace of Herbert Lewis Hadley in 1910.

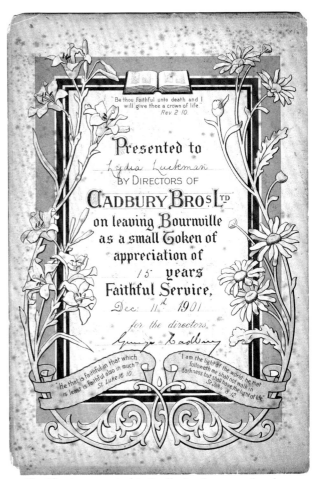

Certificate presented to Lydia Luckman on leaving Bournville. The certificate is signed by George Cadbury.

It was at Number 38, some nine years later, that their long awaited son was born on 18th April 1910. Named after his father, with his grandmother's maiden name as an addition, Herbert Lewis Hadley (HLH) arrived at the very end of the Edwardian era, a brief period of comparative peace for Great Britain after the end of the Boer War, though already there were the disturbing rumblings of German imperialism in Europe...

Herbert proudly displays his son on board his twin-steer tricycle
(dressed as for a Christening?).

Most people had to scrimp and save to make ends meet but new employment opportunities were emerging, for instance at the fledgling company started by Herbert Austin just five years previously at a former printing works in nearby Longbridge. Meanwhile Herbert Hadley, whilst still employed as an 'Engine Driver' at the Cocoa Works, had become interested in politics and involved with the Trade Union movement. With a new family to support, HCH took the opportunity to apply for the vacant position of local organiser for The Workers' Union, which he was successful in obtaining. As well as his full-time job at Cadburys, the position of Secretary for the Bournville & Stirchley Branch would be an addition to his workload but Herbert would receive a useful remuneration for his efforts.

'Brother' Hadley was to carry out these duties with some thoroughness for the next twenty-four years, bringing him into contact with many people, from management and the shop floor plus a few politicians thrown in for good measure. Though 'Bert' to the immediate family, he was always referred to as 'Herbert' in public and formal occasions. Soon after Bert junior came along and coinciding with HCH's new Union responsibilities, the family decided to move from Charlotte Road, possibly influenced by its close proximity to the Co-op dairy with its attendant early morning noise and clatter. They moved into a slightly roomier terrace house in nearby Twyning Road, still usefully located for all the local shops (and the Co-op) and the trams and later the buses that ran to all parts, via the Pershore Road. The Hadley family were to remain at number 22 for the best part of fifty years.

(Andy Lowe 2008)

22 Twyning Road, Stirchley, B30. Bert Hadley's home from 1912 until 1941.
Solidly built houses still giving good service. Original pattern bays either side.

Bert Hadley aged about two years.

(Andy Lowe 2008)

Pershore Road, Stirchley B30 looking north towards the city centre (normally very heavy traffic!).
Twyning Road is by the corner shop on the right hand side.

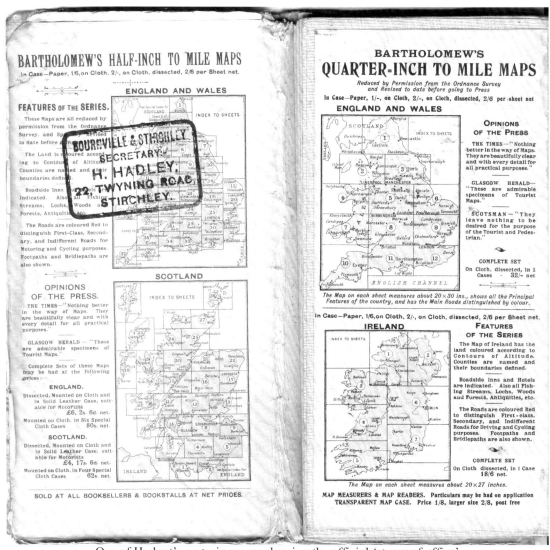

One of Herbert's motoring maps showing the official 'stamp of office'
as the local secretary of The Workers' Union.

GROWING UP

For the first two years after Herbert Lewis Hadley was born, the family continued to live in Charlotte Road, before re-locating across the Pershore Road to 22 Twyning Road. As a long-awaited only child, he had the full attention of his parents. His father gradually introduced the young Bert to things mechanical, even from an early age, the toddler no doubt holding the proverbial spanner whilst Dad fettled the family bicycles.

Developing into a stocky little lad, Bert not only had the looks of his mother, but also inherited her temperament. The youngster's wilful nature was kept in some sort of order by Lydia or, should the occasion arise, his father would take a more methodical approach in preparing his son for the big wide world. Herbert had long learnt whilst an enquiring mind was a good thing, a measure of diplomacy went a long way to achieving what you wanted, one of many reasons why he was so successful in the Union duties which he was now engaged in.

Bert took this on board and whilst his 'short fuse' lengthened over the years, it never really left him. Two other pearls of wisdom implanted by his father – *'never outstay your welcome'* and *'respect those in authority, but do not be afraid to put your point of view if you think something is wrong'*. Wise words which would serve the youngster well in later years.

Stirchley Infant School.   *(Andy Lowe 2008)*

Stirchley Junior School.   *(Andy Lowe 2008)*

Bert started his full time education in April 1915 at Stirchley Infant School. After four years he progressed to the adjacent Junior School finishing there at the end of 1923. Typical Board Schools, built in the Mid-Victorian period, they formed part of Stirchley's era of expansion, triggered by the opening of the Birmingham & West Suburban Railway in 1876. As we have seen, the establishment of Cadburys at nearby Bournville three years later also encouraged further growth as the inevitable speculators moved in. Stirchley became a self-contained township, an eclectic mix of businesses, with an emphasis on engineering and manufacturing, private and rented housing, served by a wide variety of shops.

Stirchley and its neighbours, originally in Worcestershire, were about to be absorbed into the ambitious City of Birmingham and though some aspects of the close-knit community of old no longer exist, Stirchley is still regarded locally as 'The Village'.

Being a naturally outgoing and adventurous lad, Bert and his pals found plenty of interesting places to explore, particularly during school holidays. There were a number of recreation grounds within walking distance and the Worcester & Birmingham Canal which runs alongside the Cadbury works held a particular fascination for inquisitive lads. Bert recalled larking about amongst the cocoa barges whilst these were tied up awaiting off-loading. This caused some consternation amongst the bargees who were forever chasing them off.

Herbert Charles Hadley
c.1930.

There is a link with Bert's childhood which continues to this day. Both primary schools at the junction of Charlotte Road and Pershore Road are still fully occupied with the education of today's youngsters. Meanwhile life at Bournville continued apace with Herbert busily engaged in all aspects of the engineering side of cocoa and chocolate production. With the outbreak of the Great War in the summer of 1914, Herbert was just within the upper age limit to be registered for possible enlistment. However as Cadburys were working flat out producing essential food products, Herbert would be in a reserved occupation and so found himself spared call-up. Apart from her housewifely duties, Lydia worked part-time locally and also acted as a message taker for Herbert who conducted his Union duties in his spare time from home. It was not until the 1920s that the Hadleys had a telephone installed, paid for by The Workers' Union. At a time when only a tiny portion of private houses were connected nationally, theirs would be one of the few telephones on Twyning Road for a number of years. The Workers' Union membership was mainly drawn from lower paid, unskilled people, yet paid out generous benefits despite modest union 'dues'. This was to prove the Union's undoing and by the 1930s, in financial difficulties, it merged with the powerful Transport & General Workers' Union (T&GWU). 'Brother' Hadley served as the Bournville and Stirchley Branch Secretary for 24 years and would receive national acclaim by the Union on the occasion of his retirement.

Before the Great War, what leisure time was available was often spent, when the weather was favourable, in bicycle rides out into the countryside. Cycling for pleasure was a popular leisure pursuit for lower and middle classes, much of it on an organised basis, with the formation of many local touring clubs.

A family outing with Lydia and Herbert Hadley on the right.
(Centre front) The young Bert looks the camera straight in the lens.

In the Hadleys' case, rural Worcestershire was on their doorstep, with the infant Bert initially ensconced in a basket on his father's twin-steer tricycle. A lovely set of Bartholomew's maps for 'Tourists & Cyclists' has survived in the Hadley archives covering North and South Wales, West and South Midlands and beyond. As Herbert progressed from pedal power to motorised transport, so the family ventured further afield, or rather 'adventured' as each trip would require careful preparation.

Herbert Hadley had joined the ranks of motorcycle combination owners, then the traditional low cost transport for the family man. An early 'chair outfit' was a hefty Birmingham-built 'Williamson', dating from 1919, powered by a 996cc Douglas flat-twin, rated at 8hp. Bert recalled:

'On the Birmingham to Alcester road was a notorious "stopper" known as Gorcott Hill [today it has been by-passed]. During the summer, especially at week-ends, the locals used to gather at the summit and watch the progress, or otherwise, of the various forms of motorised transport as they attempted to clear the top. Many would fail in a cloud of steam or burning clutch plates, but those who did succeed would get a big cheer from the crowd. The Williamson was a real slogger and took the ascent in its stride.'

An 8hp Williamson sidecar outfit similar to that owned by Herbert Charles Hadley.

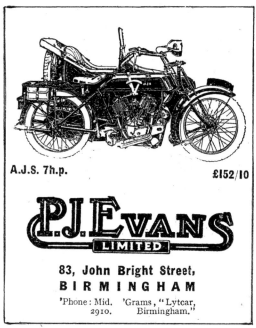

A.J.S. 7h.p. £152/10

P.J.Evans
LIMITED

83, John Bright Street,
BIRMINGHAM
'Phone : Mid.   'Grams, "Lytcar,
2910.   Birmingham."

The young Bert taught himself to ride the AJS 7hp outfit which replaced the Williamson.

A newer A.J.S. V-twin outfit (OK 3242) which took its place and rated at a mere 7hp was less 'torquey' and a great disappointment to Herbert and probably got him thinking about a transition to four wheels. However that would be for the future and meanwhile the A.J.S. took the family all over the South Birmingham area and beyond. About this time, having carefully watched his father, Bert decided to drive the A.J.S. himself. He would trundle round the back streets adjacent to Twyning Road 'disguised' in his father's 'Stormgard' all-weather motoring

"STORMGARD"
WEATHERWEAR FOR DEPENDABILITY

Any experienced motor cyclist will tell you that " Stormgard " is undoubtedly the world's finest motor cycling weatherwear. " Stormgard " were first in the field and have set the pace for years, leaving all imitators well in the rear.

Model 202.—FAWN. Motor Cycling Coat. Triple-proofed Gaberdine, with guaranteed oilskin interlining, fixed fleece lining (all-wool). Thief-proof pockets, uncreasable belt, tabs and buttons to form breeches device. Coat only 47/6.
Model 204.—FAWN. Motor Cycling Coat. Similar in design to Model 202, but self-lined Gaberdine. Coat only 55/-.
Reg. Pat. Tummipad, 3/6 extra. Reg. Pat. Stormscarf, 4/- extra (both for attachment to above models).

Model 905. — " Ixion " Motor Cycling Coat. Made from the highest quality cotton Gaberdine (Fawn), and interlined with Oilskin. Fitted with fixed fleece lining. Supplied with Tummipad. 39/6.

Model 202.—GREY. Motor Cycling Coat. Identical in design to Model 202 Fawn, but made from highest quality Grey Yarn Dyed Gaberdine with tremendous tensile strength. Coat only 55/-.
Model 204.—GREY. With detachable fleece lining. Coat only 63/6.
Reg. Pat. Tummipad, 3/6 extra. Reg. Pat. Stormscarf, 4/- extra.
(Both for attachment to above models.)

Write for illustrated catalogue of the full Stormgard range, describing over 100 Models for every purse and purpose.
STORMGARD WORKS, LEEDS.

13 year-old Bert Hadley dressed up in father's Stormgard motoring coat as a 'disguise' when riding the AJS.

coat and goggles! The sight of the diminutive youngster, still in short trousers of course and kick-starting the big v-twin engine into life must have been something to behold. It is not known if the Hadleys were aware of their wilful son's activities, but it was certainly character-building stuff.

15

As part of his Union duties Herbert was a great 'networker', something his son would later emulate. He seemed to be acquainted with a number of business people and owners of small garages in particular. One of these, Fred Preston, had an Austin agency at Fernhill Heath near Worcester. Father, with Bert on the pillion, visited the garage on the A.J.S. and talk soon veered towards motorcycles. Herbert's friend said to Bert – 'I've got just the thing for you. If you can ride it – it's yours!' The 'thing' turned out to be a tiny Ixion lightweight, locally produced in small numbers and already obsolete. Complete

IXION MODELS and Prices :

Model A. 2½ h.p., 2 str., fixed gear - - £56

Model B. 2½ h.p., 2 str., 2 sp. - - - £66

Model B II. 2½ h.p., 2 str., 2 sp. - - - £70

Model C. Sidecarette, 2½ h.p., 2 str., 3 sp. - £98 10

Model D. Ladies' 2½ h.p., 2 st., 2 sp. - £72 10

THE well-known IXION is a popular Lightweight because it is a reliable, efficient and economical Two-stroke, which, in actual service, invariably exceeds the buyer's highest expectations.

Its correct design, high-class equipment, sturdy but light build—all make for its recognised superiority and "long service" qualities.

Model B II is fitted with Sturmey-Archer 2-speed gear, kick-starter, and handle-bar control clutch. Catalogue giving fullest information gladly supplied on request.

IXION MFG. CO.
Ladywood
BIRMINGHAM

TWO STROKE

IXION

Bert's first motorcycle was given to him by a friend of HCH.

with the ubiquitous Villiers two-stroke engine and belt drive, it was typical of the many low-cost machines produced by small firms after the Great War, most of which faded into history.

Back to Bert:

'After a quick look at the controls, I wobbled off in the direction of Worcester. I had no idea of how to turn round and I must have covered four or five miles before returning. When I finally made it back to the garage, my Dad and his pal, fearing the worst, were about to send out the search posse for me.'

That is how Bert came to own his first motorised transport at the age of about 13. Of course, life was much simpler in those days, with much lighter traffic, except in town centres. Even so, a Driving Licence and eventually minimal Third Party Insurance were mandatory. The Licence, obtained at the local Post Office, cost the princely sum of 5/- (25p) – the price of a quality spark plug. At this time, there was no official driving test and new motorists normally gained rudimentary instructions, good or bad, from a friend or relative. Prospective drivers of prestige motor cars would have the option of a course of tuition from the factory or their agents. However, as more and more inexperienced drivers came onto the roads, the accident rate escalated alarmingly and the resulting carnage was on a par with today's statistics but with only a million vehicles in use by 1930. The situation continued to worsen, finally resulting in a raft of new Traffic Regulations in 1935, such as revised speed limits, designated pedestrian crossings, with 'Belisha Beacons' and most importantly, a compulsory Driving Test for all new drivers.

As soon as he was legally old enough, Bert became an 'enthusiastic' motorcyclist in the short-term, his last machine being a 500cc Norton, which he fell off 'quite regularly'. However, the young Hadley's aspirations were for something on four wheels...

Herbert, in the meantime, had taken on the tenancy of a usefully large wooden lock-up garage, situated in a nearby yard. Not only providing safe accommodation for the sidecar outfit, it would prove to be an invaluable and lucrative 'fettling' base for both father and son.

Despite his wilful ways and a penchant for attracting trouble, Bert was in fact a bright pupil and when his time at the Charlotte Road Schools ended in December 1923, he was considered good enough for a place at the prestigious Handsworth Junior Day Technical School. Starting on January 8th 1924, he was still only 13 years old. The fee per term was normally fifteen shillings (75p), but Birmingham's Education Committee exempted Mr Hadley, described as a 'Machinery Fitter' from this payment. At the time, Handsworth was considered one of the better suburbs of Birmingham, with many fine late-Victorian town houses. Today's Handsworth has changed socially, but the grandly-built Technical School stands as a monument to Victorian pride and confidence and is still in educational use.

Getting to school on time now entailed a very early start of a morning and a tram journey of some seven miles into Birmingham. The number 36 went from Pershore Road into the city Terminus on Navigation Street (where Thomas Hadley and Jane Lewis had met). From there the 74 route took Bert up through the City Centre, via the Jewellery Quarter, along the Soho Road to the Day School in Golds Hill Road. En route, there was much to interest an inquisitive youngster. One such object caught his eye and immediately sparked off his ambition to one day become a racing driver.

(Andy Lowe 2009)
Handsworth Junior Day Technical School, Golds Hill Road, showing the original main entrance.

Bert recalls:

'On Temple Street, towards the city centre, there was a small showroom, Messrs J. Heath & Co, who were displaying one of the recently-announced Gordon England "Brooklands" Sports, resplendent in gleaming polished aluminium. After some pleading I persuaded my Dad to ask the dealer for a trial run, posing as a potential customer! This he did and I even managed to charm the salesman to give me a short ride too. This would be early 1924 – I was smitten!'

[At £265 ex-works, this was indeed a very expensive Austin Seven. Apart from the narrow, staggered-seat bodywork, your money bought you a highly-tuned engine with special gearing and other desirable modifications. Each car was issued with a Certificate guaranteeing it had achieved an 80mph lap at the Brooklands Motor Course. In reality, these lightly bodied Sevens were racing cars in street-legal guise.]

The Handsworth establishment had gained an enviable reputation for turning out well-grounded boys and girls with good academic and vocational skills to give them the best possible start in life. In the 1920s, Birmingham City Council were able to offer bright youngsters an education to grammar school standard, in many cases without cost to their parents. After some 90 years of constant meddling by politicians and others, it is perhaps debatable if much progress has been made since. It was important for Bert to gain good results as he worked out his two-year stay at the Day College. Bert's initial thoughts centred around a career in journalism, the father of a school friend being the editor of a local paper, but vacancies in this field were few and far between. Guided by his parents, in particular his father, Bert's next target was to be accepted as an Apprentice at the Austin Motor Company, in nearby Longbridge.

(Andy Lowe 2009)

The ledger entry for Herbert L. Hadley's details whilst at Handsworth Technical School.

In 1925, Herbert Hadley had heeded Sir Herbert Austin's advice and 'Invested in an Austin', namely a dark blue Tourer, registered OM 7826. The running costs were only marginally greater than the old A.J.S. sidecar outfit and of course offered more comfort and space for passengers or anything else. With the side screens in place it was (almost) weatherproof.

As before, Bert decided to teach himself to drive the Austin, quite illegally of course, around the backstreets of Stirchley and in no time at all was probably more proficient than his father. Herbert, no doubt prompted by his son, became quite interested in motor sport, regularly buying magazines such as 'The Light Car' and 'Autocar'. Soon, an initial journey to the famous Brooklands Motor Course was suggested by Herbert and Lydia and as Bert later recalled:

> 'The sight of racing cars screeching round the Members' Banking was a revelation and I can say that from that moment, I was hooked. When I told my Dad that 'one day I will drive here', he didn't seem very impressed. I took some not very good snaps with my Brownie box camera but at least they preserved the magic moments'.

Always on the look-out for anything 'interesting' on wheels, Bert later recalled seeing the front wheel drive Alvis competition cars on test from nearby Coventry during his schooldays.

After the epic expedition to Surrey, the next visit to a motor sport venue of note was in 1926 and this time Bert himself drove his parents to somewhere much nearer to home. In fact it was to Shelsley Walsh, the famous hill climb near Worcester, which was to be the scene of many superb performances by Bert in later years. However, on this occasion, young Hadley was eagerly working his way amongst the drivers and cars in the paddock, so little changed today.

> 'The first competitor we chanced upon was [Sir] Henry Segrave with his Sunbeam. To be standing alongside the great man made my day. His mechanic was named Perkins and I heard Segrave address him as such. I cannot recall how Segrave fared that day, but it was of little consequence. It was seeing the man who had won so many races abroad which impressed me so much. I have always believed that Segrave was the perfect competitor – the first man to exceed 200 M.P.H. on land and over 100 M.P.H. on water. Added to that, he was so successful in road and track events at a time when motor racing was a highly dangerous sport. Tyre failures, mechanical breakages and hazardous circuits all took their toll. That first visit to Shelsley fired my enthusiasm and I determined that I would compete there one day. Nine years would elapse before I realised that ambition.'

Young Hadley continued his slightly bumpy ride through to the completion of his time at Handsworth, successfully passing his School Certificate examination with satisfactory grades. This was vital if he was to be considered for an Engineering Apprenticeship, preferably at 'The Austin' as his father had planned for him. Bert finished at the Technical School in December 1925, aged 15 years and 8 months. There is a gap of some thirteen months prior to him starting at Longbridge, but no doubt that period was spent doing something interesting, adventurous, risqué possibly. He was that sort of a lad! Apart from this, there was usually a waiting list and potential applicants would have to bide their time until there was a vacancy at the Apprentices School.

- 3 -
'THE AUSTIN'

Herbert Austin was born in 1866, the son of a Buckinghamshire farmer. After several false starts, he eventually went to Melbourne Australia, joining his Uncle Walter's engineering firm. After further training he worked at the Wolseley Sheep Shearing Company, and here the inventive Austin devised some improvements which were taken up by his employers. Impressed by his expertise, the Wolseley Company appointed him their Australian Manager. Further progress saw him eventually return to England to expand Wolseley's interests in the British Isles.

By 1900, Austin had turned his inventive mind to the new-fangled automobile and a 'voiturette' of his own design won a Silver Medal in the 1,000 Mile Trial of that year. The famous engineering firm of Vickers Sons & Maxim bought out the Wolseley vehicle interests and Herbert Austin became General Manager. He continued producing improved vehicles, but after disagreements on a future policy he resigned his position, though still retaining a connection with the Wolseley Company and with the help of outside investors set up his own venture, the Austin Motor Company Limited in a semi-derelict factory previously occupied by White & Pike, a printing firm. The site at Longbridge, south of Birmingham offered scope for future expansion which soon proved to be very necessary. It was here, in 1905, that Herbert Austin gathered a small team around him to start a remarkable journey. All the original employees were offered 'jobs for life' should the enterprise become successful. When the Great War started in August 1914 Austins were already producing around 1,000 vehicles a year and had become a public company. It could be said that the War had been good for Herbert Austin. Indeed he had been knighted for his contribution to the War effort. Through government contracts many new buildings had been built greatly increasing the Longbridge manufacturing capacity and all manner of munitions and even fighter aircraft were being produced. At the cessation of hostilities a remarkable 20,000 or more people had toiled at the site.

However, for Austin and his wife Helen, the loss of their only son Vernon on the Western Front in 1915 was a severe blow, yet probably made Austin more determined than ever to forge ahead with his ambitions. After 1918, Longbridge along with similar factories, became virtually silent overnight and Austin had to get the place moving again (and keep his shareholders happy). Having visited America before the War and admiring the production methods pioneered by his friend, Henry Ford, he decided to concentrate on one model, the Austin 'Twenty'. Whilst an admirable vehicle, it was large, quite expensive and sales were disappointing. To ease the situation, a smaller 'Twelve' was rushed out in 1921. This car was to become a mainstay of Austin production for many years but the depressed market conditions pertaining at the time did not help and by then the Company was already trading under administration.

Sir Herbert had foreseen this situation and as early as 1920 was formulating ideas for a 'real car in miniature' to capture the motorcycle & sidecar market. How this blossomed into the Austin 'Seven' has been fully documented elsewhere – suffice to say, after a few hiccups with the early cars, by 1925 production had settled down and with improved market conditions the Company was now making profits.

Herbert Austin had always been a keen advocate of proper training for young people coming into the industry. Longbridge, at the time, produced a higher proportion of the finished vehicle than most other motor companies, who largely bought in major components from specialist sources. Thus, there was a wide range of departmental skills to be learned 'on site' and an apprenticeship at 'The Austin' was considered one of the best in the industry.

The Austin Apprenticeship Scheme came into being at around the same time as the Great War and was constantly upgraded. The conditions appertaining when Bert Hadley applied for acceptance were those as revised in 1925. These make interesting reading. Firstly there was no premium or fee payable by the parent. Boys were entered for a period of four or five years, depending on the age at the start and their educational standard. Council School education of a high standard of achievement plus Night School attendance was the requirement for training in one department only as a Trade Apprentice. Secondary School education, with full evidence of examinations passed to a satisfactory standard

Come and see the famous Austins made

HOW many people wonder why the wheels go round, how all the bits and pieces were made to work so efficiently, and what there is behind the modern motor-car to make it so dependable ? If you are interested you are invited to see for yourself what it is all about.

Britain's largest and most self-contained car works are those of the Austin Motor Company at Longbridge, Birmingham, about seven miles, south-west of the city centre on the Bristol Road.

Visitors are welcomed at the special Reception Department and conducted tours of the Works commence daily, except Saturdays and Sundays, at 10 a.m. and 2 p.m. or at other times by special arrangement. Appointments should be made for parties.

Do you realise that the complete side of an Austin saloon is pressed out of a flat piece of sheet steel by gigantic presses exerting a force of six hundred tons? Have you appreciated that the wonderful sheen of your AUSTIN is a result of eight or ten coats of paint and as many hours of slow progress through the cellulose ovens?

Come to Longbridge and see the big cupolas pouring out streams of molten iron (it runs like milk) to make cylinder blocks, cylinder heads, brake drums and other parts. And a roaring steel converter sending showers of fireworks into the air preparatory to casting. Stand in the machine shops and listen to the whirr of tools shaping parts large and small, steel, iron, brass and aluminium.

Or, if you want even more of a thrill, stand in th drop forging shops and watch the drop power hammers beat white hot lumps of metal into wierd but carefully planned shapes. The glare of the furnaces, the thunder of the stamps and the vibration of the very ground will make you wonder at the skill of men who work in metals. Sixty or seventy thousand parts are made in this department every twenty-four hours — the work goes on all night.

There are 110 acres of buildings in the Austin Works and the parts are carried from place to place by mechanical conveyors, of which there are eight miles. Twenty thousand people work here.

were the minimum requirements to be considered as entry as an Engineering Apprentice, with training in various departments. This was the route taken by Herbert Lewis Hadley.

To encourage them, a complicated bonus scheme operated for all Apprentices and their progress was continuously and closely monitored. Those with exceptional abilities would be earmarked for possible Staff Posts. Day and evening release for studies at the Central Technical College and elsewhere were paid for by the Company. However, Engineering Apprentices paid a nominal Ten Shillings (50p!) per year for this facility. Apart from Educational qualifications all applicants underwent a thorough medical examination plus the usual interviews and aptitude tests. Successful applicants would receive a weekly wage starting at Five Shillings per week (25p) rising in increments of Two Shillings and Sixpence (12.5p) year by year.

Additional earnings in the form of a 'War Bonus' starting at One Shilling (5p) weekly and for those over 18, an Output Bonus was attainable worth approximately Ten Shillings (50p) a week, paid for regular and satisfactory progress at school. All these bonuses were revised monthly based on reports received from the various heads of departments and classes and particular emphasis was placed on Attendance and Timekeeping.

As was normal, there would be a three month probationary period for any would-be trainee. Bert managed to survive this and was formally signed up for a nominal four-year period from 14th March, 1927, a month before his seventeenth birthday. There were usually around 250 apprentices going through the various departments and many of these came via Austin Agents from all corners of the British Empire, in fact anywhere Austin cars were sold. Bert would be in the small minority who lived locally, the younger apprentices being quartered in a hostel block adjacent to the West Works, where there were also classrooms and sports facilities. Older trainees would live out in 'digs' provided by approved landladies.

The Apprentice Scheme provided employment for a small army of instructors with everyone under the watchful eye of Mr. Harold M. Brack, who combined the position of Apprentice Superintendent with that of the Company's Assistant Chief Engineer.

Although Longbridge was well served by the Birmingham Corporation Tramways, the journey from Stirchley involved time-consuming changes and Bert would have cycled or used one of his elderly motorcycles to get to work, along with thousands of his work colleagues. However he soon joined the motoring set at the age of just eighteen, no mean feat for an impecunious apprentice. His first two cars were not Austins, but a brace of 'Bullnose' Morris Cowleys of early 'twenties vintage. Those were popular, if plodding family cars, though not what the young Hadley really wanted to get his hands on! However, as Bert later recalled:

'I had two "Bullnose" Morris' given to me free, from friends of my father. It was not unusual for old, basically "clapped out" cars to be given away as they had little more than scrap value. The first was a four-seater tourer and within a week I had an appalling smash in Kings Heath. I was forced to swerve [in traffic] to avoid a stupid cyclist who came around the front of a stationary bus and proceeded straight at me. I hit an old chap with a large Talbot. The Morris engine, gearbox and cardan shaft [prop shaft] fell out into the road. I finished up on the back seat and a large shard of windscreen [plate glass] penetrated where I had just been sitting. The old gentleman and another witness praised me for saving, as he put it, the life of the stupid cyclist who was last seen running away with his bike minus a back wheel.

A pal whose Dad had a garage locally, arranged the Morris's removal. I eventually walked home carrying a large brass tyre pump. My dad looked up from his paper and said "where did it happen?" He must have been psychic! We went to the garage in his Austin and I sold the Morris for £6-10-00 [£6.50]. A couple of weeks later, it was on the forecourt at £27-10-00 [£27.50], having had the dumb-irons straightened and the engine and other wayward bits put back.

At the time of the accident, I had wound the car up to around 45 mph, so all in all, I was very lucky. Curiously, I was actually on my way to see the younger Stallard sister with whom I'd recently made an acquaintance! The second car was a saloon, seemingly about ten feet tall. This one did somewhat better due, I suppose, to my new "restrained" driving style. I always remember the heavy flywheels on these cars, they seemed to take ages to slow down. One had to constantly use the handbrake [which operated on the transmission] to improve progress.'

During his apprenticeship Bert spent time in ten departments within the sprawling Longbridge Works which now occupied many acres. Some of the work was naturally more interesting than others and the conditions, although some of the best by contemporary industrial standards, were pretty arduous, some quite dangerous. To relieve the boredom the young trainees would get up to the odd prank or two. Bert recalls one such occasion:

> 'Whilst working in a fitting shop, the lads placed a small innocent-looking carton in a gangway. An unpopular supervisor, known for a tidying fetish, came upon this object. Furtively looking round, he then took a running kick at it. As the carton gracefully exited through a window pane onto the road outside, the supervisor left the scene hopping about, clutching his foot. The box had contained a block of steel...'

Dated March 14th 1927

Herbert Lewis Hadley.

to

The Austin Motor Company, Limited.

Apprenticeship Indenture.

Some fifty years later HLH admitted it had been a stupid prank. Getting to know the huge Longbridge site was not an easy task for a relatively new employee but was no excuse for being late in the morning! A footbridge spanned the railway sidings at roof-top level and Bert often used this as a short cut on his way home. One dark evening on the bridge he caught up with someone he recognised, a rain-coated figure apparently bowed down with all the world's troubles. *'Hello Bert'* he croaked. *'Crikey, you sound rough.'* rejoined Hadley. *'No, I'm O.K. – it's just this rope that's choking me'.* The rope was in fact tied through the eyes of a pair of 7hp road springs which were hanging down his back, under the rain coat, hence the 'bowed' look. Bert wished him well but sped on his way, not wanting to be involved. As with most large organisations, petty theft was a common problem and though the uniformed mostly ex-military 'security' staff made regular checks, it was still possible to 'liberate' useful bits and pieces, particularly if the gateman was a neighbour. Even Bert admitted to the odd pocketful ready for a weekend's fettling. He did, however, step back from a scheme to smuggle a complete 7hp engine which someone had managed to hide awaiting 'collection'. Despite having the necessary transport, Bert declined to assist.

The reaction of Bert's relatives when he announced his intentions of becoming an apprentice at Longbridge was not what he expected. *'Going to Austins indeed – didn't you know they were always on short time?'* Later on when he was having a spell in the Foundry Department, which he found particularly interesting, he arrived home *'absolutely filthy'*, as the aforesaid relatives were visiting Twyning Road *'for tea'*. *'They recoiled in horror as if I was a throw-back from another era!'*

As he progressed through his training, he was given more responsibility. His academic work was considered acceptable as was his engineering aptitude, though his short fuse did bring him into conflict with authority from time to time. In spite of this, around 1929 found Hadley in the 7hp Engine Test House, a low-roofed concrete and steel building. Bert had four engine stands in his charge and would easily pick up a Seven engine off the floor and onto a stand.

'Short-arsed chaps like me don't suffer from back trouble, they told me, but I was to suffer later on. We had 50 engines on test at a time and would run them for two hours and then 20 minutes at full throttle. We had a special two-bladed fan bolted onto the flywheel. A wood and steel-mesh box enclosed each pair of engines mounted side by side.

The noise and heat generated could only be imagined. Some of the chaps would stand at the back to catch the breeze. Although apprenticed, I was working nights at that time, earning a very welcome additional bonus. My engine stands were full of rectified power units [this was common as engineering tolerances varied, often with piston and cylinder bore clearances, resulting in excessive oil consumption. This is borne out by surviving 7hp production records often showing several engine changes before a vehicle was deemed suitable for despatch]. As I mentioned, the cooling fans were bolted via a circular plate using the normal clutch mounting holes.

We were on "full noise" and I don't mean maybe! I completed the Test Card, hung it on the side of the cover and went to walk across the shop to get some cool fresh air. There was a "ping" behind me – I turned and there was an engine tearing itself off the stand, followed by a four gallon petrol tank mounted on top of the cover. The shop was now on fire and I had moved in the nick of time. What happened was that the flywheel on this engine detached itself and complete with fan had gone clean through a wall 50 feet away. The chap responsible got the sack because he had left the job of securing the flywheel to two inexperienced apprentices. It was so dark behind the stands, I didn't notice the tab-washer behind the flywheel nut wasn't turned up. Any modern Factory Inspector would have given birth at the sight of such a crude setup. The larger Austin engines had their individual test cells and dynamometers. I recall the "Seven" engines at that time had to pull 2,750rpm at which speed they developed around 12–14bhp.'

Some idea of the Hadley sense of humour is typified by this next account recalled by Bert:

'The chap I worked under at this particular time was a hard case. He used to stop engines by putting his hands on the plug terminals! I was determined to do this, but when I tried I thought my ankles had gone! My Dad got hold of some rubber-soled boots and one day, I did it by placing my right forearm across the four terminals. After that, nobody would approach me. The trick was to hold a plug and grab their hand! I did it on road tests too. One hand on a plug, the other on the wing. If anyone touched the car – bingo! Sometimes I wired a few cars together, but I got into hot water with Mr Brack, our Apprentice Superintendant, after a Supervisor jumped a clear foot in the air. Wouldn't do it now of course – it is necessary to be devoid of imagination. Mind you, if your hand is quite dry and you grab the plug firmly – and you have rubber soles, it's easy – or it was!'

As an out-going and confident young fellow the young Hadley had soon discovered the attractions of the opposite sex and by 1928 had met two Welsh-born sisters, Louisa and her younger sister Amy (known to their family as 'Louie' and 'Rosma'). Louie was about the same age as Bert whilst Rosma was a year and a bit her junior. The Stallard family had moved from the tiny mining village of Newtown, Rhymney Valley, South Wales following their father's underground accident. George ('Joe') had been employed in the local mine.

Amy Stallard ('Rosma')
at 17½ years of age.

With the depressed situation forcing a move to the West Midlands, Joe, who appears to have been a laid-back sort of character, found work as a millwright, carrying out factory maintenance. The real power of the family however was his wife Elizabeth, always known to as 'Marie'. Described as a 'busy little woman', Mrs Stallard had ambitions of her own. Strong women seem to form a thread in the Hadley story and 'Marie' was no exception. In between raising five children, she had graduated as a Midwife at Queen Charlotte's Maternity Hospital, London. Well qualified, she was soon in the employment of the Warwickshire Health Committee. Although mandatory training of midwives had started back in 1902, it was not until 1936 that Local Authorities were obliged to provide midwifery services.

The Stallards had settled in Kings Heath, an area adjacent to Stirchley and over the years, up to her eventual retirement, as Nurse Stallard, she had delivered hundreds of babies in the Kings Heath district. She was one of the first Midwives locally to use a small car for her daily rounds, an Austin Seven of course and was well-known and respected throughout the area.

After the escapade with the Morris Cowley, Bert was temporarily without transport, so he and an apprentice pal hatched a method of 'borrowing' a car from the Longbridge Works over a week-end and this was to continue as and when required for the next year or so. It was of course very risky and the consequences of being found out would be serious, however the chance of making an impression on the Stallard sisters proved too great and when Bert turned up in a shiny new saloon, they thought he must be worth a bob or two! He was also quite a snappy dresser with a penchant for 'natty' headgear. In fact, of course, he was only an apprentice on minimal wages.

'During my apprenticeship, I earned quite a lot of cash repairing local Austin Sevens, thanks to my Dad having the lock-up workshop. He often helped me as well. These A7s were popular with commercial travellers and company reps – one firm in Edgbaston had four and I looked after the lot. At one time, I had about fourteen on my books! Weekends meant long hours [and not much time for courting!]. In addition to breakages, de-cokes were a must due to low compression and the poor quality fuel available. About 5,000 miles between strip-downs was the norm! [Reminds the author of his apprenticeship c.1950.....].

I finally made enough cash to buy my first Seven, a 1927 R-type saloon, actually the property of Mr. Brack, our Apprentice Superintendant. It had a special hide interior and larger headlamps with a manually- operated dipping mechanism with lots of rods and levers [a proprietary accessory conversion]. I got the car for £100 and six months later, I was "persuaded" to let it go for £118, plus extra for teaching the new owner to drive it! At first Mr. Brack took a poor view of this but on reflection congratulated me on my shrewdness.'

Herbert Hadley's first Austin Seven Saloon, a 1929 RK.

The practice of borrowing Works cars came to a head on a fateful Monday morning in the spring of 1930, when Hadley and his 'accomplice' were summoned to the Apprentice Superintendant's office. H.M. Brack presented a very stern image which helped to maintain an air of authority over his charges. In no uncertain terms, they were informed their activities had been reported and as a result they were to expect serious repercussions to follow. With this news they were dismissed to await the next development, a meeting with Sir Herbert Austin – 'The Old Man'. This was too much for Bert's pal who immediately went 'sick' and stayed at home. Later, as a result of this, his Apprenticeship was terminated.

The following day, young Hadley was summoned to report to Sir Herbert's office. Here he stood in front of the man who had started the firm from scratch and in twenty-five years had built his Company into the largest vehicle producer in the country. Bald-headed, with protruding teeth and a slight speech impediment, Sir Herbert did not project the 'Headmaster' image that Brack did. However, Bert fully realised the seriousness of the moment. The conversation went something like this: *'I see you've been in trouble before*

Sir Herbert Austin at his desk - a sight which would become familiar to the young Hadley.

'adley, though your work is good'. Having perused HLH's work records, he then proceeded to give him a brief but thorough rollicking. Then he said: *'You like driving do you 'adley?'* Remembering all that his father had instilled in him, Bert looked at Sir Herbert directly eye to eye and replied *'Yes sir, it is my ambition to drive at Brooklands for the Company'*. Austin gave him a hard look and, with an *'Hmm'*, dismissed him to return to work for the time being.

Bert realised his future at Longbridge was on a knife-edge and for several days he sweated it out, trying to work as normal. He dare not tell his family what had happened as he considered he had let them down.

It was a contrite Hadley who was again summoned to Mr Brack's office a few days later. This time, whilst still retaining his stern facade, the Superintendant told him Sir Herbert wanted to see him – immediately! Naturally, Bert was even more convinced he was about to get the sack. Once again, standing before the great man, he braced himself for the worst. He was therefore greatly surprised to hear Sir Herbert say, in a quiet voice, *'I am placing you in the Experimental and Racing Department'* [this would normally be done by Mr Brack]. Austin then added, with a rare twinkle in his eye, *'don't let me down'*. Bert muttered his thanks and, promising to do his best, stumbled out of Sir Herbert's office in a daze.

This time he did have something to tell his parents.

4

'EXPERIMENTAL'

After the traumatic events of the previous week, Bert reported to the Experimental Department, situated in the South Works part of the Longbridge site. It was during the spring of 1930 and with the national unemployment figures at around the two and a half million mark, he realised what a lucky chap he was. His erstwhile colleague, who had just been dismissed, would under the circumstances find it difficult to find another decent job.

'Experimental' was housed in one of the older buildings on the site, a high-roofed single-story structure, previously used to stable the shire horses where they hauled parts and materials around the site in the earlier days of the Company. Hot in summer and somewhat draughty at other times, the sliding doors on the front were normally kept shut, mainly to keep prying eyes, even those of the Longbridge workforce, at bay.

Here Bert found the atmosphere quite unlike most of the other departments where large numbers of people were engaged in mainly repetitive jobs on production work. There were around thirty souls working in Experimental, but with others drafted in from elsewhere in the factory as required. Everyone was under the watchful eye of Alf Depper, the Foreman. Alfred Joseph Depper was one of Herbert Austin's earliest employees and as such, was guaranteed a 'job for life'. Depper did indeed take advantage of this deal, eventually to retire from Longbridge in his mid-seventies! Chief Mechanic was Leonard (Len) Brockas, who had served in the Great War as a Sergeant in the Royal Artillery.

The core activities of the Department were roughly divided into the assembly of prototype vehicles or carrying out modifications as prompted by the Drawing Office staff under the Chief Designer, A.J. (Joey) Hancock, another of the 'original' team. Road testing, dismantling and evaluating vehicles from 'the opposition' and finally, the Company's competition activities, which in 1930, were mainly concerned with racing at Brooklands Motor Course. The racing side was manned by a few selected 'regulars' under Len Brockas.

4th October 1930. Brooklands 500.
Sammy Davis and Freddie March exchange places whilst Len Brockas prepares to crank up the Austin. Bill Rogers, Arthur Waite and Ral Appleby are behind the pit counter.
20 year old Bert prepared the engine for the race, but where is he? We think he's behind the post in the centre of the picture.

As the new 'boy' and still only an apprentice of course, Hadley trod very carefully as he sized up the various characters he was now working with. To say that he was eager to learn was of course the understatement of the year but he was determined to make a go of it as his goal was to remain in the Department after the completion of his time, not a foregone conclusion by any means, but his only hope of achieving his ultimate ambition of racing for the Company.

As he settled in, young Hadley soon got a reputation for being somewhat 'cab happy' (an old Army term for someone who likes driving – anything, anywhere, anytime). Some of the staff were not particularly interested in driving, many of course could not even afford a car, so if a vehicle needed moving Bert would volunteer.

Alf Depper was a gruff sort of character, who occasionally 'flew off the handle', but seems to have left Bert largely in the safe hands of Brockas or Raleigh Appleby. 'Ral' had been one of Austin's original apprentices and was about ten years older than Hadley. Bert could not have had a better pair of mentors as he worked to becoming a fully skilled fitter and thus lessened the chances of Depper and Hadley having a 'head to head'.

As contemporary photographs show, the Experimental Department was not a particularly tidy place to work in, inevitable with a lot going on – 'bits everywhere' – a typically busy workshop scene. The racing activities were under the nominal direction of Arthur Waite, who was based at the London Sales Office. Captain A.C.R. Waite was something of a War Hero, having won the Military Cross whilst serving in the Australian Imperial Force. He had met the Austins' elder daughter Irene whilst convalescing in England and became their son-in-law in 1918. Waite was in effect to replace Vernon Austin who had shown potential as a competition driver before the Great War. Thus Waite, known to his staff as 'The Skipper' and has been well documented, was involved with competing with the Austin Seven from the outset.

In 1928, Waite and his wife were despatched to his native Australia, ostensibly to promote Austin sales over there. During their two year sojourn, he managed to famously win the first Australian Grand Prix in an early 'Ulster' prototype. Prior to this however, the lanky 'wild colonial boy' had developed a roving eye and Herbert Austin was fearful for the state of his daughter's marriage.

Bert was soon in the thick of things with occasional visits to the London Service Depot and to Brooklands itself. An early perk was a visit to the Weybridge venue with George Coldicutt, whose 'day job' was as a 7hp Road Test Supervisor. Coldicutt was a 'taciturn sort of a bloke' according to Bert but Hadley thought he was a better driver than many of his contemporaries. Coldicutt had of course driven in the famous 1929 Ards Tourist Trophy as part of the Austin Team and later also drove the 'Slippery Anne' special for John Pares. On this occasion however, their mount was an un-blown 'Super-sports'. It was a wonderful introduction for the young Bert to do some high-speed laps over the bumpy motor course.

Under the guidance of Chief Mechanic Len Brockas, Hadley was given more responsibility on the preparation of the Works competition cars. One notable car was the two-seater sports model (aka 'Ulster') entered in the 1930 500 Mile Race on a largely wet October 4th. The car was a brand new and specially lightened version of the production model.

The lead driver was Sidney Charles Houghton Davis, known to all as 'Sammy', an eminent racing driver/journalist who, as a Le Mans winner for Bentley in 1927, was initially unfamiliar with the tiny Austin. His co-driver was a quietly-unassuming fellow who introduced himself to the chaps in Experimental as 'Freddie March'. Imagine their surprise when Ral Appleby looked up from his paper during a break, exclaiming 'Blimey, Freddie's an Earl!' In fact he was Frederick Gordon-Lennox, Earl of March, the younger son of the Duke of Richmond and Gordon, whose family seat was of course, Goodwood House. Freddie later inherited the Dukedom and was the present Earl's grandfather.

It is now history that the orange No.1 car held together when the other Austins succumbed to mechanical failures and secured a famous victory at over 83mph average speed against a Bentley and a Sunbeam. Young Hadley had been given responsibility for the engine assembly under Brockas' supervision and this no doubt gave him a lot of pride and confidence for the future. In fact Bert was to become very familiar with this particular vehicle after its front-line racing duties came to an end.

The off-set single seater prepared for Malcolm Campbell's Daytona 100mph attempt. Bert built the engine then illegally tested it on the public road past Lickey Grange – the "Old Man's" residence.

Another project was the off-set single-seater car prepared for Sir Malcolm Campbell, who was off to America for another attack on the World Land Speed Record. The Austin would attempt to exceed 100mph for a new Class H record. The car was actually a re-working of the rather bulbous 'Ulster'-based machine intended for Arthur Waite. Bert was again entrusted with the engine build-up and recalled driving it on the road to Rednal, past the Old Man's residence Lickey Grange, on several occasions 'to bed it in', quite illegally of course, after all it was a racing car. Hadley remembered it as *'a curious job, very light, part fabric body, painted orange with "Austin" emblazoned on the sides'*. Some attempt to frontal streamlining was achieved, completely spoilt by the normal upright radiator cowl, presumably so it was recognisable as an Austin. HLH opined Longbridge's thinking at the time was somewhat limited as far as aerodynamics were concerned. It produced about 36bhp. In the end this output was not sufficient to reach the magic 'ton'.

Here's the Hadley take on the Campbell car:

> 'Considering the shape of the car, 94mph was creditable. There was so much space between the floor of the car and the road that it lifted at maximum speed and the steering became very light. So many much better shaped versions of Austin 7 racing cars had been made by people outside the Company before this time, it seemed incredible to me that the design people could not even copy one. I refer to Gordon England, Boyd Carpenter and A.C. Spero. As I have intimated, I found the car a bit dodgy.'

Len Brockas travelled out with the Campbell entourage to look after the car and at Daytona Beach where the action was to take place, the local press boys mistook L.B. for 'The Driver' and demanded a high-speed demonstration.

Back to Bert:

'Len had his own 7hp tourer but he was not a fast driver nor did he claim to be. Anyway, he wound the Campbell car up to near maximum on the beach, which was fine until he lifted his foot, then everything happened, spinning like a top, making life very unpleasant. He came to a standstill feeling as he put it "bloody scared". The amusing part afterwards was quite astonishing. A heavy man in a large hat rushed up to Len, showered him with congratulations and gave him a large box of cigars. "That was great," he said, "would you please do it again!?" Len was speechless. After this, the car was nicknamed "Skeedaw" in the local newspapers. It seems the big man was a local bootlegger and Brockas was wined and dined over a wide radius on the strength of his obviously fantastic driving!'

After the Campbell efforts, the Austin is thought to have remained in America, maybe waiting to be re-discovered...

It was around this time, mid-1930, that Hadley got to know Charles Goodacre, who would become a life-long friend. Charles Lindsey Goodacre was born in West Kirby, Cheshire, in July 1909. Educated at Birkenhead Public School, he joined Austins not as an apprentice but as an improver mechanic with the Experimental Department from the outset. A tall, good-looking chap with rather a debonair outlook on life, he and Hadley were like chalk and cheese, both in appearance and background. It would take some time for both of them to respect one another's strengths and weaknesses and this would be put to the test when they were later required to undertake long-term road testing together. Although only nine months older than Bert, Goodacre was already driving competitively for the Company, possibly making Bert even more determined to achieve a similar situation. As it was, he had to be content with occasional testing and convoy running on public roads. Goodacre had made his racing debut in the 1930 Brooklands 500 Mile Race as a riding mechanic with Gunnar Poppe, a big fellow who Bert considered Austins' best driver at that time. Poppe, then a member of the Longbridge Sales Department, would return the compliment a few years later! An early Goodacre achievement was his role in the 1931 Mille Miglia in which he co-drove with the Italian Francesco Trevisan to finish in 34th place.

In July 1931 Bert participated in his first full motor race as riding mechanic to Goodacre. This was the Light Car Club Relay Race which the Works team won. Driving T.T. type cars, the other drivers were Leon Cushman and Donald Barnes. Hadley seems to have enjoyed the experience despite the poor weather. By now an integral part of 'the team', though barely out of his apprenticeship, Bert regularly drove one of the T.T./'Ulster' type cars down to Brooklands which

25th July 1931. Brooklands Relay Race. Bert's first competitive event as riding mechanic with Charles Goodacre (on the left in '7C').

was then the only suitable venue for sustained high-speed testing, though they did not hang about on the roads either! Bert recalled they would leave the Works at around 5 a.m. with three or four 'noisy little orange cars, screeching through the villages, nose-to tail'. As an aside he also remembered the 'Ulsters', as raced, would survive a 500 mile race without any structural problems, though troubles with body fractures did arise during 'Double Twelve' events and record attempts due to the ever-deteriorating and bumpy Brooklands' concrete.

The Davis/March machine was retained as a development car and one of the first jobs Hadley was given on completion of his apprenticeship was the conversion of the normal Austin cable brakes to the Bendix system, quite popular on some other makes of car at the time. This employed four separate enclosed cables whilst the shoe mechanism provided a self-wrapping servo effect which could be described as 'efficient' or 'vicious' according to how well they were set up. The conversion involved much machining, manufacture of special parts, or adapting existing components and remains the only known Works conversion of this type. After much testing, unpredictable brake grabbing precluded further developments. Bert recalled an epic return journey to the Works:

'It was 120 miles from the paddock at Brooklands to the South Works entrance at Longbridge and one afternoon, against stop watches and in increasing drizzle, later pouring rain, I did it in two hours exactly. Brakes were lockable and the large bore exhaust pipe made an awful noise. There was also a 20mph speed limit in Oxford at that time. En route, I saw a chap cycling over the rise out of Henley [on Thames]. It was narrow then. I suppose he saw this "dot" with the rain cloud behind. I saw him leave the pedals, feet in the air – my lasting impression was of him going over the hedge in full take-off mode. I was miles away before it dawned on me what had happened...'

Bert remembered another occasion:

'Returning to Longbridge, I came up behind a maroon Daimler Limousine at Nettlebed, S.E. of Oxford. I thought this chap had lost his rear number plate. The noise of the Austin must have permeated the interior of the stately saloon for a lady seated in the rear turned round and gave me a wave. The Daimler seemed about 20 tall from where I was sitting and I thought "she" was a bit older than what I would be normally looking for! Two chaps sat bolt upright in the front as I overtook the vehicle. In those days one passed through a sort of forest at Nettlebed, so I went on and turned up one of the lanes. I was a bit mystified. Later I overtook the Daimler again and the penny dropped. It was Queen Mary, wife of His Majesty George V! Very nice wave again – to which I responded. She looked down on me as if from a first floor window!'

Meanwhile the Department were concentrating on a new type of single-seater for circuit racing and proposed attempts to achieve 100mph from a 750cc car for the first time – a target arch-rivals MG were also known to have in their sights. The specification was a little more ambitious than previously.

A 'Dutch Clog' or 'Rubber Duck' in its final orange-painted form with Jamieson-designed twin exhaust system. Hadley's name for it was 'Back-breaking abortion'!

For one thing, the differential was off-set to the left hand side, requiring a special assembly driving at approximately 10 degrees from normal. Suspension front and rear was also modified, resulting in a lowered chassis height and driver's seating position. Some attempt at 'streamlining' was taken this time and quite successfully too with a neat two-panel grille which must have surely inspired the later corporate look of BMW. Unfortunately, this affected cooling at maximum engine speed so was thus modified to that used on the subsequent three cars which collectively became known as 'Rubber Ducks' or 'Dutch Clogs'. Hadley was involved with the construction of all these cars at various stages and recalled the side sponsons on the original car as being so flimsy that they broke off their mountings after high-speed laps of Montlhéry. Bert was not terribly impressed by the construction of these cars and when acquainted with what was to come later on, referred to them as 'abortions'.

By this time, Bert was the proud owner of a smart Austin 'Swallow' two-seater, the first of two he would own. This particular one was a cream and green example, registered UE 6244. It was virtually new. Here's Bert's recollection of the purchase:

Stirchley 1929. Bert in his early but low mileage two-seater Swallow UE6244 outside father's commodious lock-up.

'I'd managed to make an offer I could just about afford for the Swallow which Mr Hyde of Idoson Motor Cylinder Company in Smethwick was anxious to sell as his daughter, whom he'd bought it for, was too frightened to drive. On the evening of the purchase the Hydes' insisted I should accompany the family to the Prince of Wales Theatre Birmingham! We saw "The Student Prince". However I was more interested in Mr Hyde's car, which he allowed me to drive. It was a 12/60 'Alvista' fabric saloon. I also had some "interest" in their daughter, Doris, but I must have spent too much time looking at the Alvis, as she took up with a speedway rider and eventually married him. At the time, I was working in the Longbridge Foundry, hence Mr Hyde's interest in me, as his company was casting cylinder barrels for the A.J.S. motorcycle firm'.

Nind's Garage and Store, 1516, Pershore Road, Stirchley. A wonderful picture of Bert, looking like a young James Cagney, and his pal Jimmy filling up the newly acquired Swallow Sports UE6244 whilst the Nind family stand outside their establishment.

The same property in 2010. The chapel in the background, recently re-roofed, is sadly destined for demolition. The area behind, at a lower level, was the site of the famous Wilmot-Breeden works (manufacturer of parts for the motor industry).

Amy 'Rosma' Stallard
aged about 20.

On the domestic scene, 'Louie' Stallard had married Herbert Penny and would soon give birth to a son, Peter. Bert on the other hand, had transferred his affections to younger sister Amy, known to her family as 'Rosma' and to Bert, simply as 'Rose'. This was the beginning of an epic courtship which would run for over a decade.

So the Works racing activities concentrated on the four Clog/Duck single seaters, based at the London Service Depot in Holland Park, under the direction of Stan Yeal, overseen by Arthur Waite. It was around this time that Leonard Patrick Driscoll came onto the Austin scene. Driscoll had already had a successful motor-cycle career before taking to four-wheels. With his engineering background, he was eventually allowed to make some major alterations to 'his' car including stronger connecting rods which helped with reliability. The cars made several appearances at Brooklands during the year and two cars even made it to the German Grand Prix at Avus, driven by Goodacre and Donald Barnes, another 'retained' driver. During this period, Ral Appleby joined the personnel based in London and the cars improved marginally. Pat Driscoll eventually set up a new 750cc lap record at Brooklands at 103.11mph. As Bert later wrote:

'The writing was on the wall, however, when George Eyston drove his 750cc supercharged MG "Magic Midget" single seater over the mile on Pendine sands at 118.38mph. In retrospect, I believe that Austin racing would have disappeared from the scene of major success by 1934. As it was, the situation was saved by the fortuitous appearance of "Jamie" – Thomas Murray Jamieson'.

After he had completed his apprenticeship in August 1931, Bert was gradually given more responsibilities. One of the on-going tasks within the department was the sustained road testing of new models before they came into production. Several pairs of drivers were used as it involved many hours of continuous driving in all weathers. It must be realised by younger readers that many cars of the day were open tourers and although enclosed saloons were gaining in popularity at that time, there were no interior heaters and demisters available so it could be challenging at times. However, extra payment bonuses were a welcome compensation.

Charles Goodacre, as we have heard, was quite a different sort of person to Bert, both physically and in upbringing. However, after a few rough patches, they both came to respect each other and were to remain life-long friends. 'Charlie' normally worked alongside Ral Appleby but during 1932 – 34, he and Hadley were to spend a lot of their time on the road, particularly during the winter. The test routes took them all over the country but mainly to the mountainous parts of North Wales. Basically they would set off early and try to achieve around 300 miles a day, driving as hard as conditions allowed, often on packed snow or ice – no gritting in those days. Their base in Wales, which Goodacre described as 'a home from home', was a rambling old farmhouse called 'Cefn Y Maes' at Brithdir about three miles North East from Dolgellau, then in Merionethshire.

'Cefn Y Maes' in 2009. *(Walter Lloyd Jones & Co Ltd.)*

I, the within named admit that since attaining twenty one I have adopted the within Apprenticeship Articles and have continued to work thereunder to the intent that same may be binding upon me during the remainder of the term thereof Dated this day of   One thousand nine hundred and

12.8.31.

We have pleasure in certifying that this Indenture has been faithfully and satisfactorily completed. During the period covered by this Indenture, Mr.Hadley has served in the following Departments, and has made satisfactory progress:-

Tool Room
Erecting Shop
Road Test
No.2.Machine Shop
Experimental
Engine Tests
Finished Car Test
Repair Shop.

He has also served a further year in the Experimental Car Engine Test Department.

During this period he has also attended classes held at the Central Technical College, Birmingham.

FOR AND ON BEHALF OF

THE AUSTIN MOTOR COMPANY LIMITED.

DIRECTOR

Details of Bert's progress through the Longbridge Works after successfully completing his apprenticeship as 'signed off' by Sir Herbert himself. HLH also spent time in the Foundry Shop.

It was run by Mrs Osborn, whose husband Tom tended to the surrounding estate on behalf of absentee owners, the Patterson family from Liverpool. In 2009 Mrs Ira Pritchard, the Osborn's daughter, then well into her nineties, remembered as a schoolgirl the frequent visitors whom her mother looked after particularly during the winter months.

Bert recalled the early days of the Goodacre/Hadley test team:

'Charlie had some queer ideas. After a stormy start, we got on well – at least most of the time. I was always pulling him out of some scrape or another. Trouble was, he would insult somebody in a pub, then having got them going, would disappear, leaving me to sort things out, one way or another.

As a break from road testing, three prototype 10hp engines were built. Len [Brockas] built the first, Ral [Appleby] the second. I was surprised when I was told to get cracking on the third. This was no problem to me, I was familiar with all the Austin engines at that time from 7hp to the 26hp "Six". In those days, one had to be versatile and undertake a wide range of real fitting work. Three prototype cars were built, blue, maroon and green, OV 9145/6/7. My engine was destined for the blue car. After sustained bench testing, the power units were stripped and examined. A trick I had learned on production was to ease the pistons on the 'thrust' side with a very smooth Swiss file. This made a difference to power output and on second bench testing, my engine was slightly superior to the others. The three cars were subjected to extensive night and day testing by Goodacre, Hadley and Bill Scriven who later drove in our Trials team. Virtually unchanged, the "Ten" was in production by late 1932 and was to prove a best seller.

A companion picture to one widely published, this shows HLH casting a long shadow as he 'snaps' co-driver Goodacre somewhere in North Wales.

The "blue" car was retained at Longbridge as a Works "hack" amassing a huge mileage, then found its way to another department. One day I spotted it at the Works, weighed down with iron castings and visibly sagging in the middle – what an ignominious end to an important part of Austin history.

After a hard day's testing, it was a relief to get back to Brithdir and Mrs Osborn's wonderful home cooking and in winter to the roaring log fires in the massive fireplaces. A lot of cold and wet clothes drying took place too.

Goodacre gets friendly with a member of staff at a Welsh watering hole.

One of the new models on test was the Twelve-Six, the first Austin to have cylinder block and crankcase as a single iron casting. This car had a multi-blade fan which gave it a peculiar whine and not much else. Two examples were built, one all steel and the second of composite "Weymann" fabric and wood.

Charlie was inclined to be accident prone at the best of times and one Friday evening, after I'd been driving all day and we were returning to the Works, he was driving us out of Kidderminster when, on a downhill stretch, we ran into dense fog. I knew the road and the bend we were approaching was right handed. I shouted "pull right" but he didn't – we hit a bank with the nearside front wheel going at a fair old pace, rolled twice, slid on the roof and finished up on the drivers' side. I clambered out via the window. Charlie was bawling for me to get him out. I always had a torch with me and after a quick look at the situation, said why don't you step out – there's no roof! The remains of this, leather cloth and "Kapok" wadding, was strewn all over the place. After getting the car towed to a local garage, we came home by "Midland Red" bus...

Charlie wanted to pull a fast one by telling the "Old Man" the lights had failed. I said don't be a clot, with your record he'll see through that straight away. We had a night shift on in the Department that weekend so it was possible to recover the car without delay. A second identical composite body was available and about fifteen men worked on the car over that weekend. By Monday morning all was back to "normal" and, as Sir Herbert was away, Goodacre got away with it on this occasion - as there were others! But we did have bad prop-shaft vibration all the following week which needed sorting out.

The 12-6 episode was the second 'incident' involving Charlie. Number one consisted of rolling a "Top Hat" saloon down a Welsh mountainside with a crew of young apprentices aboard. All escaped, which spoke volumes for the strength of the Seven. The third case involved losing it near Stratford-Upon-Avon in an "Ulster" which catapulted co-driver Bill Scriven over a hedge, fortunately without serious injury. The car ended up overturned, Charlie also escaped but a passing cyclist – who we didn't find for some time – he'd joined Scriven in the field - sustained a broken leg. Sir Herbert's take on these matters could be condensed as follows: "Once more to the well mate and you are out". In Goodacre's defence, I said it could happen to anybody – Sir!

On another occasion, somewhat later, a party of us were staying overnight at the Hand and Spear Hotel in Byfleet near to Brooklands. Think of sitting down at breakfast time. Goodacre opens the French windows, in winter mind you, then casually starts shooting rats with a .22 Springfield rifle. The place was infested by them and the boss of the 'Spear, an alcoholic in his own right, was very put out because he used to feed the buggers! With Alf Doody, another colleague who was also there, I took the rifle off Charlie before anyone got hurt. That pub was a fantastic place and all the "loonies" including Freddie Dixon, Percy McClure and Charlie Martin, the Riley exponents, used to be there.

I had just started racing for the Company by this time and on another trip to Brooklands, the Chief Engine Designer, Belgian-born Jules Haefeli, asked me to use an experimental "Sherbourne" 10hp saloon and drive it hard. I asked why and he explained that the steel camshaft was running directly in the cast iron block, i.e. without white metal or bronze liners. I queried this and he said, not to worry, we've increased the oil pressure. There seemed no point in discussing Coefficients of Expansion – after all he was a Senior Designer – and I wasn't! In jest I'd suggested someone to pick me up in case of breakdown. Anyway, I was on a downhill stretch near Stratford-Upon-Avon when – "ping" – everything stopped. The distributor wouldn't turn so the camshaft experiment was over. Another car came for me and eventually my weekend ended in success as I won an important race on the Campbell Circuit, despite my superstitious misgivings. A few days later I was just in time to see Joe Hunt trying to remove the camshaft from the "Sherbourne" engine with a sledgehammer, without success. It was a very nice welding job – one more bright idea up the spout!'

[Ford had long discarded separate bearing shells for in-block camshafts, but had also successfully pioneered cams made in much cheaper chilled cast iron, as against forged steel camshafts used by other manufacturers. Just another example of the brilliant 'production engineering' techniques used by Ford at the time.]

During this period Bert was regularly in direct contact with Sir Herbert on day to day matters and it was clear that Austin respected Hadley's no-nonsense opinions and that he was not afraid to express them. Bert got the impression that Austin was surrounded by a lot of 'yes' men whom Sir Herbert had little time for. On one such occasion, Bert was evaluating a Triumph 'Gloria' saloon, a quality model built in moderate numbers in nearby Coventry. Sir Herbert approached Bert and asked for a short run in the car.

> 'The Triumph had some nice features but the Old Man didn't like it because the roof interfered with his bowler hat – "what did I think?" "Well," I said, "one doesn't normally wear a hat indoors!" I realised I was steering near the wind when he asked me to stop the car, he looked at me, watery-eyed for a few moments and I prepared myself for the impact. Then he suddenly smiled and said "I see" and went off still smiling, towards his office. No, he didn't like "yes men".'

An incident occurred towards the end of the 1932 season which would have a lasting effect on the young Hadley. On Saturday 24th September, Brooklands hosted the BRDC (Brooklands Racing Drivers' Club) International 500 Mile Race. This attracted a large quality entry and three 'Ducks' were entered by the Works. No.14 to be driven by Pat Driscoll (apparently on his own), No.15 was Donald Barnes paired with Dr. John Benjafield [a 1927 Le Mans winner with 'Sammy' Davis] and No.16 shared by ex-jockey George Duller and Charles Goodacre. This last car was looked after by Brockas and Hadley.

During pre-race practice, and normally wary of 'Officer-type toffs', Bert had made the acquaintance of Clive Dunfee, one of a family of 'dashing' regulars at the track. Dunfee was to drive the fearsome 'Speed Six' Bentley which had been converted to 8 litre capacity and was owned by Woolf Barnato, the rich diamond merchant who had pumped vast amounts of cash into the under-funded Bentley outfit. This car had a reputation for being hard to handle on the Brooklands banking.

As the race progressed, the attrition rate amongst the Class H (750cc) contenders increased, but by sheer weight of numbers the MGs were able to win both Class and Team awards. Austin No.16 did manage to finish but the whole meeting was overshadowed by a dreadful accident when Clive Dunfee, in the Bentley, went over the top of the banking with fatal results. Everyone present was deeply shocked at the tragic death of a very popular man and who had only recently married. Nine years later, Bert would name his only son in Dunfee's memory.

Dunfee had made a lasting impression on Hadley. Maybe he had regarded the Longbridge brigade as normal human beings, rather than 'split-arsed'* provincial grease monkeys as was sometimes the case.

* A Hadley expression

'Every picture tells a story.'
A significant cutting from the Daily Sketch dated 23rd September 1932. Practice for the Brooklands BRDC International 500 mile race.

Hadley (baggy overalls), Brockas (on tail) and Goodacre (co-driver) push-start ex-jockey George Duller in the Clog. Dapper gent Arthur Waite observes their efforts. Behind, the ill-fated Clive Dunfee sets off on his practice run in the 8-litre Bentley.

5

'JAMIE & MONTLHÉRY' (1932-33)

May 1932, the Holland Park-based racing personnel have booked a test session at Brooklands. A Clog/Duck single-seater was to be demonstrated to invited journalists. The proceedings are interrupted by the appearance of a fully road-equipped EA Sports Austin ('Ulster') which is screaming around the track at a high rate of knots. Stan Yeal, in charge of the London staff had previously observed this white 'Ulster' in action and decided to put on a demonstration to show the press just what the Works Austins were capable of. Also present was a car-load from Longbridge, including Depper, Brockas and young Hadley. Ral Appleby was already London-based at this time. Popular myth has suggested the 'Ulster' was driven by its 'owner', an unknown, studious-looking young fellow, T. Murray Jamieson (TMJ). Furthermore, after some enquiries, Yeal informed his superior, Arthur Waite who then introduced TMJ to Sir Herbert. After further negotiations, Jamieson and 'his' modified 'Ulster' joined the Longbridge design staff. Time has since revealed this to be only partially correct and of course the story started a couple of years beforehand.

Charles Amherst Villiers (CAV) was born in 1900. His family had distant connections with the Sunbeam Motor Company and The Villiers Manufacturing Company, both based in Wolverhampton. Whilst at Oundle School, he was a contemporary of T.R. Mays, the only son of a Lincolnshire Wool and Skin Merchant and better known as Raymond Mays. He was later to co-found both English Racing Automobiles (ERA) and post-war, British Racing Motors (BRM). After Oundle, both went 'up' to Cambridge University where Mays seemed to spend the greater part of his studying time playing with motor cars and tuning these to compete successfully in the speed hill climbs of the day. He also

became very adept in the art of sand-racing, including at his local venue, Skegness Beach. The technical expertise behind Mays' success came from Villiers who was studying engineering. CAV was involved in developing the potential of most of Mays' cars, at least the ones he actually owned or were gifted by his affluent family. The first was a relatively modest Hillman Sports and then came the two famous Type 13 Bugatti 'Brescias'. From an early age, Mays realised life would be far more acceptable if he could get other people to fund his indulgences. Thus the Bugattis were emblazoned with 'Cordon Rouge' and 'Cordon Bleu', the trademarks of well-known Champagne and Cognac producers. An early example of what we now know as 'product placement'.

By 1926, Mays had graduated to an ex T.T. Vauxhall. This 3 litre car was completely re-worked by Villiers who was now in business as Amherst Villiers Superchargers Ltd (AVS) and as a result the car was eventually known as the 'Villiers Supercharge'. An early customer for the fledgeling business was (Sir) Malcolm Campbell with one of the first incarnations of 'Bluebird' of Land Speed Record fame. Villiers (at his insistence always pronounced 'Villers') continued working in engine development for many years and during the Second World War was engaged on various top-secret projects for the Government. After the hostilities, in 1945 he moved to the United States working within the American Aerospace industry on more advanced research. He finally returned to retirement in England and became a portrait painter of note, one of his sitters being Graham Hill, then F1 World Champion.

Amongst his small hand-picked team, CAV had recruited a promising young designer, Thomas Murray Jamieson. TMJ's first project was drawing up the components for the 'Blower Bentleys', the brain-child of Sir Henry Birkin (of the Nottingham lace family). This was against the express wishes of Walter Owen Bentley, who despised forced induction, at least as far as his own engines were concerned, thus it was an independent project, funded by the immensely wealthy race-horse owner the Hon. Dorothy Paget. CAV and TMJ had similar thoughts on supercharger design, particularly favouring the twin-rotor Roots pattern. By the time Jamieson got to work on the Austin Seven, he had already been made a Director of AVS, Villiers obviously keen to hang on to his young protégé.

The in-house development of the Works racing cars was reaching something of a plateau with a lot of reliability problems. Having become aware of Villiers' expertise, Sir Herbert made another of his shrewd moves and covertly arranged for a production supercharged EA sports to be placed with AVS with a brief to see what further power could be safely extracted from the basic Austin design. The blown version of the 'Ulster' employed the No. 4 version of the French 'Cozette' unit, supplied via the British concessionaires, L.T. Delaney Ltd.

After the best part of two year's development and at some expense, Villiers and TMJ had virtually re-designed the Austin power unit, with a revised cylinder head and block, crankcase, cam and crankshafts, involving many special parts, all mated up to a Jamieson-designed Roots-type supercharger driven from the front gear train. (As Bert later observed, *it was much easier in those days to get special one-off parts made at short notice – if you knew the right people!*) Development proceeded in great secrecy, no-one at Longbridge being aware of the arrangement, possibly not even Arthur Waite, who was of course based in London as was Villiers. It was probably more than coincidence that resulted in Jamieson being at Brooklands simultaneously with the factory crowd. It would be fascinating to know just how much this covert scheme of engineering and design work cost Sir Herbert, or to be more accurate, the Austin Motor Company. Apart from these costs, there would surely be a question of hefty compensation to Villiers for the loss of his star designer. Anyway, the result was quickly decided upon and Thomas Murray Jamieson B.Sc, together with all the patterns, jigs and fixtures, moved to Longbridge in the summer of 1932.

Bert takes up the story:-

'Obviously we all heard this shrieking blower. In addition, everyone noticed this was a "complete" car, with the touring wings and full-width screen, which incidentally was in use. The lap speeds of the white "Ulster" created a buzz of comment (up to 99mph). In effect, Jamieson had thrown a spanner in the works by making the Austin outfit look silly to all and sundry. Certain things were said. I had the temerity to say "We should have that engine." and I was immediately set upon by one section of the hierarchy who appeared to be about to explode. I think magenta would describe his complexion [Now, who was Bert referring to?]. Len Brockas was amused but we both agreed that poor Stan Yeal's well-meant public relations exercise had gone astray. Further nasty remarks were made. It was unfortunate that 'Jamie' was a Londoner as people from that great city were treated with grave suspicion at Longbridge. Had he sprung from a long line of chain or even nail makers, with antecedents within shopping distance from Wolverhampton, his acceptance would have been a formality.'

TMJ was born in Kentish Town, North London on 27th September 1905. His family were 'respectable, lower-middle class', father being an assistant bank manager whose clientele included members of the Guinness family. Comfortably off, but by no means affluent, they had made sacrifices in order that their only son, Thomas, received a good education which culminated in him obtaining his B.Sc. in Mechanical Engineering at Battersea Polytechnic. Incidentally, the 'Murray Jamieson' (un-hyphenated) is the joining by marriage of two families of Scottish origin in the nineteenth century. At the time he joined Austin, the family were living in Exeter Road, Southgate.

(In 1966, Bert had a spell working at the London office of the Ministry of Labour and it transpired that one of his colleagues actually lived next door to the Murray Jamiesons and had known 'Tom' throughout his formative years).

On reaching Longbridge, TMJ was introduced to the 'top brass' of the Design Department, most of whom had been at Austins since the early days. His reception was not exactly warm but on meeting the down-to earth types in 'Experimental', a quiet but noticeable air of anticipation prevailed amongst the racing personnel. Back to Bert:-

'As we got to know Jamieson, I could see it was not going to be an easy ride for him. For a start, the Design Department tried to impose conditions and exercise overall control. This situation was quite foreign to him as he had been accustomed to having a free hand and he certainly would not conform to the 9-5 theory in an environment where Timekeeping was regarded as sacrosanct as Ability. In fairness to the Old Man, he did sort that one out, making arrangements for a separate drawing office tucked away in the corner of Experimental and gave Jamieson permission to engage the services of two draughtsmen of TMJ's own choice. Sir Herbert also took financial responsibility for the Jamieson project.'

[Jamieson chose Tom Brown and Bill Appleby who were to learn a lot under TMJ's wing and both went onto successful careers in the industry. Later, a junior draughtsman, Albert Hitchman, was seconded to Jamieson and was largely responsible for the definitive body shape on the later Side-valve racers and subsequently that of the delectable Twin-cams. He too benefited greatly from Jamieson's influence and was to later return to Longbridge in a senior position.]

Bert continues:-

'Sir Herbert was still anxious to get ahead of MG in the battle for the fastest 750cc single-seater over one mile which was of considerable publicity value to the Company. It was decided that Chief Mechanic Len Brockas and I should be seconded to Murray Jamieson's control in the building of a streamliner to go for records. The idea was to use Jamieson's re-worked side-valve engine to which further modifications were made, with extensive bench testing. Eventually we wound up with a maximum output of 74.5bhp at 8,000rpm. Jamie had hoped to reach 80bhp which would have been feasible but his stress calculations indicated the need for a considerable re-design and this would have seriously delayed the project.'

TMJ sits in the newly completed Streamliner with the then-fashionable long tail fitted. Standing behind are Len Brockas, HLH and 'Redditch Ned' who crafted the elaborate bodywork. Just visible to the left of the screen is Bert's incomplete Ulster.

The chassis layout was similar to that employed on the 'Clogs', with a modified 'D' type axle-casing off-set to the left-hand side. The finished car, in retrospect, was far more elaborate than it needed to be but provided a wonderful 'showpiece' of the abilities of those involved, with the object of impressing on Austin and the pessimists at Longbridge just what Jamieson was capable of. The detailing was exquisitely executed by Brockas and Hadley, working closely to Jamieson's instructions and TMJ's ideas of airflow management were beautifully transformed into metal by one who sadly goes down in history merely as 'Redditch Ned'. Fortuitously, Jamieson designed both long and short tails from the outset and both were to be used.

Back to Bert (writing in 1985):-

'The car was a beautiful shape with a very low drag feature. The nose cone of the Austin bears a remarkable similarity to those on modern single-seaters. The underside was perfectly flat and very close to the ground. We realised even at this early stage, that in Jamieson we had a designer who was thinking accurately many years ahead of his time. It took us fourteen months to build the car, not bad when you consider the complications which Jamie had seen fit to include in the specification. It carried a battery and starter motor, horn (for signalling to the pit crew), cockpit control for the Luvax hydraulic dampers, every possible instrument including an aneroid barometer. Even the small steering wheel, which I made, was a one off. We worked very long hours, including weekends to get the job done. Eventually in August 1933, Jamie, Brockas and myself went to Montlhéry, the banked track near Paris, opened in 1924 and with a better surface than Brooklands. We were there for a total of nine weeks, based at the Hôtel de la Piste, opposite the garages built underneath the Grandstand straight.

Plenty to keep the driver occupied! The alloy dash panel and special 14" diameter steering wheel are both examples of Hadley craftsmanship.

Montlhéry autumn 1933. TMJ, LB and HLH in the pit area (note short tail fitted).

Over the years I became convinced that a string of mysterious happenings were in effect, acts of sabotage. The first thing to go wrong was the off-set rear axle. It was our custom to check each other's work, which ensured nothing was left undone, i.e. lock plates missing or wiring of parts where required. I had built the axle and finished the job with tightening and wiring the drain plug, which Len checked as per our system. The old sage in the Racing Department, Joe Hunt, used to say "A concealed mistake may cause a brave man to lose his life.", and he was so right. Anyway I think Jamie, who insisted he do the driving, took the Hour Record at 119mph when out dropped the axle drain plug, scrapping the special crown wheel and pinion. Prior to this he did have cause for alarm when a tyre tread flew off, smashing a fairing. We had made the mistake of running tyre pressures too low at 20 pounds per square inch [psi] – 38psi was the requirement on the steep Montlhéry banking. I got quite a lot of experience at this and offered to drive for serious but Jamie insisted that it would be his life at risk and no other's during the record attempts. We had a lot to learn but that drain-plug would not have dropped out unless it had been tampered with. It was a simple matter to slip the fairing off. When in position, the lower half of the diff-case was out of sight. Air stream was allowed over the top half. Jamieson was forced to return to Longbridge to personally supervise machining of new parts as there was no co-operation from the people concerned.

We had plenty to do while he was away, including sundry repairs to the bodywork, particularly problems with the long tail which kept fracturing its under-frame. Jamie's foresight in specifying a shorter alternative proved to correct, as not only did it not break up but improved the stability of the car at speed, as did removal of the front wheel discs. On his return, Jamie set up a number of records before one of the magnetos packed up, causing a power drop. Then a cylinder block cracked across the valve seats – to be a common problem. Whilst we were changing this, George Eyston's MG Midget, which was driven by the ex-jockey Albert Denly, was out smashing our records. Our garage was under the banking so we could time him as he thumped overhead – a bit depressing. It was obvious, to me at least, that Jamie was holding the car down on the banking. The presence of the rubber debris on the fairings and tail betrayed this fact. The Autodrome circuit consisted of two very steep banked corners joined by short straights, a total of 1.58 miles, plus a road circuit which extended into the countryside. Well, we worked very hard as Len and I realised that Jamieson's future depended on results. He was pleased with a maximum speed of 126mph which he reached on the level straight in front of the grandstand.

Jamieson obviously had difficulty on the banked turns, letting the car go as high as it wants to is the answer – easier said than done when learning as he was. First impressions, at a venue such as Montlhéry is being whirled around inside a bowl – this disappears with experience. The streamliner just failed to lap at 120mph. This was caused by Jamie "floating" his accelerator foot as he took to the banking and tending to hold the car down. Nevertheless it was a very brave attempt for a man with little or no experience.

Montlhéry 1933.
TMJ about to commence another test run in the Streamliner.

Apart from the MG contingent, more British personnel were present that late summer in 1933. The famous Brooklands driver John Cobb [who became another life-long friend of Hadley] had brought over the big Napier-Railton to attack the 24-hour record, the entire team having flown over to Paris, which was unusual at the time. Cobb, a fur broker by profession, was sharing the driving with Freddie Dixon, the gritty little ex-racing biker from Middlesbrough and I was to witness a hair raising accident. I seem to recall that the car had run all night and during the following day it started to rain. I was sitting on the low wall watching Dixon come off the banking to the straight in front of the grandstand. Running on the smooth "track" tyres, like most of us, the tail went down and he started to spin in great circles and I moved very smartly indeed. Freddie was going backwards at one hell of a lick when he went up the north banking. The wooden guard rail on the rim probably saved him from going over and he sheared about 100 feet off the fence before the Railton, still on its wheels, charged down to the deep sand on the infield, with a small drop off the concrete track. We ran over. Dixon was quite unhurt but shaken and obviously upset because he felt he had ruined the attempt.

Freddie was not of the usual public-school brigade, in fact he was a really hard man, short in stature [like me], enormously strong, a very good engineer and normally good humoured. I liked him, mind you, anyone who'd seen him hold up the front of one of his racing Rileys whilst the mechanics changed the wheels would think carefully before trying conclusion with him. Anyway, he struggled out of the Napier-Railton, muttered a string of dreadful Northern oaths and waddled off to the track restaurant where, I guarantee, I saw him thirty minutes later so full of brandy he was speechless. I never saw Fred drink before a race but he seemed to make up for it afterwards.

Jamieson set up a number of important records at Montlhéry but we still came away empty handed as George Eyston smashed our efforts with the MG within a few days. Nevertheless, much had been learned and Sir Herbert was pleased and readily agreed to a considerable racing car development programme for the years ahead.'

Apart from the exciting build-up prior to setting off for the Montlhéry Autodrome, it was Bert's first experience of visiting a foreign land. Not such a novelty for Len Brockas of course, who was quite familiar with Northern France and possibly Belgium too, having survived the perils and carnage of the Western Front, whilst serving in the Royal Artillery. It is also possible that TMJ had not been abroad before either. To keep costs down, the car, spares and equipment were driven down to the Autodrome, just 15 miles from Paris, in one of the converted Austin 20 flat-bed trucks used by the Racing Department at this time, with Brockas and Hadley sharing the driving. On reaching France, Jamieson had hired a Peugeot saloon which would be the 'hack' transport during their stay.

As this period stretched over two months, naturally the team became somewhat homesick. Jamie was about to become engaged to Sybil Burton, Len was of course married with two young daughters and Bert, in the parlance of the day, had been 'going steady' with Rose Stallard for several years on and off. As mentioned earlier, the team

Hôtel de la Piste.

were based at the Hôtel de la Piste right opposite the grandstand at the circuit. We have heard that George Eyston's MG contingent and John Cobb's party were also present during the Austin attempts, all billeted at the Hôtel, so it was quite a busy place particularly during periods of 'relaxation' after a hard day's testing. 'Le Patron' was very pro-British and enjoyed the company of his guests. One evening, after some wine had been consumed, he suddenly appeared with his prize possession, a Great War German machine gun, complete with tripod stand and a belt of ammunition. This he set up with great excitement on his part and pulled the trigger. To everyone's amazement the thing worked! The resulting volley of rounds peppered the wooden doors of the grandstand opposite. Luckily, being late in the day, the garages were empty of people and no damage was done to the vehicles inside. How the presence of bullet holes was explained the following day is not recorded.

The young Hadley, as we know, had a Kodak Brownie camera which luckily he had brought with him, as no official photographer was present for the record attempts, so snaps which survived are the work of Jamieson, Hadley or Brockas. It so happened that the hotel proprietor had a comely daughter who was the centre of attraction for the English guests. No photographic evidence of this 'Flower of France' has come to light, however Bert later wrote that despite the presence of all these frustrated racing folk, he finally 'made it' as he put it. He was always very competitive and could not resist a challenge! He had a rather nice leather-cased 1933 AA Motorist Diary, probably a Christmas present. There is but one entry, for January 1st – 'with Rosma'. However, in the memoranda section there are several intriguing items including the name 'Yvette Beliu' and 'Belin bien amie Birmingham vous Paris' both pencilled in a non-Hadley script.

The Streamliner in 'Experimental' with short tail offered up.
Note the 'foreigners' on the left and the general clutter.

6

HADLEY GETS HIS CHANCE (1934-36)

After returning from France with the Streamliner, Jamieson proceeded with the production of a conventionally-bodied single-seater using experience gained at Montlhéry, but still based on the production Austin Seven. The Streamliner made a couple of competition appearances including record attempts at Southport with Driscoll as the main driver, though the ongoing test work was entrusted to Hadley, he having also done this at Montlhéry. How frustrating for him as he had yet to convince Jamie he could do the job 'for real'. Later, Bert removed the engine and gearbox and the suitably spruced-up car was put on static display at the London showrooms for a time before being shown at selected Austin dealers around the country. Finally, according to Hadley, the car was systematically dismantled by himself and Len Brockas with usable parts incorporated into the second conventional race car. The beautifully crafted bodywork was not seen again, presumably scrapped.

The Streamliner ready for limited use in the UK.
(Left to right) Hadley, Brockas, TMJ and 'Redditch Ned'.

The winter of 1933-4 saw a return to a busy period of road-testing for Hadley and Goodacre, including considerable mileages in the prototype Sports 65 and 75 two-seaters. Bert had fond memories of a later 75/Speedy, *'a nice little car'*, which was retained by the Company until 1939. Various engines were tried in this car including an un-blown 'Grasshopper' unit. Registered AOG 278, it happily survives within The Pre-War Austin Seven Club.

Bert – about to test the Streamliner in 1934.
Note the mandatory Brooklands 'fish-tail' now fitted.

What with the busy racing season, often unsociable working hours including many weekends and days away up in North Wales, Bert did not have much time for a social life, but whenever they could he and Rose Stallard would spend time together though any thoughts of 'settling down' were on indefinite hold as Bert still had his sights firmly set of achieving his burning desire to race. Rose meanwhile worked in various shops around the Kings Heath area including a later spell running a newsagents.

Bert continued to live with Herbert and Lydia at Twyning Road Stirchley. Herbert was about to relinquish his Secretaryship of the local Workers' Union branch which by now was incorporated into the burgeoning Transport and General Workers' Union (T&GWU), led by their ambitious National Secretary, a former West-Country labourer who a couple of years later would enter Parliament as Ernest Bevin M.P.

During the Second World War, Churchill made Bevin Minister of Labour and he would, in effect become Bert's ultimate 'boss' when he left 'The Austin' to join the Ministry in 1941. Post-war, Bevin would achieve further fame as Britain's Foreign Secretary in the Clement Attlee Labour government.

Herbert Charles Hadley received public acclaim, at least within the Trade Union movement, for his 'twenty-four years of service to the Working Man'. At a widely-reported ceremony at The Three Horseshoes in Stirchley, Bevin presented Herbert with an inscribed mantle clock and a copy of a Trades Union Congress (TUC) publication, commemorating the Centenary of the Tolpuddle Martyrs (1834). This fully describes the chain of events which led to the trial and subsequent deportation to the Colonies of a group of honest agricultural

Herbert Charles Hadley receives his Retirement Clock from the Union's General Secretary Ernest Bevin at 'The Three Horseshoes' Stirchley.

workers who were merely asking for a fair living wage. They were comprehensively 'stitched up' by a corrupt legal system before eventually being pardoned after further years of hardship abroad. It is a fascinating and thought-provoking read. Herbert's copy survives and it is inscribed thus – 'To Bro [Brother] Hadley – With Gratitude and Affection for a Lifetime of Devoted Service. Ernest Bevin Dec 9 1934'.

Almost as a footnote, the press report concluded with the news that Mrs Hadley 'for all her years of support' was presented with – an umbrella. One can but wonder what the sharp-tongued Lydia had to say about that......

Also around this time, Herbert Hadley was about to retire from Cadbury Brothers. We know he received a silver presentation 'after 31 years service' which suggests he ceased full-time work around the age of 59. Whether this was on health grounds is not known. In fact he would survive until 1951, just one day short of his 75th birthday.

With the new Jamieson-designed single-seaters under way, initially to be driven by Pat Driscoll, Austins' leading hired driver, TMJ was also fully occupied with drafting out his ideas for a radically new design of a race car which he considered could rival anything other teams could offer, including the Continentals, particularly in the popular 1500cc 'Voiturette' class.

Working almost alone, with only those closest to him in the know, Jamieson produced outline drawings for a vehicle light-years ahead of anything currently available. Consider this:- a part monocoque chassis with independent front and rear suspension, a semi-reclined driving position, ahead of a mid-mounted all-aluminium V-8 engine with twin over head camshafts per bank. There was also provision for two-stage supercharging and a 5-speed transaxle transmission capable of being easily changed to suit different conditions. To further impress Sir Herbert, TMJ commissioned a quarter-scale wooden mock-up which showed just how low and sleek the finished vehicle could appear, with fully-ducted air intake as on the Streamliner AND adjustable aerofoils! (Jamieson had been working on a similar line to Dr. Ferdinand Porsche at about the same time, though quite independently of course. Porsche's Auto-Union P-Wagen, a less sophisticated but monster 6 litre rear-engined device was announced in early 1934.)

TMJ confidently unveiled his 'Voiturette' concept to Sir Herbert Austin. Imagine Jamieson's utter dismay when his employer rejected it out of hand, saying it was far too radical and bore no relationship to anything Austins had in production. What he wanted was a single-seater that the public could recognise as an 'Austin'. Sir Herbert still wanted to concentrate on Class H (up to 750cc) and insisted that the 7hp suspension layout of transverse front and quarter-elliptic rear leaf springs be retained. Apart from this, he would have a free hand!

Disappointed, Jamieson nevertheless buckled down to his new remit and with assistance from draughtsman Tom Brown who, not always seeing eye to eye with Jamieson, would eventually leave the project and Bill Appleby, penned a delectable front-engined single-seater, using in effect half of the proposed V-8, mated to a virtually standard four-speed A7 gearbox. As mentioned earlier, Albert Hitchman came into the design team to replace Brown. The details of TMJ's design are well-known but it is worth recording his mixture of simple and complex designs working hand in hand. For instance, the chassis consisted of two deep side members and two end pieces, either folded or hand-shaped into simple channel sections bolted together at each corner. This very basic frame is transformed into a torsionally rigid structure by a series of cast alloy cross-members plus the crankcase itself, all of which have secondary duties carrying other components. The engine of course, is something else and the surviving sectioned drawing of TMJ's masterpiece is worthy of detailed study.

Initial plans were for the manufacture of six sets of parts although whether it was ever intended to build such a quantity of completed cars is not known. Additionally, Jamieson drafted out plans for two-stage supercharging and a limited-slip differential, though none were produced. He also wanted to use hydraulic brakes, but Austins were firmly committed to rods and cables.

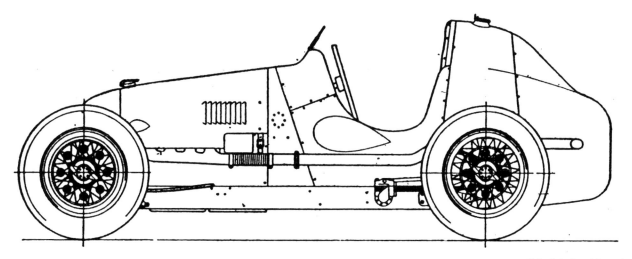

(Model Car News.)

Of course, the Austin Motor Company's Film Unit, already in the forefront amongst the motor manufacturers in using the cinema as a publicity tool, took the opportunity to record the production and assembly of the first of the three Twin-cam single-seaters. All these pre-war films are delightfully 'period' and none more so than 'The Pace That Thrills', a full 12 minutes worth of delight to the Austin racing enthusiast. Various key members of the Experimental Department feature in the film, mostly wearing clean overalls or warehouse coats, including a brief glimpse or two of Bert Hadley sporting at one stage an outsize flat cap.

As with all his creations, Jamieson insisted on doing the initial track testing of the first Twin-cam himself though Bert would often do the routine stuff when the regular drivers were not available, all adding to his experience and hopefully increasing his chances for an actual 'drive'. The history of the Jamieson single-seaters and both Side-valve and later Twin-cam in competition has been well documented elsewhere and it is not proposed to repeat it in full detail here, except where Hadley is involved.

As we have heard, Bert was a car-owner from an early age. After the two open Swallow A7s, he used several other Sevens on a regular basis. His father also continued with 'baby' Austins, buying an RN saloon in late 1931. A list of Austins with which Bert and the family owned or had associations with is appended elsewhere in the hope that there may be a survivor or two. So far nothing has turned up, but………

Rosma enjoys an outing in North Wales with Bert and his Ulster.

Those 'beguiling brown eyes'!

Forever ferreting about in the vast Longbridge complex, Bert came across an exciting discovery – an incomplete but unused EA Sports Two-Seater – an 'Ulster'. Possibly the last one ever to leave the Works, Bert, barely out of his apprenticeship, managed to blag his way into purchasing the dust-covered 'surplus' vehicle for a nominal sum, then set about replacing the missing parts, which may have included the engine. Painted a deep red, it soon sported a number of non-standard features such as a bigger bore exhaust system of which Bert was *very proud* and a handmade stone guard. According to Bert it was a production 'blown' Ulster, though the photographs show it with a starting handle. No matter, it was finally registered during 1933 as OV9386 - where are you now?

HLH wasted no time in taking Rose out for a ride - some charming photos survive of a picnic in Wales. Bert presumably sold it at a good profit after a while but the mystery remains, why did the factory not complete the car and get it sold whilst it was still 'new'?

Although Bert had gained useful experience as a riding mechanic with both Gunnar Poppe and Charles Goodacre and with some routine test work under his belt, his chances of getting a competitive drive seemed somewhat remote. He realised that, in the main, motor racing was a rich man's privilege. People who could buy their own cars and afford to maintain them properly stood a chance of some success providing of course if they could drive! Hadley greatly admired those drivers who showed not just bravery but skill also. However he had little time for those who appeared to have more money than sense.

Most works teams had a policy of inviting drivers to appear on a who-you-know basis. Bert accepted this as a fact of life and found he got on with most of the people recruited by Austin, a number becoming life-long friends. One of these was Leonard Patrick Driscoll, born in Middlesex of Irish parents in 1900 and trained as an engineer. Having cut his teeth (so to speak) on racing Norton motorcycles at Brooklands and elsewhere, he went onto Lea-Francis motor cars which he modified himself into successful and competitive machines before being 'retained' by Austins.

HLH with the first Jamieson circuit car in front of Robin Jackson's engine-tuning establishment.

At a Brooklands meeting in 1932 'Pat' was accompanied by a young man named Jack Emmott, obviously 'well-heeled' but very keen to lend a hand at anything which impressed Hadley. His father, 'Willie' Emmott had co-founded the very successful Automotive Products Group, (Lockheed brakes, Borg & Beck clutches and Thompson steering joints) and was also a racing enthusiast. Jack was not a driver but very much a background supporter of a number of motor racing projects. He and his wife Mary were to be great friends of the Hadleys. Bert felt, given the chance, he could perform as well as any of the current Works drivers.

After the 'Streamliner' was eventually dismantled, two conventionally-bodied single-seater cars were put in hand, the first one using the engine and some other parts taken from the Montlhéry car. Further improvements were incorporated, but the chassis still remained very much like the production Austin Sevens.

1934. Brooklands.
The first Jamieson circuit car in its original form.

Bert recalled:

'Early testing on the Mountain Circuit at the [Brooklands] Track revealed a serious front-end "kick" when cornering. Jamie effectively cured this by creating limited rolling movement in the newly-introduced tubular front axle, close to the left-hand stub-axle. However, the basic chassis layout cramped the potential of a vastly-improved side-valve engine and the excellent 4-speed gearbox.'

The first of the Jamieson single seaters in the cramped confines of AMCo's Brooklands facility.

Sir Herbert brought a second 'outsider' into his squad of drivers, another ex-biker and a very successful one too. Charles Joseph Pearson Dodson was a Lancastrian, born in Didsbury in 1901. He had won several Senior T.T. races on the Isle of Man and had raced successfully on the continent. Unlike Driscoll, who was inclined to make a drama out of every situation, Dodson was a small, quiet individual who in Bert's words *just got on with it'*. He and 'Doddy' got on particularly well and together they would eventually become the main race drivers for the 1938 season. They also co-drove at Le Mans together and elsewhere. Dodson had an engineering 'day job' outside of motor sport which he held until retirement. However, he always retained his love of motorcycles which sadly came to and end when he lost control whilst demonstrating one of his old racing machines at a Brands Hatch Vintage Motor Cycle Club (VMCC) meeting in 1983.

Bert continues:

'Just reverting to the side-valve engines, what Jamieson had achieved with them made a massive jump from 56bhp @ about 6,000rpm for the Clog/Duck engines to 74.5bhp @ 8,000rpm. He said that was it. No further development of note was possible. What we did eventually achieve was this power output allied to a reasonable standard of reliability. The new wedge shaped cylinder head with open water passages across each cylinder was a great improvement on the Austin design and this was held down by no fewer than 32 studs to a vastly stronger cylinder block. In spite of all the cooling effort however, the solid bridge in the cylinder block between the valves created a problem. We did have cylinder block breakages at this point, the effect of course putting one cylinder out of action. The trouble did not appear during extensive test bed running, nor did it appear during considerable mileage at Montlhéry. Mind you, we had plenty of other problems. The first block to break was at the Southport Speed Week. It was obvious that everything depended on really accurate fuel mixture setting which seemed to vary according to air temperature. Pat Driscoll drove the car and after repairs, put up a very creditable 122.74 mph for the flying kilometre. There was a prepared block at the Works, but of course when Jamie requested its transport to Southport it was not sent. Instead a second block on which very little preparation had been done was sent to us. That was the standard of co-operation afforded Jamieson even at that early stage. The 32 holes were drilled but not tapped. Ports were rough. It meant in addition to tapping the holes, all the other bits, valve guides, tappet guides etc had to be transferred. It was fortunate that the tap sizes were in our spares and all the other necessary tools including valve seat cutters etc. We worked two days and two nights. I did all the work on the block while Len relined the clutch. Poor Jamie was very upset by the Longbridge treatment which made us all the more determined to overcome our difficulties. Murray Jamieson was an academic. He lacked that little toughness needed to blast the opposition. Bill Sewell, a nice pleasant chap, was supposed to be our Team Manager for this event. He was close to the Old Man, and his duties included writing speeches. He was an ex-captain in the Border Regiment and of considerable military bearing. However he seemed to be scared of the Experimental Shop management. I told him to contact the Old Man and get them sorted out. He didn't arise to that and I became more and more fed up and angry.

We were using the garage of a man named Stephenson in Southport who had a quick Ulster and did well in racing on the Sands. A very helpful man who was very amused at my increasing belligerence. I finally exploded early one morning when still at work. The telephone rang. It was Sir Herbert Austin as he was then. Bill Sewell answered the telephone. When he knew who was speaking, he flew to attention like a Panzer corporal, allaying the Old Man's fears and rounding it off with "We have worked all night Sir Herbert". I was working close to him and I said, "You bloody liar. You have been asleep all night". This was true. Bill had been snoring his head off comfortably housed on a pile of clean sacks. The Boss must have heard me, and Bill spent some time trying to explain. We all had a good laugh about it and there were no hard feelings from Bill Sewell. He thought I was a firebrand, but we always got on well together. Southport was a success story after all the problems and very hard work. The long tail sagged again, as it had done in Montlhéry. A much shorter version was fitted after Southport as we prepared to run at Brooklands. This improved the steering, lessening the effect of side winds. Brooklands was noted for this, particularly when coming out from behind Members Hill on the Home Banking. The effect at that point could be very exciting. The Streamliner in the hands of Pat Driscoll lapped the Outer Circuit at around 114mph. We did a lot of test work with the car which was a real handful on the Byfleet Banking due to the twisting of the unsuitable chassis frame. We must have entered at least one race, but I cannot recall the degree of success. At that point, a decision was made to build a single seater with the Streamliner's engine, suitable for Brooklands and the road circuits.

(Ferret Fotographic)

AMCo's photographer Ron Beach shot this, the first Twin-cam completed, looking rather oil stained and grubby. Beyond the period 'airbrushing' is a fascinating glimpse of Experimental's cloakroom facilities.

In retrospect, it would possibly have been more efficient to have gone ahead with the Twin-cam car, thereby disregarding the fill-in role of the Side-valve single seater. Obviously if Sir Herbert had agreed to a new "proper" chassis with stiffened steering bulkhead and lowered centre line prop shaft thereby eliminating the wind-up problems of the off-set differential idea, then I think the Side-valve car would have had a longer life and a very much improved performance. At least he agreed to larger brakes, still cable operated (he was opposed to hydraulics) and he agreed to re-arrangement of the transverse front suspension, the leaf spring being located beneath a new tubular axle. The king-pin and hub assembly was new and much stronger. Centre locking wire wheels were used. The friction type dampers were used fore and aft, of Jamieson design with multi discs. We used this type of damper on the Twin-cam too. They were infinitely adjustable and superior to any hydraulic dampers of the period.

We took the first Side-valve single seater to Brooklands for testing on what was known as the Mountain Circuit. Driscoll was nominated to drive this car in competition and I was told to do what was known as 'running in', which meant restricted rpm. We did some tests with a fully locked differential which could have proved disastrous as Driscoll spun like a top at the hairpin bend known as the Fork. I found the car tried to go straight on at the uphill turn on what was known as the Members Banking where one climbed high for the swoop down to the Fork. I had visions of taking off and finishing up at Longbridge. That idea was dropped smartly. Pat Driscoll found that the front end juddered alarmingly on braking and negotiating the Fork hairpin. A second Side-valve car was in process of building at the Works by this time. Jamieson re-designed the front axle tube for both cars, introducing an arrangement which allowed slight rotational movement. The juddering was eliminated and he used the same method on the subsequent Twin-cam cars. They, of course, had the advantage of a new chassis. However, that front axle modification was regarded essential for both types.

In terms of problems with the Side-valve cars, I have mentioned the cylinder block breakages. This was eliminated when we changed to the Shell Mercedes fuel later on. A problem which we didn't really solve, principally because interest waned when the Twin-cam cars appeared, was magneto failure.

The engine had dual ignition with two magnetos, - Scintilla or sometimes Marelli. The nearside mag was located under the exhaust manifold where a Cozette supercharger can be found on the old Ulster engine. An asbestos filled shield was fitted to the underside of the manifold, but this was insufficient to preserve the magneto from breakdown. The problem could have been overcome in a number of ways, but the overall failure of these two cars was obviously of limited duration, so Jamieson simply impressed Scintilla sufficiently for them to increase the insulation strength and to re-design the distributor blocks where the heat created shrinkages and consequent breakdowns. Of course, we didn't get magneto problems at hill climbs and sprints. Long distance races sometimes produced magneto trouble. I can recall how pleased we were when Kay Petre managed thirty laps on the Outer Circuit at Brooklands as the last car in the team, to enable us to win the International Relay Race in 1937. Dual ignition was worthwhile as switching off the problem magneto dropped 550rpm.

Winter 1935 at Donington. A well wrapped TMJ takes the first Twin-cam out for a test drive.

One day in 1935 I was at Brooklands with Jamieson, Dodson and Len Brockas. We were doing some work with one of the Side-valve cars. Suddenly, Jamie said "Take it for a few laps round the circuit, Bert, and see what you can do without cracking it." We were using the Mountain Circuit. I remembered saying "With a view to what?" and Driscoll held the 750cc lap record for the Mountain by this time. Maybe still does, as I did not make an official attempt with the Side-valve, or for that matter, the Twin-cam car later. I cannot recall why this is so - possibly too busy with our limited resources elsewhere I suppose.

I borrowed Dodson's helmet and goggles and did two slow laps to get the feel of things at the Fork turn and also the bend to the Members' Banking. I had no previous experience of the Mountain at this time. On my third lap I opened up and it seems I broke Pat's record by a considerable margin. On my fifth lap I improved on this time. I did not have the impression of absolute maximum, but unfortunately, I was called in before reaching that stage. Jamie said "Did you like it?" and wandered off before I could answer him. When we went to the Club House, my mind was put at rest when Jamie told me the news. Charlie Dodson was pleased, which was nice when he added "I couldn't beat that."

When the first two Twin-cam cars appeared in 1936, I found myself entered with the Side-valve car in one of the Mountain races. Pat was down to drive the Twin-cam in the same race and Dodson was entered with the second Twin-cam on the Outer Circuit. What a day for mixed fortunes and catastrophe for Austins! In my race I was given four seconds start from Pat Driscoll. In the heat of the moment, I completely forgot that first gear was jumping out and must be held in. I had both hands on the wheel and, of course, back it went into neutral. I lost a cylinder momentarily too, while sorting things out. The side-valve engine had dual ignition i.e. two magnetos and eight plugs. Pat steamed past, giving me the rude version of the 'V' sign as he did so, prematurely as it happened. I reached the turn to the Members' Banking on full power and what did I find? – Pat Driscoll coming back towards me having spun! To avoid a major disaster I was forced to climb above him in what was rather a close call. Thereafter I went flat out and, negotiating the Fork for the first time, I overdid it a bit, slid right across the turn and made light contact with the formidable-looking guard rail. Fortunately no damage. That was my only mistake, that stupid mistake, but for which I could have won the race. Pat provided some technical reasons for his spin but I thought it prudent not to get too involved in the subsequent discussion!

(via Brooklands Society)

18th April 1936. Brooklands. HLH's first race for Austins. Getting the feel of things 'new boy' Bert Hadley in the white Side-valve 'Seven' is about to pass the stripped sports Frazer Nash-BMW of H.J.Adlington.

More drama came. While circulating the paddock with the Twin-cam for his Outer Circuit race, Dodson managed to entangle the hub cap of the near-side rear wheel with one of the steel stanchions supporting the covered car stalls. The result was horrific. The light-alloy rear axle centre case was ripped open when the steel side tube and half-shaft was forced rearwards. This in turn wrecked the fuel tank. It was bad luck for Dodson, but my sympathy went to Murray Jamieson who had pinned so much on the results of this meeting.

Back at the Works the next day, I was summoned to the Old Man's office shortly after 9am. I thought, he is going to complement me on gaining second place. To say I was naïve is an understatement of the reception which awaited me! It seemed that all other relevant members of the Austin team had busied themselves elsewhere that morning. For the sake of propriety, I will exclude Lord Austin's opening remarks. In front of him was the morning edition of the Birmingham Post and on the front page was a large photograph of the Driscoll/Hadley avoidance incident. He raved about that and became almost incoherent about the Dodson disaster. He mentioned my fluffed start but fortunately seemed to have missed my slide and near thing at the Fork. I could understand his annoyance, it had been a real catastrophe, but I didn't see why I should take the can back for other people's failures.

Finally I lost my temper and, I suppose with typical Brummie forthrightness, told him all the so-and-so smoke didn't go up his chimneys and I walked out. I collected my coat, got in my Austin Seven and drove home. The clock outside Lord Austin's office showed 10.30am. I considered I had sacked myself. Next day Charles Goodacre appeared at Twyning Road, saying "The Old man wants to see you". I said "I have finished." and told him what had happened. He said "The Old Man doesn't seem to think so." After thinking about it I went to the Works and straight to his office, to be greeted by questions on the future of the new Twin-cam cars. He made it clear that he was now in possession of all the facts about the Brooklands meeting. The Old Man asked, with a rare twinkle in his eyes, whether everything was as it should be with me. I saw no point in digging things up and said "Yes." He treated me in a kindly manner, and I was only too pleased to find that normal relations were resumed.

The blow-up proved one thing to me – that Lord Austin did not react favourably to toadyism. Later on I witnessed several examples where members of management prone to servility got a real rocket for their performances. Being a witness, albeit an unwilling one, didn't do me much good. The recipients were the sort who bided their time, or laid in wait, so to speak. I would be dubbed as "well in". I suppose it was amusing at the time but I felt that being an unfortunate witness did not augur well for my future.

It is well-known, of course, that the people in charge of Brooklands encouraged a system of the "right crowd and no crowding". I never had reason to believe that a feeling of snobbishness existed. Brooklands did have its own atmosphere and the BARC quite regularly stamped hard on any cases of rough driving. Scrutineering too was thorough, which eliminated cases of weird and dangerous motor cars. We at Austins always looked forward with pleasure to race meetings at Brooklands. The Paddock, I was led to understand, had a similar environment to that found at a horse racing venue and the line of bookmakers present on race days supported that view. "Long Tom" was one bookie I can recall. At one meeting he quoted 16 to 1 against the Austins. I think it was the International Relay Race of 1937. This seemed too good to be true. One of our mechanics removed his overalls and placed a tenner for me. We won that race.'

1936 Brooklands.
Thomas Murray Jamieson, just out of his twenties, with the first Twin-cam.

After the satisfaction and excitement of finishing his first motor race in April 1936, Bert had to play a waiting game before his next chance came. The month of May saw the JCC (Junior Car Club) International Trophy Race. All three T/C (Twin-cam) cars were now ready and entered for Driscoll, Dodson and Goodacre. Bert was the nominated reserve driver for all three. In the event they all started as intended but were to retire with various problems, the most serious being a connecting-rod failure on Driscoll's car.

Bert also missed out on the next Shelsley meeting. The Twin-cams were entered with the usual line-up and the two Side-valves were driven by guest drivers, Sammy Davis and the German Walter Bäumer, with HLH acting as his 'nurse-maid'. Bäumer actually established a new class record and made second fastest time of the day (FTD) to Fane in a Frazer Nash. Another mixed public appearance by Sir Herbert's team. (Austin was about to be ennobled as Daron Austin of Longbridge). June saw the Austin team out in force for the County Down Trophy Race, 30 laps on a country Northern Ireland circuit of 3.8 miles. Hadley was part of the support staff once again. All three Twin-cams retired suffering various mechanical maladies, but not before Dodson created a new lap record whilst ahead on handicap, only for a piston to fail, probably due to mixture problems which were to prove a regular occurrence. Another disappointing result, though the potential was certainly beginning to show.

After Bert's eventful race debut in 1936 and with all three Twin-cams up and running, the winter was taken up with periods of sustained testing at Donington Park, the Leicestershire circuit being handily placed to Longbridge. In addition to this, Fred Craner, the Derby garage owner who was now running the circuit, had arranged for some outbuildings adjacent to Coppice Farm (now the present-day Circuit Office) to be converted into a number of lock-up workshops. Situated on the inside of Coppice Corner, these basic buildings were promptly leased by Austins and would prove very useful.

Whilst the chance of a 'reserve' drive in one of the Twin-cams was still in the offering, Bert reckoned a Side-valve could obtain a better handicap plus reliability of the Twin-cams was still in doubt. The long-term aim was to win the prestigious Nuffield Trophy Race in the following July. Jamieson agreed to Bert spending considerable time preparing 'his' Side-valve for the purpose. January testing was enlivened by the crankshaft breaking whilst flat-out around Coppice, the resulting lock-up causing Hadley to spin wildly into the outfield, fortunately without further mishap. Another lucky escape!

Having consequently rebuilt the engine, plus the gearbox and back axle and further concentrated testing, HLH was looking forward to the race with keen anticipation. Imagine his chagrin to be told in the run-up to the event that the well-known Siamese driver Prince Birabongse ('B. Bira') was to have a guest drive in 'his' car. To rub it in, the car was to be repainted and trimmed in Bira's pale blue colours, driving position adjusted as necessary and furthermore H.L. Hadley was to provide His Serene Highness with any help and advice required. The deal was apparently arranged by Bira's cousin Prince Chula who acted as his manager. At the time, Bert thought that Bira must have known he'd 'pinched' his drive, but in fact this turned out to be untrue. Bert's faith in Austin as a firm but fair man took a severe knock as he considered he'd been deprived of a glorious opportunity to do something worthwhile, both for the Company and himself.

(John Skeavington)
Sans Serif: The Art Deco 'A' used on the wheel spinners of the Jamieson single seaters and embroidered in green on the mechanics' overalls.

He could not really blame the Siamese, but as he later wrote:-

'Here was a man with three racing cars, two ERAs and a 2.9 litre Maserati, all capable of winning this particular race, but preferred, as I saw it, in influencing Lord Austin into a publicity exercise. Jamieson had not agreed with the Old Man's decision and was quick to point out what had been lost, after the race. It was disheartening for him as all three Twin-cams were beset with further troubles.

4th July 1936. Donington Park Nuffield Trophy.
Prince Birabongse asks Bert for advice on how to drive the Side-valve.
Dennis Buckley (left rear) and Bill Sewell (wearing cap) listen intently.

Before the race, I had the job of instructing Bira, including how to switch off the nearside magneto in the event of misfiring. Well, it happened in the race and he got it wrong. Out of Bira's pit for just a few moments, I returned to see his own mechanics changing all the plugs, which was quite unnecessary and I blew my top at them but by then the time had been wasted. I think the engine was just a "noise" as far as he was concerned. Then the exhaust pipe joint slipped. As it happened it was the only part I had not assembled, our "pipe king" Bill Martin did the job. Of course, Lord Austin seemed to infer that I should have seen it. Bira had made a fuss because the cockpit became hot. I told Austin that, if I had driven the car, we could have won the race.

Now I suppose we could bathe in a little adverse publicity. When Lord Austin got over the shock of that and I recovered from the knowledge that my outburst had not caused premature retirement, he grunted what appeared to be agreement and that was the end of it.

A curious revelation came about when I discovered a pair of expensive goggles belonging to Bira lying in a pool of oil on the cockpit floor. I washed them in petrol and re-assembled them and in spite of furious polishing I couldn't see a thing through them. Then the penny dropped – the lenses were optical. Almost at the same time the blue Bentley turned up [this was at the Works] and Chula and Bira appeared in a great hurry. They asked about the goggles "Had I seen them?" "Yes," I said "I have fixed them, but I find they are no good for me." Looks of consternation, so I said I knew the problem but be assured the information will not get past me. I didn't mention it even to my closest friends. It is all history now so it doesn't matter. Bira was obviously very short sighted. The medical people must have known, so why did he not wear spectacles when he used a crash hat and a visor in the rain, even in the poorest light conditions?

It was a bad time for me and I found it difficult to keep calm when talking to Lord Austin. What really hurt was the fact that he too had started from the bottom of the ladder so to speak and I felt he should have recognised where I stood. In any case, everybody else concerned, including Jamieson, took the view that I would win and Bira would most likely fail as he did not understand the peculiarities of the car. That in fact is what happened. One of my colleagues, I think it was Charlie Dodson, said perhaps the old boy has ideas of winding up in a palace in Bangkok? Anyway, I did have reason to believe that Lord Austin was subject to the sort of human frailties that I as a young man was surprised to find in a leader of industry. Well, my black mood did not last long and I have to say that after the Bira episode he gave me lots of support right up to the outbreak of war in September 1939.

As for the Side-valve, it was a delightful little car and certainly gave a great improvement on any earlier Austin racing car. It was limited by too-flexible a chassis, but one learned to live with that. The Side-valve was equally at home on the Mountain Circuit at Brooklands as it was at Donington Park and elsewhere. I have often been asked how the Side-valve compared with the Twin-cam. Well, it was like getting out of something which, on full noise required maximum concentration, particularly in corners, to a single-seater which by comparison had no vices and seemed to steer itself. Of course, one had to recognise limits as with any single-seater.

A lot has been written about how many Side-valve [Jamieson] single-seaters were built. The true answer to that question is THREE (a) The white Streamliner (b) Two subsequent road circuit cars. Confusion may have arisen as a result of a series of appearance modification of the two cars.

(Left) TMJ in the newly completed Streamliner at Longbridge September 1933.
(Right) Bert – 'cab-happy' in the first Jamieson Side-valve outside the 'tuning village', Brooklands 1934. The engine and some running gear from the Streamliner were used in its construction.

(Left) Hadley and Jamieson watch Walter Bäumer off the line at Shelsley Walsh 1936. Other Austin personnel in the background. This is the 'Phase 2' look with the bird-cage grill and higher tail.
(Right) 3rd July 1939 Shelsley Walsh. Journalist Tommy Wisdom guest-driving in the surviving Side-valve in its final 'sprint' form.

The first example was untidy – we knew that. What followed was a smoothing process. Then there was the problem of the extra filler caps. Photographs appear showing filler caps sprouting fore and aft, giving rise to the belief that a whole series of Side-valve cars were built. This untidy appearance (and the bought-out caps were dreadful) appeared when two fuel tanks were fitted for long distance races. In fact the first, or No.2, Side-valve had two fuel tanks as Jamieson intended to use the car for long distance races from the start. For short races, hill climbs and speed trials the tanks were removed and a sprint tank was fitted and the holes were filled in. I drove my Side-valve in sprint appearance. The body is detachable and I used a light gauge shell with one coat of paint. As time went on it became the custom to spray paint on paint. Out of curiosity, I had the body shell weighed as it seemed heavy, then the paint shop removed all paint and the weight saving was remarkable.

The cars did not always conform to the event in terms of tanks. Bäumer for example drove a Side-valve at Shelsley sprouting filler caps. So did Driscoll. All a bit confusing I suppose, but rest assured, only two cars for road circuits etc were built. I can recall a spare engine and gearbox early in the process. This was loaned to Alec Issigonis and was the first engine he used in his Lightweight Special. Later on he used other engines. I was at Shelsley about three years ago when I met Mrs. Dowson, widow of George Dowson, the co-builder of the Lightweight [Special] with Alec. She was with her son Geoffrey who competes at Shelsley. It suddenly occurred to me that our engine did not return to Longbridge when Alec had finished with it. I mentioned this to Geoffrey Dowson and much to my astonishment he said a friend had just completed a re-build of the engine in Jersey.

Looking back, one can say that the Side-valve car provided a worthwhile stepping stone in the development while awaiting the building of the Twin-cam and it certainly provided a mobile test bed for Jamieson's improved design of what had gone before. Austins had certainly reached a point in their racing engine version where further improvement was beyond their thinking. It was not an easy road for Jamieson and it is obvious that had he been given a clear, unfettered path, the results would have been outstanding, but then it's not a perfect world. The results were good in spite of all the problems.'

Bert's next competition drive was at the West Country speed venue of Backwell Hill in late July. Often misquoted as 'Blackwell', this was a picturesque though infrequently used estate road bordered by large trees. A little known factor was that the owner would not allow the usual two practice runs to take place, a situation which probably had a bearing of what was to come.

Pat Driscoll (LPD) was to use the meeting to demonstrate the latest Austin racing car to the spectating public. Bert was the only official Works entry, driving a Side-valve. Despite a wet and slippery track, Hadley managed 2nd place to an MG in the Racing Car Class. Having run before Driscoll's demonstration run, he was parked up at the top of the hill so was not a witness to what befell his team mate. It was intended that Driscoll's drive was for publicity purposes only, with directions from Jamieson to take things easy. As was often the case, LPD had other ideas, with disastrous results. Once the news reached Longbridge, the rumour-mongers had a field day, with suggestions that a (Murray Jamieson designed) steering joint had failed.

Here's the Hadley version:

'We had some twin rear wheels. They used 5.25 x 16" tyres. The hubs were not offset. They had a wide space between them. One can imagine the increase in the rear track. I tried these wheels on our near circular track at the Works and I didn't like them. I told Jamieson so. I said they would only be safe in a straight line. Dodson and Driscoll did use them, I think at Madresfield Speed Trials which was a straight run. I used the Side-valve using single wheels. We won the team prize, and as I recall the OHC cars were only fractionally faster. It was a very wet day and the Twin-cam cars looked decidedly dicey. I thought that their tyre pressures were also much too low.

25th July 1936. Backwell Hill Climb.
Bert achieved 2nd in Class in his Side-valve, now re-painted in green.

When we went to Backwell, Pat again ran on the twins and low pressures. The whole thing was a ghastly mistake. Pat, unfortunately tried to put on a big show when really it was not on. It was a dangerous hill in the wet in any case, with overhanging trees dropping whatever they drop and adding to the slippery conditions. There was a longish left-hander where Pat lost it. The car just glided off and hit a tree. He was not wearing his crash helmet (nor did I for that matter) and he struck the tree, causing a depressed fracture on the right forehead.

After the event, I went with Jamieson to the hospital where I saw the injury as Pat was waiting for surgery. Murray Jamieson was a brilliant designer and a wonderful colleague. Unfortunately, he was not the type of man, up to that point who could give orders or put the boot in when he met resistance. As it was, Pat and others tended to push their own ideas, often in defiance of his instructions. The trouble started at the onset when Jamieson joined the Company in 1932. Had Lord Austin outlined Jamieson's terms of reference to everybody things would have been much better. I have always believed too that control and directions should have been essentially in the hands of Arthur Waite, who after all, had started the competition activity in 1923. Lord Austin seemed to hang onto control, but how could he do that effectively and know everything which went on behind the scenes, while discharging so many other duties?

I drove to the hospital in Bristol, using Pat's blue Buick which I intended to return to the Driscolls' London home. Jamieson said he would stay overnight with Pat and would I visit Lord Austin the following morning, which was a Sunday, and explain what had happened? I didn't really relish the job, but agreed to do so. I met Lord Austin at Lickey Grange and outlined what had happened. His first reaction was to talk of stopping the job. I said we had to expect accidents to happen in motor racing though they could be minimised with careful preparation. He asked if anything broke on the car and if not why did Driscoll crash? To that I said that I had just left the factory where I had a second and closer look at the car on my own. In spite of all the damage, bent chassis and steering arms etc. the movement between the steering wheel and front wheels was still there. All the ball ends were intact and I told him I was sure the low pressure twins were to blame.

Incidentally, I have seen photographs at Backwell showing the car both with twin wheels and single after the crash. The explanation for that is the twins were removed to facilitate loading into the covered trailer which we used that weekend. I then suggested to Lord Austin that he would perhaps like to look at the car himself to corroborate what I had told him. He said he would do that. I spent quite a long time with him that Sunday morning during which time he telephoned the hospital in Bristol to learn that surgery had been successfully carried out and Pat was comfortable. That information obviously pleased him.

Looking back, I suppose I should have voiced my knowledge of the campaign to discredit Murray Jamieson which I knew was afoot. I don't know what his reaction would have been. At the time, I thought probably disbelief. But Len Brockas and Hadley, who had worked with Jamieson from the start, knew the facts. We hoped it would dawn on the Old Man in the not too distant future.'

Driscoll's racing career ended at Backwell and it was to be some time before he was anything like back to normal, though he did eventually make a good recovery and lived until the age of 82.

August 3rd saw Hadley back in competitive mode, managing a 3rd place in the 2nd Brooklands Mountain Handicap at the BARC Bank Holiday meeting. Later that month, he won the 1500cc class at a Southsea MC sprint held on a new unopened stretch of public road.

A week later, Bert made his first appearance at the Lewes Speed Trials, watched by an enthralled schoolboy Denis S. Jenkinson, who was to become a life-long fan. This time, he was beaten into second place by Alain Maclachlan in his Special, built at Cresta Garage, Worthing and on this day, using a Jamieson side-valve engine. There was just 0.03 of a second between the two of them.

22nd August 1936. Hadley's first appearance at Lewes Speed Trial in one of the Side-valve cars. Amongst the spectators on the left is schoolboy motoring enthusiast Denis Jenkinson.

Austinews

FOR FAVOUR OF
EDITORIAL MENTION

From the PUBLICITY BUREAU, LONGBRIDGE, BIRMINGHAM (Priory 2101)

AUSTIN SEVEN TRIUMPHS

IN SOUTHSEA SPEED TRIALS

In the Southsea Motor Club's speed trials held recently at Southsea, the Austin Seven put up a brilliant performance.

Driven by H. L. Hadley, the supercharged special secured first place in the 750 c.c. and 1,100 c.c. classes and was third in the 1,500 c.c. class, competing with cars of almost double its capacity.

The meeting, which was the first of its kind to be held at Southsea, attracted an entry including some of the most famous racing drivers and cars and the Seven, the smallest car competing, made the fourth fastest time of the day.

——: :——

RECORD DEMAND FOR NEW AUSTINS

PRODUCTION SPEED-UP AT LONGBRIDGE

We are informed by the Austin Motor Company that, following the announcement of their new programme just over a week ago (on August 11th), the demand for the new Austin models is unprecedented.

As a result the great Austin factory at Longbridge, Birmingham, where nearly 20,000 workers are employed, is working at full pressure, and production is being speeded-up to meet the rapidly increasing volume of orders.

An indication of the public interest aroused by the new Austin is provided by the demand for descriptive literature which the Publicity department at Longbridge reports to have been a record one.

Interest naturally centres on the new Austin Fourteen, but the new Ten and Twelve models are in exceptionally keen demand.

No. 86

Hundreds of thousands of Austin Owners are interested in AUSTINEWS

An official Austin press release including a report on the Southsea Speed Trials
15th August 1936.

At the very end of August, Hadley, plus one of the Side-valves now painted dark green and accompanied by Bill 'Wizard' Rogers crossed the Irish Sea to Craigantlet, the hill climb just five miles north-west of Belfast. It was in fact Bert's second visit, having accompanied Pat Driscoll the previous year. HLH had fond memories of his visits and his detailed account appears later. Suffice to say, on this occasion, he set a new course record.

As the 1936 racing season neared its conclusion, HLH achieved a Shelsley time of 46.91, his best so far. At the BRDC 500 Mile Race, Bert was nominated as a second driver to Charlie Dodson but he did not get a drive. Back at Brooklands for the Autumn Meeting, he drove the Side-valve but without featuring in the results.

Apart from being present when Dodson took some Class H records at a bleak October Brooklands that was it for the time being. However, during the year, HLH had become a regular member of the newly-constituted Works Trials Team, but we will leave that for Bert to tell in his own words later on.

Brooklands October 1936. Charlie Dodson's attempts to take Class H records were eventually thwarted by high winds. Len Brockas (centre) oversees the project. Note the various non-standard features on the Austin.

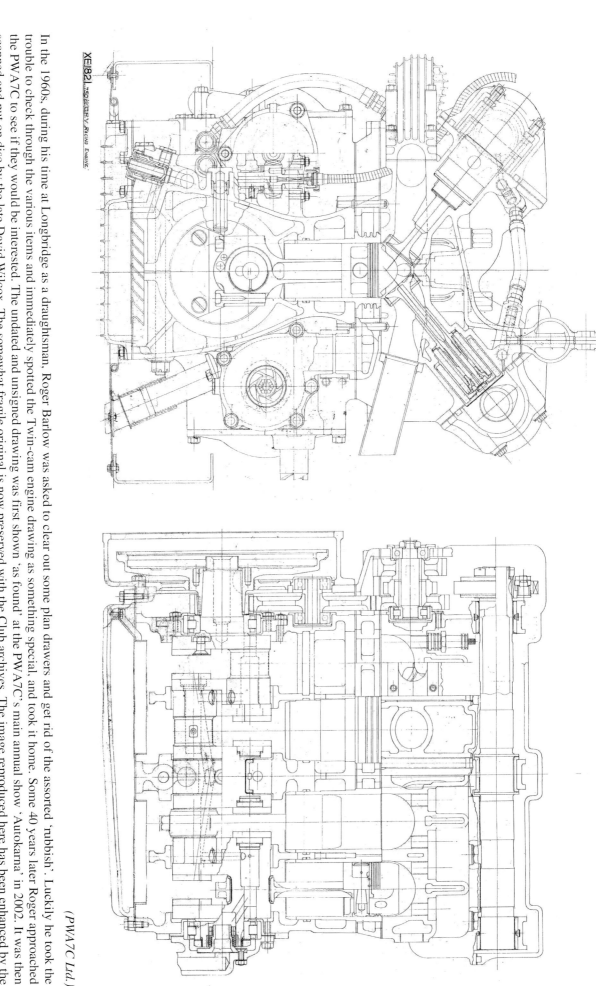

XEI182I.'750 cc O.H.V. Racing Engine'

(PWA7C Ltd.)

In the 1960s, during his time at Longbridge as a draughtsman, Roger Barlow was asked to clear out some plan drawers and get rid of the assorted 'rubbish'. Luckily he took the trouble to check through the various items and immediately spotted the Twin-cam engine drawing as something special, and took it home. Some 40 years later Roger approached the PWA7C to see if they would be interested. The undated and unsigned drawing was first shown 'as found' at the PWA7C's main annual show 'Autokarna' in 2002. It was then scanned and put on disc by the late David Wilcox. The somewhat fragile original is now preserved with the Club archives. The image reproduced here has been enhanced by the wonders of modern technology.

- 7 -

HIGH AND LOWS OF MOTOR RACING (1937-39)

After a season of consolidating his position within the team, HLH was looking forward to 1937 with some anticipation. By now employed on a 'staff' basis, he was still subjected to the restraints dictated by the management, though mostly working alongside Jamieson. TMJ was feeling frustrated by the niggling problems which had precluded the Twin-cams obtaining the results Lord Austin demanded and by the continual lack of co-operation from the 'old guard', who were always seeking opportunities to discredit Jamie's reputation.

The motor sport industry has always been a close-knit community and Jamieson's unsettled situation had not escaped the notice of Humphrey Cook, major share-holder in English Racing Automobiles Ltd (ERA). He was keen to further the marque's image by marketing a high performance sports car and he saw TMJ as the ideal man to design it.

On a personal level, Bert and Rose were spending as much time together as his employer's activities permitted, which of course included trialling events during the winter period. Factory entered cars were not officially allowed so cars were entered as private ventures, including those from Longbridge, thus the individual drivers (and passengers) would become members of Invited Clubs, in Hadley's case the Midland Automobile Club (MAC) and the Sutton Coldfield and North Birmingham Automobile Club (thankfully abbreviated to SUNBAC!). The MAC of course continues to thrive but the latter outfit seems to have folded just recently. During the pre-war period, the MAC had their own suite of rooms at the Grand Hotel on Colmore Row in Birmingham city centre and as a special treat Bert would escort Rose to Saturday afternoon tea at The Grand, the height of middle-class sophistication. Healthwise, apart from occasional backache, his main pre-occupation was trying to keep his weight in check, something he would have to contend with during his lifetime.

Along with a majority of the population at that time Bert was a smoker, though in later years he was very anti-smoking and, sadly with good reason, used to chide his son Clive about it. Meanwhile Herbert and Lydia were enjoying a quiet retirement together and probably very proud of their son's successes, though mindful of the possible dangers he might face. They also wondered if Bert and Rose would ever settle down to family life. They would have to wait a few years more.

Lord Austin, always publicity conscious, hit upon the idea of bringing one of the leading women drivers into the racing team. As a result of this, he announced that Mrs Kay Petre would be joining the team for the 1937 season, driving one of the Side-valve single-seaters.

63

Born in 1903, in Toronto, Canada, Kathleen Coad Defries, from an early age showed a great talent for gymnastics and ice skating, whilst being something of a tom-boy. Dark-haired, very petite and always immaculately turned out, she attracted attention wherever she went. Henry Aloysius Petre DSC MC on the other hand had been an eminent pioneer aviator before the Great War and later commissioned in the Royal Flying Corps. During the 1920s he flew competitively as an amateur pilot at the Brooklands Flying Club, winning several air races. He later took up yachting with a boat based on the River Hamble. A 'confirmed bachelor' type and known to his friends as 'Peter the Monk', it was a great surprise when he returned from Canada with a vivacious young bride on his arm, almost young enough to be his daughter!

The new Mrs Petre soon got into the swing of things and persuaded her husband, a wealthy solicitor, to buy her a Wolseley Hornet 'Daytona Special'. Having had some success with this, she quickly progressed to several Bugattis, setting up a new Ladies' Record. In 1935 she achieved a Brooklands lap of 134.75 mph bravely driving Oliver Bertram's huge V-12 10.5 litre Delage, gaining a coveted 130 mph Badge. Thereafter she drove other potent machinery including the famous 'White Riley', forerunner of the ERA.

1937 Works driver line-up.
How did Goodacre ever fit into a Twin-cam cockpit?

When Kay Petre was introduced the rest of the Racing Department, the 'lads' were very intrigued by this young female but soon learnt to respect her. Lord Austin sent for Hadley and informed Bert that it would be his responsibility to make Mrs Petre 'at home' and provide her with any assistance she might require as regards the cars or any other matter!

Bert could not believe his luck, though he wondered what words of wisdom he could impart on someone of her racing experience. Like his employer, who had provided Kay with a brand new Austin Big Seven painted in her favourite powder blue, Bert was somewhat smitten with this very feminine newcomer and of course the 'nudge-nudge' brigade were soon wagging their tongues. Even the press were printing mild innuendos as they were often pictured together. Bert recalled the situation:

'Having got through the preliminaries, I found that I liked Kay – a lot. If she had been single I might well have taken things further, but she wasn't and in fact I met her husband quite regularly and I respected him. However, Kay and I were 'close' – she was that sort of girl and a very courageous lady.'

What Rosma Stallard thought about the innuendos being bandied about is not known, but it must have been unsettling for her, even if there was no substance in the rumours.

Jamieson was renting a house in Moseley, Birmingham but he was still inclined to work at odd hours. Bert had realised that his boss would often miss a meal or two and it came about that TMJ became a frequent diner with the Hadleys at Twyning Road. How the middle-class academic Londoner and his 'Brummie' hosts all got on is a mystery, but they certainly did and in subsequent letters from TMJ (then at ERA) he fondly remembers Bert's parents. Their conversations must have made fascinating listening.

A rare photograph showing a Twin-cam engine connected to a Heenan & Froude dynamometer used to measure power output. Len Brockas in charge.

A lot of testing took place during the pre-season period, now centred on Donington of course. The Twin-cams were getting more reliable apart from the almost daily need to adjust the fuel mixture settings, a constant worry as the slightest sign of weakness would burn a piston. The problem would not be overcome until after the arrival of the German racing teams for the Donington Grand Prix later in the year.

Over the winter Charles Goodacre had decided to leave Austins and took a position with an Austin main dealer, Parish's of Hull, but this did not work out and with the help of Bert Hadley he 'charmed' his way back into Longbridge, and so became available to drive again.

The opening meeting for 1937 was the British Empire Trophy race at the extended Donington Park on April 10th when Kay Petre made her official debut for the Austin team in one of the Side-valve cars. The two Twin-cams were to be driven by Charlie Dodson and Hadley and Austins were hopeful of a successful outcome. However it was not to be. For one thing, the weather turned out to be pretty miserable and the race was run in the wet which caused various fuel and ignition maladies. Hadley had problems and fell back and Mrs Petre encountered trouble with fuel as well. After the meeting and back at Longbridge, the remains of a cigarette butt was found in the Twin-cam's fuel feed pipe. How this obstruction found its way into the system was anyone's guess. Again, there were strong suspicions, but crucially nothing was ever proven.

Meanwhile, Charlie Dodson whilst hanging on to a slim lead had pulled in to sort out a misfire. In an article he later wrote for the Vintage Motor Cycle Club, he recalled what happened next:

'It did rain soon after the start causing a plug to oil up and forcing me into the pits. Unfortunately, one mechanic had thought I wanted a fill up [from the old-fashioned churns then in use] and most of this went down my neck! At the same time the ailing plug was found with the engine still running. As I switched off – up went the flames including me. In my haste I grabbed the hot exhaust pipe, adding to the fact I was truly in flames. I ran [across the track!], rolled on to the grass – the next thing I could hardly breathe as a fire extinguisher was emptied over me, not to mention a large mac [raincoat] still containing its large owner which finally put out the flames and almost me.'

Dodson in fact received some nasty burns around the face and neck and his left hand, but despite these, recovered sufficiently to be fit enough for his next outing. However, Lord Austin was not impressed by the day's proceedings and the adverse publicity generated. As for Tom Murray Jamieson, who was not present at Donington on that day, the whole debacle was sufficient for him to finally resign his position at Longbridge. By the following month he would be commuting to Bourne, the Lincolnshire headquarters of ERA, as their new Chief Designer.

10th April 1937. Donington British Empire Trophy. Hadley chases an MG around Hairpin Bend. He finished in 12th place. 'Jamie's' fuel mix makes an effective paint stripper!

With Jamieson's departure and the return of Charles Goodacre, the running of the Works racing cars took on a different tack. Any further development was limited to what parts where available in stock. TMJ had drafted out various goodies, such as two-stage supercharging and eight-plug heads, but there was no funding available for major changes.

Since Jamieson's arrival at Longbridge, Lord Austin had undertaken to pay for the major outings related to the racing programme out of his own pocket – he received little or no support from the majority of his fellow directors in this matter. It has to be said that they were influenced in some part by the anti-Jamieson faction within a section of senior management. Goodacre became a sort of team leader, but it was Bert Hadley who kept in covert contact with TMJ, providing regular updates on the team's progress or otherwise and receiving invaluable advice in return.

The next major outing for the team was May 12th, the appropriately named Coronation Day Meeting at Donington Park, celebrating the crowning of King George VI and Queen Elizabeth, something to cheer their loyal subjects after the hiatus of the Abdication. The meeting consisted of four races, all run as handicaps, which Austins favoured and culminating in the 100 mile Coronation Trophy Race. It was a brilliant return for Goodacre who won *all* four races, a unique achievement. Kay Petre, in her second outing for Austin, finished in 6th place. Hadley, who had lapped consistently with Goodacre, providing a fine spectacle for the spectators, was not in luck, his engine succumbing to overheating problems. He must have felt somewhat jaded, considering all the trouble he'd gone to in helping Goodacre's return, only to see Charles take all the glory. A mere two days later, however, Bert was back on form collecting a Premier Award in the MCC Edinburgh Trial.

A week later HLH returned to the infamous Backwell Hill climb where he and 'his' Twin-cam cleaned up with a class win and fastest time of the day (FTD).

The busy period continued with the popular International Meeting at Shelsley Walsh on 5th June. Lord Austin had entered both Side-valve cars, Kay Petre in her regular mount and a guest drive for the successful Derby privateer, Rodney Turner. Also present were Walter Bäumer, driving the Goodacre/Dodson Twin-cam and HLH in his. Hadley, in fine form, was seconds ahead of the others, setting a new class record on his first timed run. Lord Austin had arrived to see his team in action.

Bert remembered the day:

> 'Austin had brought over the German driver Walter Bäumer who had driven both the Side-valve and Twin-cam single-seaters following some success with his own "Ulster" two-seater. It was a curious thing but it was assumed that a foreign driver was bound to overcome any local lad from the UK. It seems to happen even today but I am told they come bearing bags of gold and even I can understand that key to fame.
>
> It was clear to me that Bäumer was expected to wipe the floor with Hadley and Goodacre but I cannot recall giving much thought to that expectancy. In earlier conversations with "Jamie" I had suggested that we should approach 40 secs with the Twin-cam and I based my beliefs on times with the Side-valve cars. They were friendly little cars in the right setting but a real handful if one tried anything spectacular at a rather bumpy [as it was then] Shelsley. Driving the Twin-cam was child's play by comparison.
>
> I felt that I had made a reasonable run first time and was pleased to note that my approximation to 40 secs had been reasonably correct. I was astounded to learn that Walter was over 2 secs adrift, which is a tremendous difference in a short climb like Shelsley. There was a lot of huffing and puffing

going on in the Paddock with Bäumer and the Works interpreter occupying the star roles. The assertion was that I had a better car, more power and different gear box and final drive ratios. In point of fact the cars were identical in this respect. Moreover we knew that Bäumer's engine was giving slightly more power at the top end. Both engines had been on test a few days before the event.

5th June 1937. Shelsley Walsh Hill Climb.
Hadley won the M.A.C. Challenge Trophy and £25 for his efforts.

I could see his point of view and suggested that I should drive his car for the second run. I said I would be quite happy to make the change to prove to him we had nothing to hide. I realised it would not be in the Company's interest if Bäumer went home full of complaints. I asked for my seat and throttle pad to be installed in his car and the conversion was on the way before Bäumer looking crestfallen said he wished to apologise. Bill Rogers, the mechanic on my car, hailed from the inner enclaves of Birmingham with usual direct approach and laconic turn of phrase. He said to our Walter "Make up your bloody mind" and he added some other pithy remarks. When Bäumer got the gist of all that he laughed and the uneasy spell was broken.

Having discussed Bäumer's methods with him we walked up part of the hill together. I told him to use the offside of the start line which pointed the car correct at Kennel. The bend could be taken on full noise when the right line was applied. We discussed step off revs and it was obvious he was using too much power, resulting in wasteful spin. I told Bäumer to use full noise up to the Esses and how to miss the disconcerting bumps at the Crossing, with a partial lift off for the left hander at the Esses. My humble opinion was, and still is, that early or late heavy braking destroyed the smooth line, an essential ingredient. I cannot recall whether Bäumer improved on his second run.

Liking Bäumer was not difficult. He was a happy-go-lucky type and we remained friends in spite of my persistent denunciation of Adolf Hitler who I described variously as a first class shit. Walter protested but we always found something to laugh about.

Bill Sewell, our team manager, was well suited to ward off the verbal insults frequently launched by his Lordship. Came the moment when they met in the Paddock and the opening remarks were on the lines of "Why have you spent so much money bringing this fellow over? – Hadley has wiped the floor with him." Bill pointed out that it was the Old Man's idea in the first place, whereupon he received a blasting for smoking. His Lordship hated smoking and drinking i.e. alcoholic beverages. To me later on he said "Congratulations you have done a good job for the company. It will not be forgotten." All very encouraging of course in the heat of that afternoon. One of the mechanics, a wag in his own right said "Trouble is, he has a bloody poor memory in some respects, that's a well known fact!" He may have been right as I cannot recall being given a car in my favourite colour as had happened elsewhere. No, it was business as usual on the following Monday. Mind you it was good to see the Old Man so happy. As I was Longbridge material, man and boy, he was something of a father figure and I continued to regards him as such in spite of being subjected to remarks like "He has got you on the cheap mate." After all without his support, and the confidence invested in me by Murray Jamieson, my ride would have gone to some other outside driver.

Money accumulation has never coloured my thinking to any extent. I loved motor racing. It seemed to suit my temperament and I didn't suffer unduly from pre-race nerves. I used to wonder why some chaps drove at all as they seem to be torturing themselves.'

Once Bert had got his feet firmly on the pedals of the third of the Twin-cams built (second surviving), he wasted no time in 'customizing' it. There were several modifications made, all of which remain with the car today. Bert altered the accelerator pedal, changing this to a pendant type, which enabled proper 'heel and toe' operation. The steering wheel position was altered to suit Bert's reach. Probably the major change was re-covering the seat in a patterned fabric as used in some Austin saloons (still available - to order - from the Yorkshire supplier!). Cloth was less slippery than leather and also gave Bert a cooler ride over long distances. Additionally, the padding was revised to hug the Hadley thighs – he said *"a single-seat racing car should fit the driver like a good shoe!"*

Lord Austin did not forget, though Bert would have to wait until December until he was sent for.

'He said "I had done very well and my efforts were of great value to the Company." I remember thinking "How do I spend that?" As if to read my thoughts, he passed a sealed envelope across his desk with a rare smile. I was pleasantly surprised to find it contained a cheque of considerable value [Actually £120.00 – in today's terms about £6,800!].'

The **Motor**   *June 15, 1937.*

IN THE NEWS . .

Personal

MADE TO MEASURE for the cars they drive. H. L. Hadley and Mrs. K. Petre, photographed at Shelsley, who will handle Austins at Le Mans next week-end.

12th June 1937. Donington Nuffield Junior Handicap.
Standing behind left to right are 'Wizard' Rogers, Depper, Ral, Len and Bob.

It was a busy week's preparation for the next event on June 12th, the Nuffield Trophy meeting at Donington. The first race was over 25 miles and Bert and Goodacre set off in great style and headed the field throughout, Hadley winning the race (his first win).

Great hopes were expected in the Nuffield Trophy event again run on handicap. Goodacre set the pace initially whilst Hadley was having fuel delivery problems. Kay Petre in the Side-valve had to retire with a major oil leak and Goodacre had a delay in the pits.

All the Works cars eventually retired from this much publicised event.

1937 Nuffield Trophy. Bert is nearest the camera.

1937 Nuffield Trophy. The race gets underway.

Continuing this busy period a contingent from Longbridge made the trek down to Sarthe in France where 'Les 24 Heures du Mans 1937' for sports cars was to take place on the 19/20th June. The previous year's race had been cancelled due to industrial unrest throughout France so it was now back to normal for the Automobile Club de l'Ouest who organise the event to this day. Austins had entered a team of three of the trials-type cars. These were from the later COA registered series with door-less bodies on the low chassis, with un-blown engines.

AUTOMOBILE CLUB DE L'OUEST

Bert recalls the event in some detail:

'I shared one of the Austin two-seaters with Charlie Dodson. We were great friends when driving the Austin Twin-cam single-seaters. Three cars from the Works ran in the 1937 race. The second was driven by Charlie Goodacre and Dennis Buckley and the third by Kay Petre and an Irishman, George Mangan.

Jamieson had taken a small part as much as he was allowed in the prep of the three-bearing engines. The cars were similar in appearance to those which ran, not very successfully in 1935, but this time they had lighter bodies and maybe not so wide. No attempt was made to streamline or reduce the frontal area. Jamieson had suggested a prototype streamlined coupé, similar to the German Adlers, but he didn't get very far with that which was a pity. In any case, he had left the Company before the race, having become completely fed up.

Before he did, however, he produced a better head, improved camshaft and Laystall crankshafts for the 1937 race cars. He wanted to improve the ports and fit twin SU carbs, but I think the regulations got in the way so we were left with one downdraught carb (Solex or Zenith). Ral Appleby tested the engines and the maximum reached was 28bhp at 5000rpm. An additional 10bhp would have been useful. Jamieson specified flexible, braided internal oil pipes, but after he had gone, Alf Depper overruled him and fitted solid copper pipes. That put us out of the race, they broke and all three cars went out during the night with clapped big end shells. Before this happened to Goodacre, he or Buckley managed to run out of fuel somewhere. They did get going again, having worn themselves out running miles with a small can and fooling the chaps who seal the tanks at refuelling only to be bitterly disappointed when the oil pipe broke.

We had landed at Boulogne and Dodson and I drove gently to Le Mans without pause. Sitting in the lounge of the Hotel Continental drinking coffee, when perhaps an hour later, the rest of the party arrived and from the look of it they had stopped at every watering hole en-route. Depper's face was puce and he launched into an unprintable harangue directed at Dodson who appeared bewildered. We had rushed on ahead, apparently to pinch the best rooms. Of course, we had not done any such thing. In fact Dodson had said to me "This is a bloody crummy hole." I thought so too. Madame was a very large lady who sailed through the place like a battleship, followed everywhere by an unpleasant pimpish looking little bloke in a very loud check suit. Bill Sewell described himself as our Team Manager and Dodson told him to get the Old Man on the telephone as he wanted Depper recalled and an immediate apology. Some semblance of peace was restored without recourse to Longbridge. Curiously, Alf did not include me in his grievances. When Kay Petre joined the Austin team to drive the Jamieson Side-valve car, Lord Austin sent for me and told me I was to look after her and teach her all about the car, since I had been competing with it. Well of course, one has to obey instructions from the Gaffer and I did my best, in the process of which I discovered that I liked Kay very much. I was single then, but I did of course realise that Kay was married. Nevertheless, we had a nice innocent friendship which the press tried to push. My colleagues thought there was more in it than that, so Kay thought it would be great if *we* pushed it a bit. The result was very funny while at the Hotel Continental. I knew Charlie Dodson was smitten by Kay's good looks. I would go to bed fairly early and it was not long before Charlie felt he should visit my room "just to check if I was alright." "Yes, fine Charlie. Goodnight." Next Bill Sewell would pop in with a similar enquiry. Then Charlie Goodacre, the same question. To which I said "Is it Kay you are seeking? She is in room so and so." All very funny. Bill Sewell's wife was with us. She was on watch too, but some of her time was taken up watching Bill.

During the night practice, I found that our car pulled a few more revs than the others and I told Charlie. He dreamed up the idea whereby we could win a few bob. Did I think I could lap both other Austins during the first stint of 4 hours? I thought it was going to be a bit tricky, but could be interesting. I said see if they will accept the challenge.

19th June 1937. Le Mans 24 hour.
Kay Petre in COA 119 just before the race.

Goodacre jumped at it and Kay too thought I couldn't do it. Ten quid was the stake – quite a sum in those days. We of course paid up if I failed. In the race I was away first and I drove flat out down the hill to the Esses, first lap. I knew I would have to take chances in the corners. That was where I thought I could build faster laps. It seems they stayed close together for the 4 hours. Everybody who passed me, and most did, I jumped in behind to get a quick tow. I remember Robert Benoist coming behind me on the banked (as it was then) left hand corner at Arnage. For some reason, this corner was bricked in those days, like Indianapolis and was called the "Brickyard" too. When Benoist eventually got past in his streamlined Bugatti, he waved both fists at me, streaking away at the same time. I met him during the race and found him to be a really nice fellow. He was executed during the war for Resistance activities.

At the end of the first hour, Ral Appleby, by arrangement, gave me a signal which said "two miles" which represented my lead. I realised it was going to be tight. I had expected Ral to give me my lead in seconds. It seems he had approximated distance against lap times. Not a bad guess as it happens. I managed to get one or two decent tows towards Mulsanne, then late in the fourth hour, I spotted the other Austins going away from Mulsanne corner. At the end of the lap I got the come in signal. Well, I was with them at Arnage and I overtook both of them on the downhill stretch towards White House, which in those days had a tight right and almost immediate left bend. I took a quick look at them. I don't think Goodacre could believe it.

Less than a kilometre and I pulled into the pits. Five quid each was worth the effort. Goodacre said "How the hell did you do it?" I said that I had read somewhere that Nuvolari hardly ever used the brakes so I copied him. There was nothing really remarkable about my private "race" with Kay and Charlie. I knew they had been advised to think in terms of finishing. No such restrictions were placed on us. "Doddy" would not have stood for it. It was all good fun.'

With the disappointment felt by all the team with the engine problems and the news that the popular English driver Pat Fairfield had died of injuries received when his Frazer Nash – BMW collided with a pile-up of other vehicles at Arnage on lap nine (which the Austin team luckily managed to avoid) the mood in the camp was not of the best. Bert decided to see what had caused the big ends to fail. He and Dodson tipped COA 121 on its side and removed the sump. It was then that the 'Ruby' pattern copper oil-feed pipe was discovered, fractured at one of the 'formed' ends. Bert was livid at this, knowing what Jamie had specified and set about repairs. Using some rubber tubing and new big-end shells (carried as spares in the car) they completed the job in 90 minutes and departed on a 'local' road-test. Upon their return and satisfied all was well, Hadley and Dodson gathered their gear together and departed for the ferry, leaving the rest of the team to sort themselves out. They completed the homeward journey without any further problems.

The busy June period ended back at Brooklands on the 26th for the LCC Relay Race. Ten teams of three cars apiece took part with 'Austin' represented by Bert and Charles Goodacre in the Twin-cams plus Mrs Petre in the Side-valve. Hadley took the first stint and cracked on, lapping at around 120mph (best 121.18mph). Goodacre was slightly slower but Kay Petre maintained a steady 95mph.

Kay Petre later recalled:

'The Austin team were on scratch. I, having the slowest car, went last. Bert and Charlie drove their cars flat out trying to catch the leaders. When I took over as car "C", victory looked possible if the Side-valve ran without trouble. A leaky pipe developed, spraying hot oil all over my legs. I wriggled and squirmed about, trying to avoid it. "Poor little thing, she's getting badly burned." Bill Sewell in the pits said, "Call her in." Both Bert and Charlie assured him I didn't really mind and that I would come in if it got too hot. That I considered a great tribute from my team mates who knew I would hate to be called in for a thing like that. We won the race at 105.63mph.'

A heavily posed publicity shot featuring 'Mrs Petre in her Austin'. Bill Rogers and Bob Simpson try to look interested.

10th July 1937. Brooklands Campbell Circuit Races.
The National Long Handicap. Bert negotiates The Fork by the famous Vickers Ltd shed.

July was a busy month for the Racing Department – Brooklands on the 10th was wet but Bert managed to win the National Long Handicap on the Campbell Circuit, beating Arthur Dobson in the 1.5 litre ERA by a car's length. For a change, the following week-end was taken over to some 'gentle' rallying, though not without incident for Hadley and his intrepid passenger Bob Simpson.

We will let Bert elaborate later on.

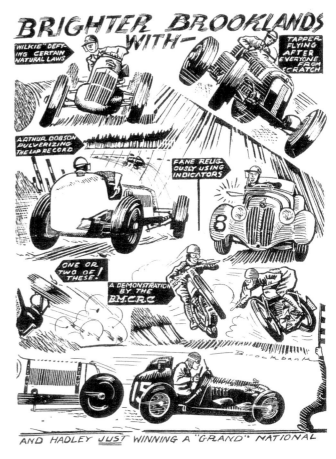

Russell Brockbank's impressions of the 10th July 1937 Brooklands meeting.

10th July 1937. Brooklands Campbell Circuit Races.
Sir Malcolm and Lady Campbell pass the time of day with Alf Depper and HLH.

24th July 1937. Donington 12hr Sports Car Race.
One of the three COA series Grasshoppers entered enjoys a pre-race practice session. Note the trees!

On July 24th, Donington Park was the venue for the 12 Hour Sports Car Race. After the Le Mans debacle, Bert was determined to produce a result. Using COA 121 again, which he prepared himself, he undertook a *twelve-hour* test session at the Park before he was satisfied that all was well. In the race, he and Charlie Dodson finished in 7th place overall and 2nd in their class behind a Singer.

Behind the scenes, much work was being put in to make the Twin-cams more reliable. A major problem was fuel and mixture settings. Using the fuel formula set up by Jamieson, i.e. 50% Methanol, 40% RDI (leaded racing fuel), 5% acetone and 5% water, it was found that mixture strength had to be re-set on virtually every occasion, ambient temperature and/or humidity having a critical effect, with any sign of a weak mixture resulting in certain mechanical failure, usually piston damage. This ongoing problem would not be resolved until the visit of the mighty German state-funded teams later in the season. Bert was in constant touch with Murray Jamieson, who was by now married to Mabel Sybil Burton, but still living at Goodby Road, Moseley. It was here that HLH assembled a batch of TMJ-designed ERA superchargers from parts made by the David Brown gear people. They worked in their spare time in a bedroom converted into a small workshop. Jamieson obviously preferred Hadley to do the final fettling on these units, someone he could trust implicitly.

Returning to Hadley's 1937 race season, the short but tortuous Crystal Palace meeting on 14th August provided Bert with a fine win in the 30 lap main race. He kept 'Bira' and Reg Parnell, both in ERAs, at bay through sheer hard work and concentration.

The month ended with a fine set of runs at the Craigantlet Hill Climb, five miles outside of Belfast. It was Bert's third visit to the hill and the first with a Twin-cam, though it was not 'his' car. He set a new record for the hill and he would return again in 1938. We will revisit Craigantlet later on for Bert's own memories of his visits to Ulster.

28th August 1937. Craigantlet Hill Climb.
Bill Rogers attends to the car as it is Goodacre's.
Bert wears the hand-knitted pullover presented by 'an admirer'.

1937 Craigantlet. Hadley tries the wide twin wheels – he didn't trust them and so ran with normal singles later on.

Shelsley Walsh Autumn Hill Climb was Bert's next event. Hadley, back in his own car, and Kay Petre in the Side-valve were entered by Lord Austin with support from various privateers to aim for the Team Prize as usual.

Bert was experimenting with the optional twin rear wheels as used originally by Pat Driscoll at Backwell. Whether he was under pressure to try them we do not know but he was not entirely convinced that they were of much advantage, in fact Goodacre in the other Twin-cam was faster.

11th September 1937. Shelsley Walsh Hill Climb.
Hadley has a eye problem as a concerned Alf Depper looks on. Note the use of twin rear wheels this time.

On Bert's second run, his clutch expired in a cloud of smoke. The late Hugh Dunsterville, a member of the 'design' team that created the famous 'Freikaiserwagen' hill climb Special which was competing at the same meeting, recalled:

1937 Shelsley Walsh.
Oh "bother"! Bert's clutch expires.

'Bert Hadley outraged the proprieties of the times with carefree abandon. He was sitting on the start line with the revs rising when his climatic moment of departure fizzled out with a burnt out clutch. He switched off the engine and in the deathly quiet, in ringing tones for all to hear, volunteered the concise and expressive sentiment "Oh fuck it!" One just didn't swear publicly like that in 1937.'

Despite this glitch, the Austin team collected the Fray Challenge Cup and Kay Petre the Ladies Challenge Trophy. Sadly, it was to be her last outing in an Austin single-seater.

September 18th was the next date on the Austin calendar, the BRDC '500' (mostly on cost grounds, the '500' was changed in 1937 from miles to kilometres). Hadley and Goodacre plus Mrs Petre were entered and the team were in a confident mood and looking forward to putting on a good show for His Lordship.

As so often happens, fate stepped in to decree otherwise. Kay was practicing on the Friday for what would have been her eighth race outing for the team. As she was circulating on the damp track she was overtaken by the Derby driver Reg Parnell who had elected to take a higher line on the banking. What happened next was to effectively end Kay's racing career and almost cost her life. Parnell lost control at the very point of overtaking. The tail broke away and his MG slid down nose first into the side of the lighter Austin, causing the latter to overturn several times, throwing Mrs Petre out onto the concrete track. Parnell, who had been previously penalised for 'wild' driving on other occasions, received minor injuries and shock. Kay was not so lucky and was rushed to Weybridge Hospital. Apart from multiple bruising her tiny frame had escaped serious injury, however she was unconscious and was to remain in a deep coma for a full five weeks. Things looked so bad that she was not expected to survive the weekend and last rites were administered.

Naturally, the whole of the Austin team, as well as the wider motor racing world were devastated by this news, but Lord Austin, after discussions with the drivers, decided to run the other two cars as a tribute to Kay. In the event both Twin-cams had to retire. Before the start of the '500', there was a two minutes silence which had many of the team in tears, such was the expected outcome.

In fact, Kay did not die as had been predicted, but it was a long haul back and during the ensuing weeks Bert made time to regularly visit the hospital where he met up with Henry Petre and Kay's brother John Defries who happened to be visiting England from his native Canada. Kay eventually regained conscious and after a period of convalescence made a good recovery but with some facial scarring and nerve damage. She did briefly return to motor racing in one of her own cars but eventually decided to end what had been an outstanding racing career.

As for Parnell, he was censured by the Royal Automobile Club (RAC) as 'unfit to hold a Competition Licence' and despite appeal, which included support from Kay Petre who in no way blamed Parnell for her misfortune, would not be able to resume racing until the 1939 season. After the War, Reg Parnell would play a leading role in the revival of British motor sport, both as a courageous driver and as a successful team manager. He died at the early age of 53.

September 1937 Brooklands.
Prior to Brighton, Hadley hones his standing-start techniques. Note the 19" wheels.

Hadley's season continued with a visit to Brighton where the famous Speed Trials continue to be held on Madeira Drive to this day. Having set a new course record, he ended up third fastest overall. Alain Maclachlan, using a Jamieson-type engine, was in brilliant form to take top honours on the day.

25th September 1937. Brighton Speed Trials.
Bert speeds down Madeira Drive past a Morris 8 parked under the familiar arches.
1st in 1100cc and 3rd in 1500cc classes.

October 9th saw a return to London's Crystal Palace with Hadley and Goodacre in the Twin-cams. The Imperial Trophy was run as usual with two heats and a final, as handicaps. For once, Bert did not make the final but Charles Goodacre did, finishing in a steady third place – his final race for Austins. Bert recalls:

'I was leading as I approached the Ramp Bend on full noise, changed down on the run in and was conscious of a new feeling in my hands. Anyway, I negotiated the turn to the winding uphill stretch to the Terrace Straight, I was 8,000 rpm in third when to all intent, etc. the steering disappeared, the steering wheel spinning, and the near side front wheel flapping about. Braking was out because had I done so, both front wheels would have pulled inwards. I went towards the crowd on the outside of the bend to the Terrace Straight then I think I must have made some movement with the offside front wheel, the car turned sharply and finished up in a ditch on the inside of the corner with the tail still on the road. Raymond Mays, who was chasing me, came into sight, his mouth open in disbelief. He managed to edge his ERA out to miss the tail of the Austin by a whisker. After that I baled out very smartly indeed. That near catastrophe was caused by a milling machinist who had taken too much metal out of the axle swivel at a critical point leaving it paper thin. At the time I was annoyed about losing the race for such a stupid reason. Losing my life, or the possibilities of it, didn't occur to me until later when we were considering the number of events, including Shelsley, where I had participated successfully with the same faulty component. I mention Shelsley because loss of steering there would have been a disaster. By this time I was fed up with so many unnecessary failures and I made my position clear to those I held responsible. Lord Austin saw my point of view in the ensuing shemozzle and things did improve but of course, I realised that I had made some enemies in the process. My quarrel was not with the mechanics - they were excellent colleagues.'

A week later on the 16th, Bert drove in the 10 lap Siam Trophy race on Brooklands' Mountain Circuit. With the encouraging news of Kay Petre's ongoing recovery and raring to go, Bert led from the start but mechanical problems intruded and once again, Hadley had to retire from the race and indeed the meeting. More frustrations!

However, an event of some significance had taken place at Donington Park on Saturday October 2nd. Fred Craner, the Derby garage owner and energetic Secretary of the Derby & District Motor Club, had achieved 'the impossible' in persuading the mighty German factory teams of Auto-Union and Mercedes-Benz to participate in the International Donington Grand Prix, along with the cream of British and Continental drivers. Lord Austin had connections with German industry, plus the fact that AMCo had service buildings at the circuit, so it was only natural that one of the German teams would avail themselves of the facilities. Thus Mercedes, with four cars entered, would be at Donington, whilst Auto-Union, with three cars and a smaller retinue would be based in nearby Melbourne village.

Either way, the standards of organisation were far ahead of anything previously seen in England before, a foretaste of what is the norm in today's Formula One scene. The actual cars, which had been winning all season were awesome machines, particularly the Auto-Unions. Described as 'the most unconventional racing car in the world' and designed by the well-known Dr. Ferdinand Porsche, it featured a mighty 16-cylinder supercharged engine of no less than 6,000cc mounted in the rear of an independently suspended tubular chassis. Apart from the sheer size of the thing, the layout was not dissimilar to that proposed by Tom Murray Jamieson and rejected out of hand by Herbert Austin in 1934.

The four Mercedes were more conventional in design, though brimming with technical features. The front-mounted engine was a straight-eight of a mere 5.66 litres. Both designs were reputed to generate in excess of 500bhp. All this was against the background of increasing Nazi imperialism in Europe and it was no secret that both teams were heavily subsidised by the German Government as part of Adolf Hitler's propaganda campaign.

Bert being Bert, lost no time in getting himself to Donington, whilst perhaps not exactly unlocking the premises for the new temporary occupier, as a leading member of the Austin Racing Department, he was allowed access to the inner workings of the mighty Mercedes set-up. What he saw amazed him. The equipment and facilities brought over with teams of smartly attired technicians, tyre specialists and so on, all convoyed from Germany in a fleet of purpose-built Mercedes trucks and workshop vans.

He also had the opportunity to view the cylinder head off one of the team cars, noticing how 'happy' the valves and combustion chambers looked, plus the appearance of the piston crowns. With the fuel mix Austins had been persevering with, these parts always seemed to have a 'dry' and 'lean' look about them. Not all the mechanics were out-and-out Nazis, though there were plenty of 'Party' officials about – these were easy to spot – and Bert managed to speak to several

technicians. As a result of this, he found that Shell-Mex were supplying both German teams with a special fuel. Knowing Shell's U.K. Competition Manager, Jimmy Simpson, a former T.T. motorcycle rider for the A.J.S. Company, Bert approached him for details of the 'brew' with a view to trying it in the Austins. Having received this, Hadley immediately contacted TMJ at Rutland Terrace, Stamford, where he and Sybil were now renting an elegant Georgian town house. Jamie liked the idea and arrangements were made to obtain a supply of the fuel and try it out during winter testing, as there would not be time whilst the current fixtures were being run.

Tom and Sybil Murray Jamieson at home in Stamford.

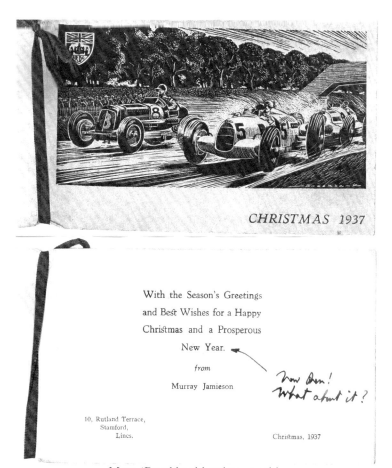

CHRISTMAS 1937

With the Season's Greetings
and Best Wishes for a Happy
Christmas and a Prosperous
New Year.

from

Murray Jamieson

Now Bert!
What about it?

10, Rutland Terrace,
Stamford,
Lincs.

Christmas, 1937

More 'Brockbank' artistry on this
1937 BRDC Christmas card from TMJ.

Bert's meeting with the Germans also revealed the drivers were using talcum powder in their driving gloves. Ignoring the remarks of the Longbridge wits, HLH tried this for himself and was pleased to discover his hands remained cooler and reduced soreness, particularly over longer distances.

Another event for the trials team took place on December 4th, the demanding 'London to Gloucester' with Bert collecting a Second Class award.

1937 ended on a happier note for HLH when Lord Austin personally thanked him for his efforts on behalf of the Company and presented him with a cheque for £120, a very useful sum with which you could have then purchased a new small car.

Winter in Experimental 1937/38. Len Brockas gives the Goodacre/Dodson Twin-cam an in-depth 'fettle'.
The chap on the right in smock and flat cap could be Hadley.

After the Christmas break, the traditional MCC 'Exeter Trial' took place on the week-end of January 7/8th 1938. The Austin team was well represented with Bert amongst the Premier Award winners, a very plucky effort on his part. It would be his last trial until the following November.

Whilst Austin employees were driving competitively on the Company's behalf they were always heavily insured. As a result, Austins made available the best medical treatment of the time, particularly after an extended race or gruelling trial. Bert had been experiencing severe back pain which had probably started back in his apprenticeship when lifting Austin Seven engines on and off the test-beds, aggravated whilst testing the bone-shaking Ducks/Clogs on the bumpy Brooklands Track plus determined driving in every event he took part in.

7th/8th January 1938. MCC Exeter Trial.
Hadley and Simpson on their way to a Premier Award.
BOA 60 is now on a high chassis.

A leading specialist examined him and decided an operation was required. Even today spinal surgery can be critical, in 1938 it was very risky. As Bert recalled in 1986:

'The start of 1938 saw me in Selly Oak Hospital, Birmingham, for an operation to my back. I was quite ill but made a complete recovery, being determined to be driving again at the first meeting at the Palace in April. Lord Austin visited the hospital to present me with a suitably inscribed gold pocket watch which includes a stop watch. I still have it to this day. One revelation was to witness Lord Austin literally melting to the charms of the nurses. I thought to myself, the old so-and-so is human after all. Mind you, I had beaten him to the punch by this time! I did drive at the first meeting [Crystal Palace Coronation Trophy April 2nd 1938] and gained a place, albeit completely exhausted at the end.'

For the Austin Racing Team, it was important that Bert was fully operational again, not only as their lead driver but also for the fact that he was effectively running the team, reporting to Lord Austin on a daily basis. This was because Charles Goodacre had got itchy feet during the previous autumn and finally left Longbridge for good, joining the Associated Ethyl Corporation as a technical manager. Apart from the War period, he would remain with them until retirement.

The enforced convalescence had given Bert the opportunity to reflect on the misfortunes and near disasters which had accompanied the running of the Jamieson cars.

'Perhaps not all bad luck because I am convinced many incidents which happened were pre-arranged. The rear axle drain plug episode at Montlhéry comes to mind, but the loss of steering whilst racing at the Crystal Palace was *not* funny. At a Shelsley meeting, Jamieson suddenly spotted a drop-arm on my car almost in two pieces, seconds before I was to make my run. If he had not been so sharp-eyed, I would not be writing this today. The cigarette end stuffed in the fuel line was another example. Of course I had many successes too, but it all seemed to be against a background of intrigue, jealousy and foul play.'

During the close season Brockas, Rogers and Appleby gave the two Twin-cam cars a thorough overhaul whilst Bob Simpson fettled the Side-valve. The other Side-valve in which Kay Petre had her accident was in fact not too badly damaged and could have been rebuilt, but such was the pressure on the Racing Department to keep costs down, it was merely put aside for spares if required. As soon as Bert was fit enough, some pre-season testing was arranged at Donington Park. Some of the Shell-supplied fuel was available for the first time and initial tests were very encouraging. Previously, Austins (i.e. Hadley!), had mixed their own 'brew', a not particularly pleasant task, in view of the ingredients involved and it was subject to variation. The new fuel, which came in sealed drums, consisted of methyl alcohol 86%, nitro-benzole 4.4%, acetone 8.8% and sulphuric ether 0.8% and smelt 'like burning shoe polish'. One particular advance was the absence of the previous requirement of constant mixture adjustment – once set it would now remain stable – a tremendous improvement. Later, examination of the combustion chambers revealed a much healthier appearance of the critical components which augured well for the coming season. In addition, both engines improved their power output on test.

Following the Crystal Palace Trophy on 2nd April, HLH achieved a determined 6th place in the Empire Trophy Race at Donington on the 9th.

26th/30th April 1938. RAC Rally Austin team.
18hp Norfolk (Sewell), Big Seven Forlite (Hadley), 14hp Goodwood (Buckley).

The next event for Bert was to be the RAC Rally held over the 26th-30th April 1938. In those days the Rally was not at all like the events of recent years but more of a reliability contest with some driving tests along the way. A Concours d'Elegance was also included at the finish.

Austins entered a team of three cars, an 18hp Norfolk driven by Captain Sewell, Hadley and Dodson in the Big Seven Forlite DOV768 and Dennis Buckley in a 14hp Goodwood.

All three cars would have special accessories fitted and have non-standard paintwork, the two larger saloons being finished in a metallic silver, quite unusual at that time.

1938 RAC Rally. Austin team en-route.

Bert leads the Austin team through the
Honister Pass and past a stranded Singer.

You <u>can</u> do it in a Big Seven! Bert hustles DOV through
the driving tests in the 1938 RAC Rally.

The rally started from the Ace of Spades
Garage, Hounslow, Middlesex and ended four
days later in Blackpool, via Wales and
Scotland.

Bert's car was somewhat modified and of
course carefully prepared and proved to be a
brisk performer. Bert described it as 'a
delightful little car' and it was to be part of
Bert's life for a number of years, eventually
becoming his own property.

ROUTE CARD — LONDON

Starting Point : THE ACE OF SPADES GARAGE, Great West Road, Hounslow

ITINERARY.	MILEAGE		Intermediate Time Allowed H.M.	Periods during which Controls will be open.
	Intermediate	Growing		
LONDON (Start)				
OXFORD BY-PASS	50			
GLOUCESTER	48			
BRECON	60			
TENBY (Control)	76	234	234	9·0	6.20 p.m. to 8.50 p.m. Tues.
Royal Gate House Hotel				
TENBY				
LLANDOVERY	55			
CROSS GATES	36			
SHREWSBURY	53			
NEWCASTLE-UNDER-LYME	34			
SHEFFIELD	48			
DONCASTER	19			
YORK (Control)	34	279	513	10·44	5 a.m. to 7.30 a.m. Wed.
Royal Station Hotel	—			
YORK				
KENDAL	89			
KESWICK	30			
ROSTHWAITE (Check)	6	125	638	4·49	9.50 a.m. to 12.20 p.m. Wed.
Scawfell Hotel	—			
ROSTHWAITE				
BUTTERMERE (Check)	7	7	645	16	10.5 a.m. to 12.35 p.m. Wed.
Victoria Hotel	—			
BUTTERMERE				
COCKERMOUTH	10			
CARLISLE	26			
DUMFRIES	33			
STRANRAER (Check)	67	136	781	5·14	3.20 p.m. to 5.50 p.m. Wed.
George Hotel	—			
STRANRAER				
AYR	51			
LARGS (Control)	31	82	863	3·9	Open on Wed. to each competitor for one hour after his schedule time of arrival.
Hollywood Hotel	—			
NIGHT STOP			12·51	
LARGS				
CUMNOCK	42			
DUMFRIES	44			
CARLISLE	33			
KENDAL	45			
BLACKPOOL (Finish)	48	212	1075	8·9	For 1 hour after each competitor's schedule time of arrival on Thursday.
	Total Time Allowed 54·12			

THE
ROYAL AUTOMOBILE CLUB
RALLY
26th—30th April, 1938

ROUTE BOOK

For Competitors starting from

LONDON

THE ACE OF SPADES GARAGE
Great West Road, Hounslow

RALLY   NUMBER

This Route Book must be carried throughout the journey,
and must be handed to all Control and Checking Officers
for their signature and stamp. It must also be signed by
the drivers and passengers at each Control, but not at the
Checks.

Bert was due to be the sole Austin driver to take part in the Junior Car Club (JCC) International Trophy meeting at Brooklands on May 8th. An excellent field of the leading drivers had entered and with the Track's method of handicapping by means of artificial 'chicanes' in operation, Bert thought he had a good chance of an outright win. That was the plan but fate stepped in to decree otherwise.

Bert takes up the story:

'During practice however, my engine blew up without warning. A valve dropped in, smashing the piston, and a conrod came out through the side. I was flat out coming off the Members Banking just after the famous bump. The Twin-cam has a transverse steering arm arrangement operating via a small light alloy casting bolted to the chassis offside. There is very little clearance between the arm and the horizontal magneto. The conrod smashed the magneto and the debris locked the steering, fortunately with a few degrees to the left. Inclination to the right would have meant hitting the fence on the Railway Straight. I couldn't possibly have walked away from that. As it was, I finished up in a tuning bay at the end of the straight. John Cobb had the Napier-Railton located there. He said jokingly "Don't tell me that was a broken oil pipe!" When he gathered what had happened he said "You are a very lucky chap." We had two cars running at that time. The second car was in Germany on loan to Walter Bäumer and no real effort was made at the Works to build a new engine, this in spite of the fact that sets of parts existed in the Experimental Department stores. We were forced to withdraw from a race which had tremendous possibilities for the Austin Twin-cam.

Showing the close proximity of the steering arm to the right-hand magneto. Not much room for re-arrangement!

Lord Austin was abroad at the time, which allowed full rein to the anti-everything clique. I telephoned Murray Jamieson at his home in Stamford and told him we were out. He was understandably annoyed. He had written to me to say he would be going to see the race and that he had a very special pass. He pinpointed the place where he would be taking photographs. I told him on the telephone that I would meet him there and we would be able to use our pits.

I travelled from Birmingham to Brooklands on the day of 8th May. I was held up by heavy traffic on the way and found a second hold up at the Paddock entrance gate where Jack McCann was officiating. It seemed a chap was trying to get in without the necessary pass, but Mr. McCann was not the type of man to be fooled by anybody. Anyway, by the time I reached the Paddock, the race had started. Crossing the bridge over the old Finishing Straight I met Bill Anderson who was Competitions Manager for Wakefield's Oils at that time. He told me about the crash, saying "Bad luck about Jamieson, he was knocked down and seriously injured."

I went to Weybridge Hospital immediately and found Humphrey Cook of ERA there. He was in a terrible state. He obviously had a lot of time for Jamie and his wife Sybil. The best medical attention available could not save Murray Jamieson. Humphrey mentioned the sports car project at ERA, current at that time and designed by Jamieson. Without Jamieson, he said, the project could not be completed.'

The disaster naturally made lurid headlines in the daily papers with calls for safety procedures to be improved or even for an outright ban on further racing. What actually happened was succinctly reported by eye-witness, Rodney Walkerly, 'The Motor' magazine's 'Grande Vitesse':

> 'After the first lap, the leaders streamed around the hairpin at The Fork.........close behind in a pack came the rest of the field – and then we saw Joseph Paul's V-12 Delage was blazing. As it passed me, slowing down, the Delage pulled over to the left, crossing the nose of A.C. Lace's sports/racing Darracq. As I watched, Lace's car slammed the tail of the Delage, which instantly shot up the earth bank and plunged into the crowd, packed four deep at that spot.'

Amongst those present was Kay Petre, naturally very shaken but luckily unhurt. Nine people were rushed to Weybridge Hospital with one immediate fatality. The one person who *wasn't* there was of course Bert Hadley who, but for the delays in getting into the circuit, would have without doubt been standing alongside his friend and mentor 'Jamie'.

Tom Murray Jamieson died without regaining consciousness on Tuesday May 10th, aged just 32, leaving his young widow Sybil and their five week old son, David.

---

14 1938

BLAZING CAR AT BROOKLANDS

JURY AND PROTECTION FOR PUBLIC

Verdicts of "Death by misadventure" were returned by a jury at Weybridge yesterday, at the inquest on the bodies of Thomas Murray Jamieson, of Stamford, Lincolnshire, a racing car designer, and Miss Peggy Williams, 23, of Wembley Park, who were fatally injured when a blazing racing car crashed into a section of the crowd within two minutes of the start of the International Trophy Race at Brooklands last Saturday.

The jury added a rider that "We consider that some steps should be taken to afford more protection to this section of the course, and until this is done that section should be closed to the public".

Mr. D. Lloyd-Lowles said that the Brooklands Automobile Racing Club (for whom he appeared) had already decided to close that part of the course to the public until further protection had been afforded. He added that Mr. Jamieson was not in the public enclosure at the time of the accident.

"A LAP OF FLAME"

M. Joseph Paul, the driver of the car, was wheeled into Court on a chair. Giving evidence through an interpreter, he said: "After I made the first turn at the end of the finishing straight and entering the Campbell straight I felt moisture on my back and 20 or 30 metres on I noticed flame. After leaving the corner I accelerated first, but finding more moisture I braked. After that I was enveloped in flames. I continued to brake in order to reduce the speed of the car. I was practically

asphyxiated. I did everything I possibly could." He added that he had to be lifted out of the car and did not know anything more.

M. Paul said that the rule of racing was to overtake on the left. He looked to see if he were inconveniencing anybody and pulled to the left. There would have been a holocaust if he had pulled to the right. He could not possibly get to the right as there were cars there which prevented him. He did not remember touching anybody or anybody touching him. He had no idea what lit the petrol. In theory it might have been a "lap of flame coming out of the exhaust pipes."

"COLLISION INEVITABLE"

Mr. A. C. Lace, of Staines, said that as far as he could remember Paul accompanied him throughout the rolling start and was in a position half-right of him and slightly ahead. There were about half-a-dozen cars in front of Paul. "I did not notice anything the matter with his car until he had taken the first hairpin into the Campbell straight," said Mr. Lace. "I saw a burst of flame—so far as I could see, from the extreme tail of the car. It seemed to envelop the entire tail. From that moment Paul continued straight for a matter of 25 or 30 yards. His car then appeared to pull off slightly to the right. I thought then was my opportunity to accelerate and pass him before anything happened, but unfortunately his car swerved left. I thereupon left the track and ran on to the grass verge. I realized that a collision was inevitable, applied my brakes and switched off. Paul's car then struck mine a glancing blow amidships. I did not know whether Paul was in the car or out of it. I was covered with burning petrol which splashed on to me, and my clothing caught fire."

At the time of the impact it seemed to him (the witness added) that Paul's car was completely out of control.

LEAKAGE OF PETROL

Mr. H. P. McConnell, official scrutineer at Brooklands, said that he examined the car after the accident. The fire was obviously caused by a leakage of petrol and either, accepting the driver's suggestion, a flame from the exhaust pipe or a loose electrical connexion. The only way he could account for the petrol being on

Paul's back was that the petrol from the rear tank surged forward into the side tanks and so overflowed up through the filler caps. He would never have thought that sufficient petrol could have got through. Mr. McConnell said that he accepted M. Paul's theory of flame from the exhaust rather than the electrical theory. There was no suggestion of fire on the engine side of the bulkhead.

William Ernest Humphreys, a racing driver, who was also taken to hospital, said, "All I remember is that Mr. Jamieson was behind me. We were walking together, not looking at the cars but in conversation. Then he knocked me over and threw me forward and went up in the air over my head, and we both landed together at the bottom of the grass verge. Some car, I do not remember which, cut across my shins."

MRS. THOMAS'S ESCAPE

Mrs. Eileen May Thomas, who was to have driven in the race but whose car was scratched, said that she saw the blazing car coming straight at her. "I just dropped on my face," she added, "and the car went right over me. I was picked up rather alight."

Mr. Harold John Griffiths, of Hersham, said that he extinguished the flames on Mr. Lace's car with a sheet. He would say that the speed of M. Paul's car as it left the track was about 40 miles an hour. He did not think that either M. Paul or Mr. Lace could have done anything more.

Mr. A. Percy Bradley, clerk of the course at Brooklands, was asked by the CORONER whether a jury's rider in a previous case—that there should be stricter supervision with regard to racing—had been carried out.

M. Bradley replied that it was carried out in many directions. What happened last Saturday was in an entirely different set of circumstances. Special precautions were taken for the race at other spots thought possibly dangerous.

Mr. MONTAGU.—If there had been an iron fence these unfortunate people would probably be still alive?

Mr. BRADLEY.—I am afraid the whole question of safety banks is a very difficult one, because there is always the danger that if a car went into a very stiff bank its tail might go up and it might somersault right into the people.

(via David Murray Jamieson)

14th May 1938. Donington Coronation Trophy Meeting.
(Left) A pensive Hadley prior to the race, wearing an armband in memory of 'Jamie' who had died just four days beforehand. *(Right)* Bert gave his all when racing for the Company as this photo shows after he had to retire five laps before the end of the Trophy event.

A mere 4 days after Jamie's death it was back to racing at Donington for the JCC Coronation Trophy meeting. One can only guess Hadley's state of mind after the tragedy of the previous week, but Charlie Dodson was back in support in the other Twin-cam and they had three races to contest. Bert won the first two 5-lap races followed home by Dodson on each occasion.

14th May 1938. Donington Coronation Trophy Meeting – 5 lap Handicap Race.
Hadley takes the win with 2nd placed Dodson in the distance.

Hadley, driving in Jamie's memory, was expected to win the main event but despite showing mastery of the by now wet and slippery conditions, had to retire five laps short of the finish. Dodson had also dropped out earlier.

Two weeks later it was back to Shelsley Walsh. It was a superb day for Bert, settling a new class record of 40.09 seconds. Dennis Buckley, the son of AMCo's Sales Manager drove the surviving Side-valve. Their combined efforts ensured Austin received the team prize. The event was beautifully recorded by 'The Motor' magazine's staff artist, Frederic Nevin whose pencil and poster paint illustration appeared in the following week's issue on the Tuesday. They did not hang about in those days! Featuring several other competitors but with Nevin's dramatic impression of Bert 'on full noise' as the centre-piece, the original artwork graced the Hadley living room for many years thereafter (see back cover).

There was then a full month's breather for the team to re-fettle the Twin-cams and try and sort out the niggling problems still being experienced.

A Great Try
Bert Hadley (below) drove with as much determination as ever and got down to 40.09 sec. (second fastest) with the 750 c.c. Austin. He did not use twin rear-wheels.

28th May 1938. Shelsley Walsh Hill Climb.
Note the leather seating at this stage.

Ron Beach snapped his friend HLH in his Twin-cam, prior to the 1938 Nuffield Trophy meeting.

July 9th and it was back to Donington for the Nuffield Trophy race. As usual it was to be run on a handicap basis. The Longbridge team had to pick their events with care, only entering those where they had a chance of success. This was vital to keep the race programme afloat, the budget for this almost down to a pittance level.

9th July 1938. Donington Nuffield Trophy Handicap.
(Left) Hadley going flat out down to the Melbourne Hairpin. *(Right)* Note the marshals sitting casually trackside.

Bert and Charlie worked wonders to keep the larger opposition at bay but 'Bira' (ERA) took the lead from Hadley with eight of sixty-four laps to go. Bert held on to 2nd place, Doddy was 4th.

Bert enjoys some refreshment after the Finish. Brockas, Appleby and Freddie Bonham look happy.
Captain Sewell *(centre)* enjoys a quick 'snifter'.

20th/23rd July 1938. Welsh Rally.
1937 DOV768 has now been updated with 1938 running boards.

For August 27th it was across the Irish Sea for Craigantlet Hill Climb. As Bert will tell in his own words, the mile-long hill just outside Belfast was one of his all-time favourite venues along with the wonderful hospitality of the Ulster people. On this occasion, he had the 'right' car and had high hopes of lowering his existing record time for the hill (1min 21.25secs or 1min 4secs – depending where you read it – Irish timing?). Unfortunately it rained and despite his best efforts, which had the sodden crowd enthralled, he remained two seconds adrift (though still fastest on the day). His record would stand until 1948 only to be beaten by Bert's nemesis – Thomas Raymond Mays.

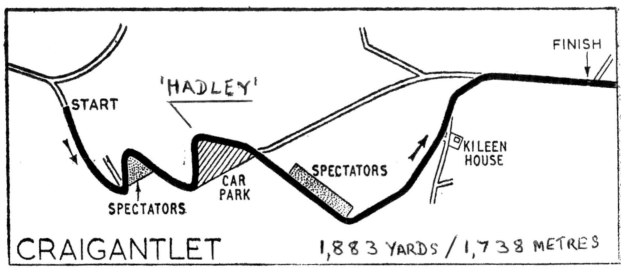
Craigantlet c.1938. (The 4th corner was dedicated to HLH after the war.)

September 10th at a dry and sunny Shelsley Walsh, Hadley, Dodson and Buckley in the Side-valve are raring to go. Bert was able to just shave his existing class record with a storming 40.05 seconds to gain 2nd FTD only beaten by Mays, whose ERA was now stretched to 2 litre capacity.

After his successful Shelsley outing, Bert's remaining season was centred around Weybridge. The Dunlop Rubber Company was celebrating its fiftieth year of trading and as a result of this sponsored an entire Brooklands meeting on September 24th. Both Twin-cams were entered and for HLH, it resulted in him winning the Dunlop Jubilee Trophy, a 10-lap scratch race and coming a close second in the 4th Road Handicap event.

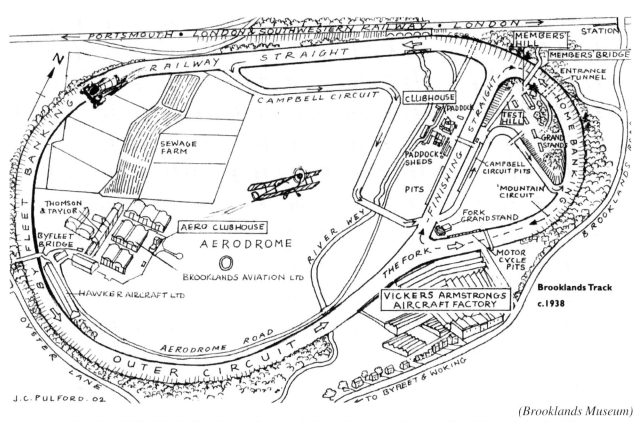

(Brooklands Museum)

Brooklands c.1938. John Pulford's excellent 'period' modern map of pre-war Brooklands in its final form.

Meanwhile, the International situation was not improving, with an increasing number of people belatedly realising that the antics of Hitler and his cohorts were for real and that appeasement was not the answer. Prime Minister Neville Chamberlain perhaps, in hindsight, unfairly berated for his 'futile' efforts to reach a peaceful solution had returned from Munich – emerging from his hired Lockheed Electra waving that famous piece of paper, declaring 'Peace in Our Time'.

The Donington Grand Prix, originally scheduled for October 1st had been cancelled at the last moment, with the German drivers and their entourages scuttling back to the Fatherland for fear of internment. The event was hurriedly re-scheduled and eventually went ahead on the 22nd. Interestingly, in early 1938 Bert had casually asked Lord Austin if was war likely, to be told in no uncertain terms 'not to be a bloody fool and listen to idle chit-chat'. Of course Austin knew otherwise – after all he headed various committees involving the leading industrialists and Government ministers and had full knowledge of the situation as it developed.

Austins had been the first of the larger employers to provide its workforce with underground shelters for possible air raids (the Longbridge tunnels were planned as early as 1935) and of course, the new Flight Shed, much publicised as the widest open-span structure in the country, was hardly constructed for the manufacture of pea-shooters.

The final Brooklands meeting for Bert took place on October 15th but it was not to end in glory and in fact fizzled out as he had to withdraw with mechanical problems whilst contesting the Siam Challenge Trophy. So ended another eventful and reasonably successful year (for Hadley), with him regularly featuring in the motoring press and receiving rave reviews for his heroic efforts, usually against greater opposition.

Perhaps more gratifyingly for Bert was the respect handed out by his peers and the fact that several of the major works teams were showing an interest in him. Engineer-drivers who were capable of fast and consistent performances were always in demand and there were times when Hadley had thoughts of taking his chances with another firm, particularly when he encountered problems within the Longbridge 'system'. In the end, he decided to stay loyal to Lord Austin and to the memory of his mentor Murray Jamieson, at least for the foreseeable future.

Bert and Rose Stallard were still an 'item' but with his continuing ambition to further his racing career there was no way he could commit himself to matrimony. Rose accepted this, though their families would have liked to have seen the couple 'settle down' like their siblings.

The 1939 season started for Bert and Bob Simpson with the January 6th/7th Exeter Trial. Their vehicle however was not one of the usual trials cars, latterly called 'Grasshoppers', but the Austin Big Seven driven by Bert in the 1938 RAC Rally.

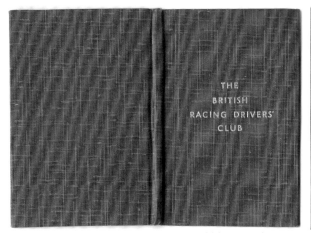 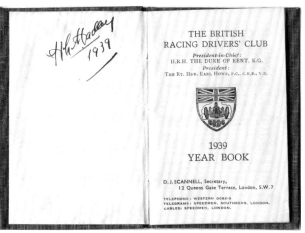

1939. Part of 'The Establishment' – at last!

For the Colmore Cup event in February, COA 119 replaced 'old faithful' BOA 60, which had been sold. By this time, Bert had become elected as a member of the British Racing Drivers' Club and purchased a new set of white 'Grenfell' cloth overalls from 'S. Lewis of London' to proudly display the distinctive club badge thereon. Some racing drivers were beginning to be aware of the dangers of motor racing and purchasing 'proper' helmets – Hadley was one of these and bought a 'Herbert Johnson' helmet which he painted a sort of Air Force blue. By modern standards these helmets were little more than 'hard hats' but were better than nothing.

S. LEWIS

Racing, Flying & Motor Clothing Fame

27 Carburton St., LONDON, W.1

'Phone : Museum 4793

WHITE RACING SUITS, button front, all round belt	22/6
" " " fitted Zip front, all round belt	27/6
UNBLEACHED SUITS, Zip Fastener	22/6
CAR CRASH HELMETS, our super quality, all colours	42/-
" " " cheaper quality	32/-
WHITE LINEN HELMETS, perfect fitting	8/6
RACING GOGGLES, fitted Triplex Lenses, Rubber	
Eye Pads	45/-
MEYROWITZ GOGGLES .. .. 45/- and	85/-
AVIATION MASK GOGGLES, fitted Triplex Lenses	16/-
" " " Duplex Safety Lenses	8/-
F.W.T. PATTERN GOGGLES, Clear Triplex Lenses	13/-
" " " Duplex Lenses ..	6/-
RACING VISORS, any style made	6/6

We make Racing Suits in any Colours to own requirements for a few shillings extra.

Over the years, the appearance of the Twin-cams had seen a number of detail changes – the body was made in separate sections unlike the one-piece effect of the earlier cars. For 1939 the 'Hadley' car would have a revised front cowling. The peripheral slots surrounding the air intake were louvered and the wire-mesh stone-guard retained but the nine 'Staybrite' vertical slats were omitted. To further encourage the air to flow through the intake rather than over it, an 'eyebrow' deflector plate was attached to the cowling, just below the 'Wheel on Wings' badge. The ex-Dodson car was unaltered. 'Ex–Dodson' as Charlie was not retained for the new season and would be plying his driving skills elsewhere. In fact, the racing budget was so drastically cut that Bert on his own would contest just four circuit meetings, supported by Dennis Buckley (already on the Longbridge payroll of course) in speed events. Such was the general opposition at Board level that Lord Austin himself partly funded the '39 competition programme out of his own pocket. With a new Works Director, Leonard Lord at the helm, Herbert Austin was gradually having to cede various aspects of the Company to others. In addition, having reached his seventies, Austin's health was not so robust as before.

The possible availability of Bert's services for other races was not un-noticed by other teams, including the German outfits, as both Bernd Rosemeyer and the Englishman, Dick Seaman had lost their lives the previous season. At home, the only other British team with purpose-built race cars, ERA, was now under the full control of Humphrey Cook and had conveniently relocated to Donington Park. There were also two new 'E-type' ERAs available and Cook had plans for Hadley to team up with Arthur Dobson for the Albi Grand Prix in July. At the Italian event only the Dobson car ran, which retired with mechanical problems. Correspondence survives in which, having been approached by Cook, Lord Austin declines *'a loan arrangement as a matter of principle ....I hope however you will be able to get someone equally as good as Hadley'.* Of course, Bert knew nothing of this until he found out via 'the grapevine' what had gone on. He was naturally upset at not being kept in the picture, though of course he was merely an Austin employee. Nevertheless, Bert confronted Austin about the matter in his inimitable, 'diplomatic' way and his Lordship saw the Hadley point of view and actually apologised for not keeping Bert informed. However his decision remained unchanged.

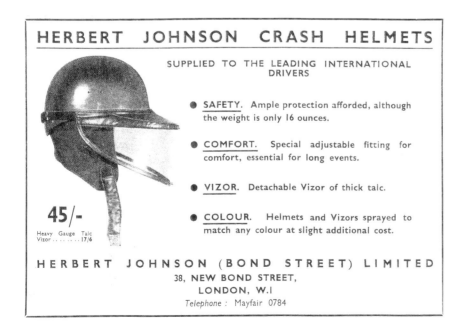

HERBERT JOHNSON CRASH HELMETS

SUPPLIED TO THE LEADING INTERNATIONAL DRIVERS

● SAFETY. Ample protection afforded, although the weight is only 16 ounces.

● COMFORT. Special adjustable fitting for comfort, essential for long events.

● VIZOR. Detachable Vizor of thick talc.

● COLOUR. Helmets and Vizors sprayed to match any colour at slight additional cost.

45/-
Heavy Gauge Talc Vizor 17/6

HERBERT JOHNSON (BOND STREET) LIMITED
38, NEW BOND STREET,
LONDON, W.I
Telephone : Mayfair 0784

Bert was obviously looking forward to his future as a racing driver on a full-time professional basis although was becoming increasingly frustrated with the situation at Longbridge. By the late summer Austin had finally agreed that Hadley would be released to drive for ERA in the 4th Donington Grand Prix already scheduled for the forthcoming October. Of course the 'international situation' put paid to this.

The next outing for Bert was on April 1st for the customary British Empire Trophy Race. An excellent entry had been gathered with most of the leading British drivers participating. Run over 64 laps (200 miles), Bert battled his way through into a secure second place to Tony Rolt's ERA, only two laps adrift.

1st April 1939. Donington BRDC British Empire Trophy.
Hadley (No.1) leads under the Dunlop Bridge. Bert eventually finished 2nd to Tony Rolt (No.19) in ERA R5B, right behind Bert in this picture.

As usual, Bert had worked hard for his place, years later admitting that he often took chances 'and got away with it'.

Bert occasionally suffered upper leg cramps during the longer races which manifested itself in later years as painful sciatic nerve problems. But as he also said, it was the memories of his mentor 'Jamie' which provided a large amount of his motivation.

1st April 1939. Donington BRDC British Empire Trophy.
(Left to right) Con Pollock 3rd, Bert 2nd, Tony Rolt 1st (behind the trophy).
Dodson, who was forced to drop out, joins them on the podium.

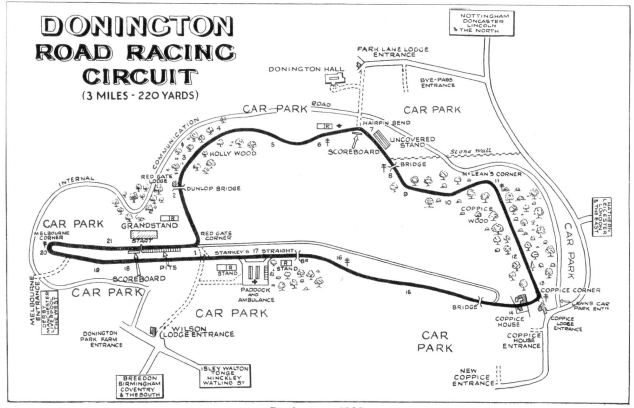

DONINGTON ROAD RACING CIRCUIT (3 MILES - 220 YARDS)

Donington c.1939.

No competitive motoring for HLH until June 3rd for the next Shelsley Walsh meeting. The bigger gaps between meetings meant that the single-seaters, particularly Bert's car of course, could have as much time and attention paid as was necessary to keep them in perfect order. The team, such as it was, were literally running from event to event and it was essential that a good showing was achieved on every occasion. Bert did a lot of the preparation himself, along with Ral Appleby and Bill Rogers, leaving Len Brockas free for more urgent production projects.

25th/28th April 1939. RAC Rally.
HLH debuts the new Austin Eight Saloon on Brighton's Madeira Drive.

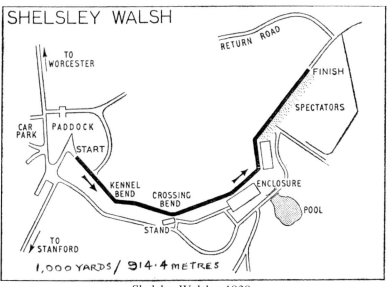

SHELSLEY WALSH

1,000 YARDS / 914·4 METRES

Shelsley Walsh c.1939.

At Shelsley, Bert was joined by Buckley in the other Twin-cam whilst motoring journalist T.H. Wisdom had a guest drive in the Side-valve. Some twelve years later, Bert and Tommy Wisdom would be team mates again in the Jowett team. Bert's best time on this occasion was 40.56 secs, ending up 4th FTD.

10th June 1939. Donington Nuffield Trophy.
Bert finished in 8th place behind six ERAs and the Maserati driven by Charlie Dodson.
Note the revised front cowling on Bert's car.

Back to Donington a week later for the Nuffield Trophy Race, the Hadley/Austin combination could only muster 58 out of the target 64 laps, finishing in 8th place, but with all those ahead of him in bigger-engined cars.

1939 Nuffield Trophy. Bert leads Pollock (ERA) into Hairpin Bend.
Note the closeness of the spectators – and the trees!

10th June 1939. Donington Nuffield Trophy.

An evocative view of the circuit with the Hall in the distance. HLH and Peter Whitehead (ERA R10B) battle it out.

1st July 1939. The Crystal Palace Cup.
H.L.Hadley in pristine white overalls and new
BRDC badge. Note the inset Dunlop 'Fort' twin
tyres on the rear.

July 1st and it was down to London for the Road Racing Club's Crystal Palace Cup meeting. As usual it was run as two heats plus a final, with handicapping on engine size. Bert won Heat 2 with no problems and the Final provided the enthusiastic spectators to a superb spectacle of close racing between Mays, Hadley and 'Bira'. Bert 'drove his socks off' to keep the two more powerful ERAs apart and it was considered to have been the finest race so far witnessed at the tortuous venue. Although Mays won (on the last corner of the final lap!) it was Hadley who made the headlines in the press reports.

For some time, Bert had been giving considerable thought on how to obtain more performance out of his car. The developments planned by Jamieson were all at the blue print stage and some components had actually been part-machined. The limited-slip differential assembly would have been particularly beneficial, but there were just no funds available for this. Bert had even considered converting the front suspension to Porsche-type independent springing as used on the Auto-Unions. Perhaps a more likely change would have been to hydraulic braking which his friends the Emmotts would have been delighted to arrange via their Lockheed Company. None of this happened and if any improvement was to be obtained it had to be down to perfect preparation and HLH's driving ability. Let Bert continue the story:-

'The need to produce "results" was such that I could not stop the racing programme to introduce any major modifications. However, I did wonder if I could improve my lap times at the Crystal Palace – full of corners but ideally suited to our cars – if I could work out a way to overcome the persistent wheel spin and reduce the tendency to slide, both due to a high power-to-weight ratio. In the early days we had used twin rear wheels as had others. I tried them at Craigantlet and Shelsley and found them highly dangerous. It seemed obvious to me they were too wide and promoted rear-end steering, a situation which contributed to Pat Driscoll's bad accident in 1936.

I decided to have another go with the twin rears. I had in mind a tyre with twin treads with a space between them. I tried Dunlop, but they would not play so I contacted Pirelli at Burton-on-Trent. They agreed to look into my suggestion. Obviously I had to keep the Old Man informed of my plans. Unexpectedly he said 'you cannot go ahead with your idea with Pirelli as we have a binding contract with Dunlop [this was certainly the case as the Du Cros family, who owned Dunlop, had bank-rolled Herbert Austin's company since the early days and were major share holders]. By chance, a little later I happened to mention my ideas to Geoffrey Taylor, whose firm were producing Alta cars in small numbers. He said "Let me have a drawing, I know a place in London which will make them." With Albert Hitchman's assistance, I provided Geoffrey with a blueprint on which I specified narrow 4-50 section tyres on 17" rims. I did discuss this with Dunlop's Competition Manager who was horrified when I told him there would be no space between the tyre walls. He was very set in his ways, like many other competition "reps" in those days. In my design the hubs were inset so that the inner tyre was almost touching the suspension. The new wheels were a first class job and I fitted standard Dunlop "Fort" tyres straight out of the Longbridge stores. After a terrific bashing on our test track at the Works, they neither moved or overheated or even flew off as people had forecast.'

The Bugatti Owners' Club meeting at Prescott on July 30th had an International flavour to it and was billed as such. Star attraction was the French 'ace' Jean-Pierre Wimille driving the 4.7 litre Bugatti, accompanied by Jean Bugatti himself. Hadley and Buckley were both present with the Twin-cams, fitted with the new rear set-up. Buckley had set a new 750cc racing car record the year before in the Side-valve but it was Bert's first outing at the picturesque venue and the only Prescott appearance of the Twin-cams, so the good crowd of spectators had plenty to look forward to despite damp conditions. Bert's recollection of this meeting is a bit hazy and for once his otherwise very good memory let him down. However, the Bugatti Trust's archives contain a comprehensive report on this meeting which clarifies the sequence of events as far as Bert's day went.

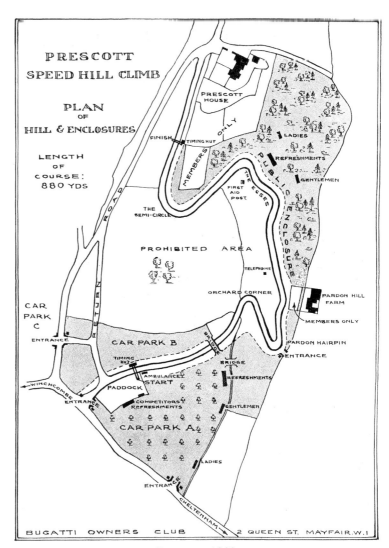

Prescott c.1939.

(© Bugatti Trust)

During practice Bert cut the last right-hand corner too close. The right-hand rear wheels hit a small wooden stake which completely removed the outer tyre and tube which went on to land in a tree near a marshals' post. HLH later said he never noticed this and knew nothing until Ral Appleby pointed it out on his return to the paddock. Although the rim was slightly damaged, Bert was able to continue thanks to the organisers altering the running order to enable a wheel assembly to be shared between both Twin-cams.

30th July 1939. Prescott Hill Climb.
Bert sets off on his first run of the day
and is caught by the camera of
Jean Bugatti no less.

30th July 1939. Prescott Hill Climb. A wonderful shot of Bert as he aims for the other cameraman by the tree, whilst Earl Howe, Jean Bugatti and Jean-Pierre Wimille stand unconcernedly amongst the weeds.

As it happened Bert had three runs, the first one not being recorded. Having already set a new class record on his re-run, his final time was 47.76 secs, 0.09 seconds under the course record! Of course this spurred Mays to post 46.14 secs. (2 litre ERA) with Wimille, Beadle (Alta) and Fane (Frazer Nash) followed by Hadley. So the fastest five cars were separated by 1.62 seconds. All were supercharged and apart from the Austins, of 1.5 litre capacity or over. A splendid achievement by the Longbridge representatives (Buckley was under 50 seconds) and well recorded by the photographers. There is even a colour ciné film of the event made by A. F. Rivers Fletcher, but don't blink or you may miss the Austins!

The Motor

October 18, 1939.

Last week, "Grande Vitesse" reviewed the racing performances of Johnny Wakefield, Raymond Mays, Arthur Dobson, Reggie Tongue, H. L. Brooke, Kenneth Evans, Lord Howe and Robin Hanson. Here are the achievements of a few more well-known men. At the foot of this page we repeat the full list of drivers and their 1939 placings.

Bert Hadley, the works Austin driver and a very fine man to have behind any wheel, has again had a good season, seeing that the little car could only be run in a few selected events. As usual, he was terrific—and terrifying—at Shelsley, where he was fourth fastest, irrespective of engine size. Then there was the famous Crystal Palace Cup race in which he made second place, not a length ahead of Bira, who was somewhat disgruntled about it, and after running fifth at Prescott he won the Imperial Trophy in a canter, driving as usual without making a single mistake and giving nothing away. A man to watch, is portly little Bert. And what a genial grin.

(Ferret Fotographic)

30th July 1939. Prescott Hill Climb.
Bert passes under the original footbridge.

Back to Bert:

'I thought it was now time to look hard at the axle ratios in use. We had got into a rut on this issue. There was one ratio we used for the Outer Circuit at Brooklands and a second which was used for all other events (3.43). In addition there was a third and very low ratio (4.26) which had been used only for the standing start records. Deemed too low for anything else by everybody, I thought there would be no harm in trying it out at the Crystal Palace.'

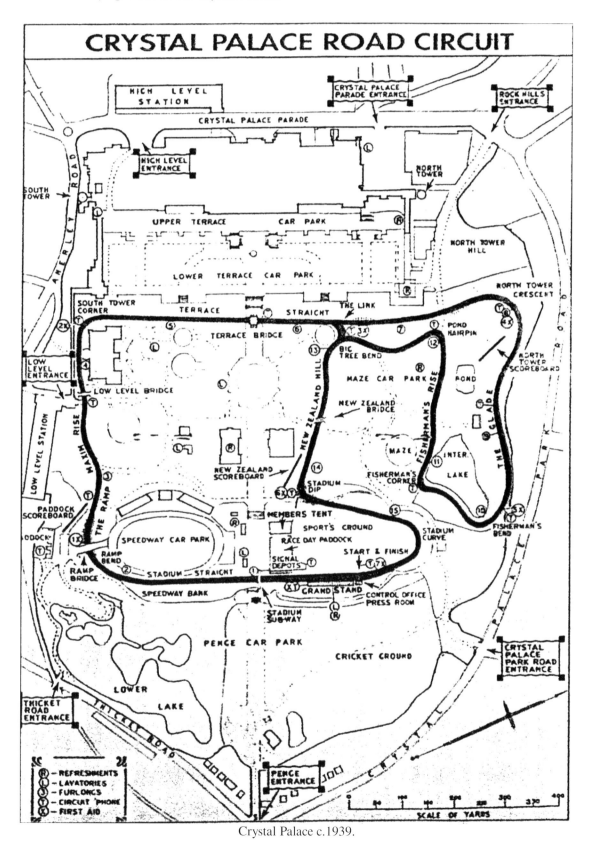

Crystal Palace c.1939.

At the August 26th RRC Imperial Trophy Meeting Bert was determined to put up a good show for Lord Austin and to the memory of Jamie.

'During practice, I had fixed a stopwatch to the steering wheel and I timed it myself on start and finish points, out of sight of the Official Time-Keepers. The result was quite astonishing for I found I was fractionally inside the lap record for the circuit [Mays ERA – 60.97 mph]'.

26th August 1939. Crystal Palace Imperial Trophy.
Bert thrills the packed spectators with a faultless performance.

Conditions at Sydenham were good and Bert, driving in Heat 1, won comfortably. Heat 2 was a scrap between Mays (1st) and Arthur Dobson, both ERA mounted. A full house of enthusiasts lined the two-mile circuit and was treated to a superb display of precision driving by Hadley as he scorched into the lead, leaving the opposition vainly trying to keep up. Back to Bert – in the driving seat!

> 'During the race, the car handled in a way I had not experienced before. It was quite extraordinary. I could not induce any break-away action in the corners and the low final drive allowed me to go right into corners without severe braking, the deceleration was so rapid. It seems incredible that we had achieved so much for a relative small outlay in time and effort.'

Hadley was reported as 'driving like a man inspired' or 'going like a bomb' and ended the race nearly two minutes ahead of 2nd placed Dobson, who driving at the limit, could not better Mays' lap record – the latter having retired with a puncture. As it happened, it would be the final race held on the two-mile circuit and what a corker! Bert switched his engine off at 4.30pm and it would not run again for over half a century.

26th August 1939. Crystal Palace. Bert takes the chequered flag to win the Imperial Trophy Race.

Amidst wild acclaim from the crowd and much praise from his peers, Bert stepped up to the podium to receive the splendid solid-silver Imperial Trophy for his efforts. He was of course interviewed over the 'Tannoy' system and even made a (short) speech in reply. Naturally, Lord Austin was delighted with HLH's success on behalf of the Company, but of course, had much graver matters on his mind.

Back at Longbridge, the Twin-cam was thoroughly checked over prior to the next event, the much awaited Shelsley meeting scheduled for September 9th, just two weeks away. The engine was partially dismantled to make sure all was well internally, in particular the state of the big-end bearings. Although the recently introduced 'Thin-Wall' detachable shells had been tried, the team were persevering with Jamieson's original direct-metalled connecting rods. They followed conventional practice of using a high quality white metal alloy, but on the Twin-cams the amount of metal was incredibly thin and had to be renewed at specific running intervals.

A tired but happy HLH on the dias with the splendid Imperial Trophy in his hands.

Bert recalls:-

'During practice for the earlier Shelsley meeting, I had arranged (with Ral Appleby) for comparative times to be taken for both Mays' ERA and my Austin between the exit of Kennel Bend and the last possible glimpse of The Esses. We discovered that I was at least a second faster than Ray on this section, although his superior bhp and resulting pace on the finishing straight gave him the overall edge. I was sure I now had the answer and certain I could lower Mays' record time. I worked out I had to find 2.68 secs to equal his best of 37.37 secs established at the June meeting. I was really looking forward to that meeting on the 9th, but it was not to be.'

- 8 -
WAR - AND NEW RESPONSIBILITIES (1940-45)

Behind the façade of 'normality', the Government had been preparing for a possible outbreak of hostilities for some time. By 1937, Air Raid Precautions (ARP) plans were secretly drawn-up and partially implemented (the Longbridge Tunnels for example), based on some ideas originally proposed in 1924! In the summer of 1938, as the situation worsened, trenches were dug in public parks, gas masks issued to all civilians, including babies, whilst in London, sirens were tested, as were anti-aircraft barrage balloons. Sand bags appeared, protecting public buildings. Hitler had annexed his Austrian homeland but the 'appeasers' and there were many, hoped that the Nazi regime would not further their territorial ambitions. At the time it was not general knowledge that the Nazis were already planning the methodical extermination of Jews and other 'undesirables'.

A raft of legislation was pushed through Parliament, including the Emergency Powers (Defence) Act, giving the Authorities permission to make any regulations for Public Safety, Defence of the Country, support for all Services and Maintain Public Order. Countless regulations would have an immediate impact on basic wages and working practices in the drive for maximum efficiency towards the War Effort.

During that same week-end when Bert was thrilling the crowds at Crystal Palace, Poland, under increasing threat from their Teutonic neighbours, mobilised its small defence force and the British and Polish Governments signed a Mutual Assistance Treaty. On September 1st German Troops marched into Poland. Hitler having ignored Prime Minister Neville Chamberlain's request for dialogue the United Kingdom, Australia and New Zealand, plus the French declared War against Germany on Sunday September 3rd. 'Black-out' regulations were immediately enforced, as was the Military Training Act under which all men between 18 & 41 had to register for military service. Back at Longbridge a state of 'organised panic' prevailed as the Works prepared for War Production. Bert recalled seeing a freight train full of steel scrap parked in the Longbridge sidings clearly marked HAMBURG! A few months later a German high-explosive bomb would fall on virtually the same spot killing Hubert Overend, a millwright who he knew well.

All motor sport had been cancelled forthwith and Bert was instructed to clear the Competition items from the Experimental building which was now required for other use. He eventually found a suitable and secure space within the North Works complex. Here, the three race cars plus the entire spares inventory, including at least three unused Twin-cam crankshafts, were moved in. In addition, the ex–Kay Petre Side-valve car was included. As previously mentioned, the Brooklands accident had put paid to her racing career, the car however had not been badly damaged and was certainly repairable, but for various reasons it had just been put aside. By the Tuesday after the Crystal Palace outing, the piston and connecting rod assemblies had been removed from Bert's engine for attention prior to the next outing at Shelsley on which Hadley had such high hopes of beating Mays. In addition, the clutch had been relined. The loose parts were all carefully wrapped up and labelled. There may have also been one or two Trials cars included though, according to Bert, most of these were out 'on loan' never to return to Longbridge. Hadley's personal tools and his note books were also amongst the many items locked-up for the duration - something he would later regret.

With HLH likely to be called-up anyway, he immediately volunteered to be trained as a fighter pilot with the Royal Air Force (R.A.F.). The Air Ministry in their wisdom thought otherwise decreeing that at the ripe old age of 29 his reflexes would not be up to the required standard, and not only that, they were not even willing to give him a chance to prove himself. This attitude infuriated Hadley and he expressed his feelings in no uncertain terms! He really wanted to leave Longbridge as he was becoming increasingly frustrated with his situation.

Vehicle production was steadily moved over to those complying with War Department specifications, such as 4 and 6–wheel–drive trucks, K2 ambulances, 10hp Utilities ('Tillies') and a spartan version of the Austin Eight Tourer. A few saloons would also be produced with basic trim for Ministry duties. Meanwhile in the huge Shadow Factory, Fairy Battle monoplanes had been in production for several months plus sub-assemblies for Miles Master training aircraft. In service the 'Battle' proved vulnerable to the superior firepower of the Luftwaffe and losses were high. This was not necessarily the fault of the designers nor of the brave men who crewed them, rather it was down to the Air Ministry Specification they were built to. Whitehall was notorious for its dithering and procrastinations when it came to making decisions and aircraft were often obsolete by the time they came into service. The tunnels eventually stretched for a remarkable three miles under Longbridge and were put into use for the production of Bristol radial engines, being assembled largely by women. In fact, Bert had a cousin, Bill Bedford, who was in charge of the Airframe Section at the Shadow Factory.

Bert was eventually seconded to the Aircraft Works and was now in a Reserved Occupation, thus being exempt from immediate call-up. Such were his talents recognised, he became a 'Rate Fixer'. Most of the production workers were on piece-work, paid by results. Thus Hadley had to get to grips with the 'black art' of Time and Motion Study and several of his books on the subject have survived. As time went on, Hawker Hurricanes were added to Austins' contracts, the Hurricane becoming the most successful British fighter aircraft during Battle of Britain, though popularly overshadowed by the more glamorous Spitfire. As an aside, one of the author's heroes - Sir Tom Sopwith - made a decision which probably saved Britain. During the Great War fighter planes bearing his name had played a vital part on the Western Front. Later his company became Hawker Aircraft, named in memory of his friend and pilot the Australian Harry Hawker who lost his life whilst testing.

Although the Hurricane had impressed Air Ministry officials as early as 1935 the orders were not forthcoming and Sopwith, fully aware of the German menace, decided to go ahead for production of 1,000 aircraft. In so doing, invaluable manufacturing time was gained before the hostilities actually began.

By the middle of 1940, production of the Short Stirling was underway at Longbridge. The first of the RAF's heavy bombers, these four-engined aircraft were far too big to take off from the Flying Ground, so these were transported to nearby Elmdon (now Birmingham Airport) for assembly and dispatch.

This then was the everyday world of work now occupying Bert's thoughts. He continued to live with Herbert and Lydia at Twyning Road and 'Rosma' Stallard with her parents. Despite being an 'item' for over a decade, they were still not officially engaged. Not a great deal happened on the 'Home Front' during the so-called 'phoney war', but after the hurried withdrawal from France and the miracle of the Dunkirk evacuation, Great Britain really was standing alone against the Nazi hordes, as the German invasion barges were assembling over in the Channel ports.

HLH continued to be in regular contact with Lord Austin, who at 74 was declining in health and it grieved Hadley to see the upper management types hovering around Austin 'like vultures' as the Old Man's faculties diminished. Whilst doing his best for the Company – he knew no other way – Bert kept reminding Austin of his wish to move on. Because of the regulations referred to earlier, he could not leave his position at Longbridge unless offered alternative employment of similar importance to the war effort. To this end Austin personally provided references addressed to both Ministry of Supply and Ministry of Aircraft Production. Neither of these interviews came to anything so Bert continued working at the 'Aero'.

By January 1940, both food and petrol rationing were in place, though the latter would be withdrawn completely with fuel only available to essential users. After Dunkirk it was only a matter of time before the expected German Invasion by sea got underway, supported by squadrons of Junkers JU 52 transport planes, each capable of carrying 18 fully-armed paratroops. To carry out such a task the Nazis needed control of the air and Field Marshal Hermann Göering declared his Luftwaffe pilots would destroy the Royal Air Force in a week. History and the Battle of Britain were to prove him completely wrong and by September the invasion, 'Operation Sea Lion', was postponed indefinitely.

As the R.A.F. took on the might of Germany over the skies of Southern England during that summer of 1940, as well as producing new Hurricanes for the conflict, many battle-scarred Spitfires came to Longbridge for urgent airframe repairs. By November the Luftwaffe started to concentrate on sustained night bombing of industrial centres throughout the country. One of the heaviest onslaughts was against the city of Coventry, less than 20 miles east of Birmingham, which was effectively destroyed including its famous Cathedral, the ruins of which still stand as a memorial to all those who lost their lives.

Birmingham also suffered several heavy raids within days of each other. The raids could last up to eleven hours in duration with wave after wave of bombers droning overhead. On the 22/23 November six hundred separate fires were recorded, with over 800 fatalities and thousands more injured. Much of the south of the city escaped, apart from isolated damage, Stirchley coming off fairly lightly. However neighbouring Kings Heath, home to the Stallards, did suffer quite badly. Bert recalled driving his future mother-in-law on her rounds during one such attack. Bombs or no bombs, babies could not wait! HLH regarded Nurse Stallard not only a determined lady, but also a very courageous one, far braver than he. The morning after revealed the steel sunroof on her 1938 Austin 'Ruby' saloon peppered by shrapnel damage.

To cope with the situation even more legislation came in to force. Sir William Beveridge, later to achieve fame for his 'Beveridge Plan', which included the founding of the National Health Service, had been appointed head of the Manpower Requirements Committee. An emergency survey had showed there would be insufficient able-bodied people to man the Armed Forces *and* maintain War Production. Radical and compulsory re-organisation of available labour, including females, was the result. The Registration of Employment Order and the Essential Work Order covered four and a half million workers of all trades. It was this last piece of legislation, signed by the Minister of Labour & National Service, Ernest Bevin, no less, in March 1941 which would dictate H. L. Hadley's future career path.

There were over 100,000 individual manufacturing firms, large and small throughout the land and it would require an army of knowledgeable people to oversee the directing of these companies

THE MINISTRY OF LABOUR AND NATIONAL SERVICE

towards maximum output of essential production. Lord Austin, still serving on various Government Committees would be fully informed of all the developments and realised it would be a challenge to Hadley to make a go of it. Shrewd to the end, Herbert Austin saw in Bert that potential to make a success of a new job, possibly a new career. Thus Austin put forward Bert's name, personally recommending him for the position of an Inspector of Labour Supply in early May 1941. Shortly after this, Lord Austin fell ill with pneumonia, which combined with a heart condition resulted in his death, aged 75 on 23rd May. His funeral was, of course, a major affair attended by dozens of dignitaries and thousands of Longbridge workers, including Bert. A sad end to HLH's time at Austins but now another new challenge awaited him at the Ministry of Labour and National Service District Office at Cheylesmore, Coventry.

Around Christmas 1940, a time of great uncertainty at both family and national level, Rosma Stallard announced to one and all that (by 'design or accident' – we can but speculate) she was pregnant! After an epic courtship which had started way back in 1928 this was something both sets of parents had hoped for – another grandchild – but perhaps not under these circumstances.

The Hadleys appear to have been rather upset that the conception had taken place out of wedlock – attitudes then were somewhat different from those prevailing today. The Stallards on the other hand took a different view, particularly Mrs. S, who as an experienced Midwife had 'seen it all'.

On a short honeymoon, Rose models the latest fashion in maternity wear!

During his racing career, Bert would not have wished to commit himself to the responsibilities of marriage, let alone fatherhood, because of the inherent risks he took. Rose, being the quiet, patient soul she was, accepted this.

So, four days before his 31st birthday, Herbert Lewis Hadley and 29 year old Amy Stallard were married on 4th April 1941, at Birmingham Register Office with Mr & Mrs Stallard as witnesses. The Hadleys do not seem to have been involved, at least not 'on paper'. Neither does living at Twyning Road (where there was ample room) seemed to have been an option for the newly-weds.

Interestingly, Amy / Rosma / Rose is described on the Marriage Certificate as a 'Chauffeuse'. We know Bert taught her to drive, though she still had a Provisional Licence as late as 1938. Unfortunately we do not have details of any 'professional' driving duties she may have carried out prior to her marriage.

Bert was formally issued with his Certificate of Appointment as an Inspector of Labour Supply on the 18th June 1941 and it must have been a daunting period for him, acclimatising himself to the ways of the Ministry, with everything following set procedures and quite probably written down in triplicate. Commuting daily to and from the Coventry Office and also doing his rounds of manufacturing firms, he was on the road a great deal, using the ex-RAC Rally 'Big Seven' saloon he'd bought off the company several years before. DOV 768 had been up-rated by a 'sportier' camshaft, bigger valves and carburation by Bert himself when it was new so it was a brisk performer, especially with HLH at the wheel! It would serve him well until around 1943 when, after an incredible mileage, it was replaced by a 1939 Morris 'Series M' Ten saloon which boasted an overhead valve engine and Lockheed hydraulic brakes – years before Longbridge started to use these features on their passenger cars.

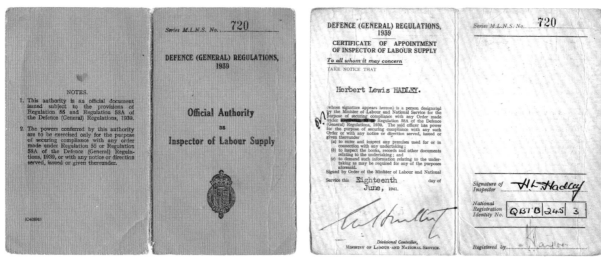

H.L.Hadley's Warrant Card 'Inspector of Labour Supply'.

He had not long been into his new duties when, travelling in DOV on a country road in broad daylight, he was startled by a short burst of machine-gun fire as a German intruder aircraft, possibly a Messerschmitt ME 110, flashed overhead into the far distance. Bert pulled up obviously shaken but completely unhurt, as was the car, but it was a stark reminder that, at the time, danger could be lurking around anywhere.

Meanwhile, in between his increasingly busy work schedule, Bert was actively searching for somewhere to set up home with Rose and their yet unborn child. Empty or vacant properties of any kind had to be registered with the Authorities who were constantly requiring accommodation for key workers and military personnel. As her daughter's time was approaching and mindful that at nearly 30, a first pregnancy could be critical, Nurse Stallard arranged for Rosma to enter 'Avonside' at Bidford-on-Avon in the Warwickshire countryside. Being 'in the trade' Mrs. S. knew this would be the best place for her daughter to be before the event, being one of Warwickshire County Council's main maternity homes. Today, 'Avonside' is a beautifully-maintained private residence. Rose seems to have been at 'Avonside' for quite a time. Bert was worried about Rose and chasing leads for a possible house, and of course, Rose was concerned for his safety, with the threat of intermittent air-raids still about.

Four letters have survived, all undated, one on Midland Automobile Club (MAC) notepaper! Bert is then staying at 40 Mayfield Road Ashbourne in Derbyshire, the home of Bill Butler and his family (of whom, more anon). Bert writes of *'being at school today'*, *'still going to it'*, *'addressing the boys to volunteer for Rootes Securities'* (an aircraft 'shadow' factory in Coventry), *'Just like old times at*

Handsworth Tech'. He mentions someone at Austins' aerodrome going after a furnished house for him *'tonight'* – it didn't happen but – *'we have to score sometime'.*

Communication by telephone seems to have been difficult so the letters continue. *'Busy with thousands of reports'*, *'It's a hell of a life arguing all day, getting people to work who don't want to'*, *'How are you getting on this week – any nearer?'*, *'Bill is trying to get us a house – we may be lucky'.* Meanwhile, Bert is being persuaded to do ARP duties at the week-end.

Later Bert received a letter from Rose, complaining about 'pains'. In reply, HLH hopes it's 'the start' – he will be glad when it's all over. Meanwhile, he has pains in his back and sides! Bert mentions he is *'taking over a big factory to find all their labour requirements'.* This gives an indication of the sort of responsibilities he was taking on. As an aside, *'going to that farm for some butter and a rabbit – if I can shoot it.......'.*

Eventually, after all the waiting, Rose gave birth to a healthy boy on 28th July 1941. Bert made a brief visit to see his son and then it was back to work. The final letter starts:

'How is he looking now – I have been thinking of you both all day – seems too good to be true.......The greater difficulty will be finding a name, at least that's the concern of the Butlers, they are delighted with the news. Told someone at the office – now it's all round the place – even the Boss conveyed his somewhat austere congratulations! It's great to know you are both ok. There seems to be a tendency tonight to wet the baby's head. I pointed out I didn't bring your mother's ten-bob note with me so won't be able to pay.'

1942. All smiles. Granny Hadley with young Clive at Twyning Road.

The 'boy' was eventually named – Clive Lewis Hadley. Bert had recalled the dashing 'Bentley Boy' Clive Dunfee who had made such an impression on him at Brooklands all those years ago. The middle name of Lewis was, like Bert's, included in the memory of Jane Lewis who had married Thomas Hadley in 1870. Rose eventually left 'Avonside' to return to her parents' home at Kings Heath with the new grandson. Bert was busy commuting between Ashbourne, Coventry and Birmingham, whilst still searching for a permanent home for his family.

Bert had met William Cornelius Butler (WCB) whilst taking part in a trial in 1935. It was an early outing for Bert and Bob Simpson in BOA 60 (later to be known as Grasshopper II) and in between sections they came across a fellow competitor with a Singer propped up on bricks in the pouring rain. The driver, a tall chap with thick glasses was scrabbling about under the front of the car, trying to fix the exhaust. Hadley and Simpson offered what help they could then continued on their way. It was the start of a life-long friendship and when Bert needed a temporary base whilst Rose was in 'Avonside', Bill Butler and his wife Ann, together with their young sons Douglas and Brian, were only too pleased to help out. Bill had built up a successful garage business, 'Harcourt Motors' on Stafford Street in Derby. He had also bought into a small machine shop in Ashbourne, not far from their home. Upon the outbreak of war, both these premises would be commandeered for the manufacturing of small parts for Rolls-Royce 'Merlin' aero-engines.

Back in 1935, Butler had purchased the Singer, a 1.5 litre 'Le Mans' 2-seater, registered AOG 1 from the Patrick Motors Group in Birmingham whilst obtaining second-hand stock for his forecourt sales. He became a regular on the Trials scene and he and Ann also took part in the 1937 RAC Rally as did Bert in an Austin 10hp Cambridge. Bill continued campaigning Singers up to the outbreak of hostilities. Through the 'grapevine', WCB had discovered there was an empty cottage on North Avenue in the town and this is where the Hadleys finally settled and made their first home together. During the summertime this was a very pleasant place to live, situated 13 miles west of Derby just off the A52 and surrounded by typical Derbyshire countryside. The two-bedroomed property, 'Beechcroft', stood on its own within a spacious cottage-type garden with ample space to grow fruit and vegetables to augment the basic food ration.

Bert commuted to Coventry each week staying near his office, mainly to save time and petrol, though he would endeavour to get home during the week if he could. Of course there were no motorways in those days and the strictly-enforced 'black-out' made driving often difficult particularly in bad weather and with only the one masked headlight allowed.

At about the time the Hadleys settled in Ashbourne, work commenced on the construction of R.A.F. Ashbourne, on the flat farmland adjacent to the Derby-Leek road and by the autumn of 1942, No.42 OTU (Operational Training Unit) had started training bomber crews. The former peace and quiet was now constantly interrupted by low-flying Whitleys, Blenheims and Ansons. At least they were 'friendly' and not carrying bombs! Ashbourne, in the main has not changed all that much and remains an attractive market town, with many interesting Georgian properties. The levels of the area rise sharply and North Avenue runs high along a ridge across the back of the town, the centre of which lies below, thus all accesses from the town are up fairly steep hills, which must have been hard work for Rose with Clive in the pram, whenever she needed to reach the shops. In winter it would be virtually impossible. Winters in general were far worse than we experience today and Derbyshire was particularly prone to heavy snowfalls as it still is. Bert recalled drifts of up to 20 feet deep not uncommon and he would regularly become stranded in Coventry or at home.

Wintry Ashbourne. Rose with one of her pet Dachshunds.

Despite his commitments to his new job, Bert regularly kept in touch with his motor racing contacts. Humphrey Cook, owner of ERA, had found some heated premises in Coalville, Leicestershire, opposite a Meredith & Drew biscuit factory. With Fred Craner's assistance, the ERA cars and spares had been moved out of Donington Park as the War Department had requisitioned it all for vehicle storage. Knowing of Bert's concern for the Austin single seaters at Longbridge, Cook suggested there was ample room at Coalville, where it would be more secure. Bert did approach Arthur Waite about this, but sadly nothing was done about it. As Bert later observed, Britain's future was looking grim and there were more important matters to consider.

A view of Ashbourne, Derbyshire.
North Avenue runs across the top of the town.

Amongst other people he kept in contact with were Francis Curzon, otherwise known as Earl Howe, who at that time was President of the British Racing Drivers Club (BRDC) and a great admirer of Bert's racing talents. Howe regularly corresponded with HLH during the war, all hand-written, but unfortunately (for us) the letters 'went missing' in the move to Kenilworth in 1950.

F.J.Findon, long-term editor of 'The Light Car' magazine and fan of HLH, outside Vox Villa at Shelsley where he pioneered outside broadcasting of motorsport during the 1930s.

He was also in contact with another pre-war acquaintance, F. J. Findon, who was known as 'Eric', the long-time editor of 'The Light Car' magazine from 1932 until its demise in 1956. Herbert Hadley had been a regular reader of this since Bert was a small boy. Findon had pioneered public address broadcasting at Shelsley Walsh since 1931, based in a wooden shed known as 'Vox Villa', still a feature of the famous venue. He also commentated on the BBC and at the inaugural televisual broadcast from the Crystal Palace meeting in October 1938.

During the war, 'The Light Car' soldiered on as a slim monthly publication, largely filled with historic articles and snippets of news concerning well-known motoring personalities. The December issue in 1943 contained news from 'another famous racing driver' – Bert Hadley - who writes: '*After meteoric promotion, I am now a very serious (and much wiser) person. I am a member of a Manpower Board.*' Bert is also 'a proud father' which explains the picture of Clive Hadley on the next page. Bert also adds his bit to a subject aired elsewhere in this issue – namely 'Government Support for Motor Sport' '*If people (and I mean self-satisfied industrialists) had realised the propaganda effect of motor racing before the war, they might easily have contributed towards a change of Hitler's plans.*' Instancing the ignorance which then prevailed, he says that he was asked by a prominent industrialist who stood alongside him at the start of the 1938 Donington Grand Prix, whether the '*Works Austins were as fast as the Germans*!' The gathering of detailed information regarding Bert's Civil

MINISTRY OF INFORMATION

FREE
FILM SHOW
AT

THE ELITE
ASHBOURNE
ON

WEDNESDAY, 24th SEPTEMBER
1941

Commence at 2.30 p.m.   Doors open at 2.0 p.m.

WOMEN'S WORK IN THE WAR
AND OTHER EXCITING WAR FILMS

Children only admitted if accompanied by an adult

NO COLLECTION

Service records seems to have resulted in previous data either being destroyed or locked away for eternity. This little gem from 'The Light Car' gives an indication of just how quickly Bert adapted to his new career.

The Hadleys continued to enjoy the relative peace of life at 'Beechcroft', the modest cottage they rented in Ashbourne. Only the constant flying activity and the harsh winters spoilt an otherwise tranquil existence. During this period Bert continued the weekly commutes to his Coventry base, though later he was able to transfer to the Staffordshire office which enabled him to spend more time at home.

(Author)

'Beechcroft'. The two-bedroom cottage rented on North Avenue, Ashbourne.
On the right is 'Beechcroft' in 2010, showing parts of the major extensions added in the 1960s.

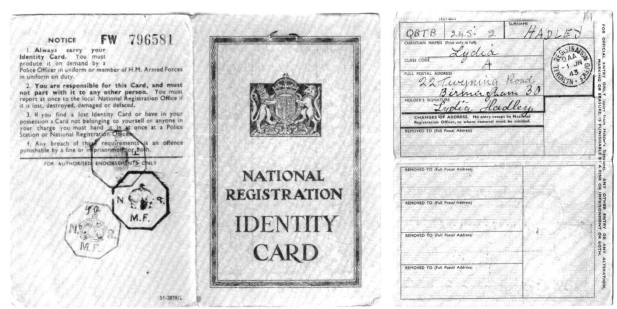

Lydia Hadley's Identity Card issued in 1943.

One major incident almost ended Bert's career, but once again fate was on his side. A former gypsum mine outside the village of Fauld near Tutbury in Staffordshire, had become R.A.F. 21 M.U. (Munitions Unit), a huge underground storage facility. On Monday 27th October 1944 a subterranean explosion occurred. An estimated 4,000 tons of bombs and ammunition blew up – the fourth greatest blast ever recorded during the Second World War. It happened at 11.11am, just about the same time Mr Hadley of the Ministry of Labour and National Service was due to see the Officer Commanding regarding a shortage of suitable supervisory staff. R.A.F. personnel, civilians and Italian prisoners-of-war were employed on the site. Bert was unable to keep the appointment, simply because his car would not start. The incident which claimed the lives of around 75 people was said to have been caused by the incorrect handling of a batch of already primed high explosive bombs. The crater is over 90 feet deep and covers some 12 acres. Even today it is a danger area and out of bounds to the public.

THE FAULD EXPLOSION

At just after 1100 hours on the 27th NOVEMBER 1944, the largest explosion caused by conventional weapons in both the world wars took place at this spot when some 3,500 tons of high explosives accidently blew up.
A crater some 300 feet deep and approximately a quarter of a mile in diameter was blown into the North Staffordshire countryside.
A total of seventy people lost their lives, with eighteen bodies never being recovered.
The 21 MU RAF Fauld disaster is commemorated by this memorial which was dedicated on the 25th November 1990, some 46 years after the event. The stone, which is of fine white granite, was a gift, organised by the Commandante of the Italian Air Force Supply Depot at Novara, a sister depot of No 16 MU RAF Stafford, from the firm of CIRLA & Son. Graniti-Milano.

(via Neville Barr)
A memorial to the many people who were killed
in the 1944 disaster.

Another incident, much closer to home, occurred three weeks later on 18th December. R.A.F. Ashbourne was still fully occupied in training bomber crews and was operating around the clock. A twin-engined medium bomber, Armstrong-Whitworth Albemarle, P.1554, had been flying in and out of the airfield since 6 a.m. the previous day and was returning to base at 4am on the 18th with a trainee pilot at the controls. The five crewmen aboard were very tired by this time. Given permission to land on the south-easterly runway, the pilot positioned the aircraft which entailed flying towards the town from higher ground behind North Avenue. It would then drop down directly over the town centre towards the aerodrome for its final touch-down.

An Armstrong-Whitworth Albemarle bomber (actually the prototype) of the type which crashed into the Hadley neighbour's house at Ashbourne.

Even in daylight, such an approach required intense concentration on the part of the pilot and his crew. With the 'black-out' still partly in force, the town was in virtual darkness below. One of the features of the Albemarle was its nose-wheel or 'tricycle' undercarriage, a 'first' for a British warplane and it was this which was to prove the undoing of P1554. As it approached North Avenue the aircraft dropped too low, the undercarriage hit a tree and the bomber ripped into the roof of a large Victorian house, 'The Mount', sweeping away several upper bedrooms, luckily without casualties, though the house was otherwise fully occupied.

Apart from the kitchen garden and some trees in between, 'The Mount' was next door to the Hadleys' home and it being a week-end, Bert was at home with his family and was one of the first on the scene. After hitting the house the Albemarle was literally stopped in its tracks and dropped nose-first behind the dwelling with its tail sticking up at roof level. Partly of wooden construction and with petrol venting from a fuel tank, fire or explosion was highly likely.

Bert would be very aware of this of course and with his help, the injured crew members were helped out of the wreckage before anything could happen. Unfortunately the navigator, in the nose of the aircraft, was thrown clear and died immediately. Several others were badly injured but later recovered. The aircraft having been made safe was quickly dismantled by R.A.F. ground staff and removed from the site. Whilst the incident was the talk of Ashbourne for a few days, the event was not reported to the outside world, such were the constraints of censorship at that time. Today, 'The Mount' has a flat roof which together with its castellated parapet looks remarkably 'original'. 'Beechcroft' has also survived, though during the 1960s it was greatly extended and is now a rather smart residence with an impressive garage block.

When Bert left Longbridge in 1941, he vowed never to return. In fact he did a few times during the war but only as part of his official duties. Soon after the surrender of Nazi Germany in 1945, he decided to see how the cars and equipment left 'secured for the duration' had fared in the North Works premises. After five years of flat-out production for the war effort, Longbridge was in some disarray. Having located the building HLH noticed the locks appeared to have been changed and sure enough what confronted him made his heart sink. All the cars and carefully stored spares had been disturbed and scattered and his own personal toolboxes had been broken into with many items including his notebooks missing, presumed stolen.

He attempted to find someone responsible for this lamentable state of affairs with little or no success and left, upset and very angry at the way the efforts of 'Jamie' and his team colleagues in promoting the company had so quickly been forgotten. Eventually space was cleared in the now redundant tunnel complex and the surviving cars were unceremoniously dumped therein, to gather more damp and dust. This was confirmed by historic racer Barrie Williams who recalled visiting Longbridge as a schoolboy in 1947 with his father, then an Austin retail dealer, and seeing the 'hush-hush' cars in the gloom. Of course by this time any loose parts or new spares had gone. Bert established some years later that the majority of these went for scrap. A few 'choice' items found their way to people 'outside Longbridge'.

Rose and Clive c.1946.

HLH was utterly disgusted by all of this, but turned his thoughts to maybe indulging in some form of competitive motoring, once the petrol rationing situation eased and motor sport could return. He was of course in a very secure position with the Ministry and had been promoted to Technical Officer, a role which offered further scope for advancement as well as having a very good pension. However, he felt he still had much to offer as an engineer/driver and had kept contact with many of his contemporaries from the pre-war racing scene.

Rose was not quite so keen. Whilst she had been made welcome by the Longbridge racing team whenever she was present, she had never felt she was a part of the scene. In any case, she wanted them to concentrate on their son who would soon be starting school.

- 9 -

PEACE – A RETURN TO MOTOR SPORT (1946-55)

Bert's return to the sporting scene came early in 1946 and from an unexpected quarter. Before the war, Robert Kirkwood Nicol Clarkson, generally known as 'Roy' had become Scottish Hill Climb Champion, usually driving Ford V-8 Specials, which were popular at the time. An article in 'The Light Car' featured AOX 4, one of the earlier AMCo trials cars now owned by Clarkson and to which he had fitted one of Leslie Ballamy's 'LMB' swing-axle independent suspension conversions. Apart from this, the car was largely in its pre-war configuration, complete with retro-fitted Centric supercharger. The magazine praised its lively performance and general handling.

By some means, Clarkson, now plying his trade as an ambitious dental surgeon in Essex, had tracked down HLH with a view to the latter driving his car in the forthcoming 'Colmore Cup' trial, a prestigious event run by SUNBAC and a happy hunting ground for Hadley and Bob Simpson before the war. Bert recalled Clarkson's appearance in some detail:-

'A curious chap, he arrived without warning on our doorstep at North Avenue. Before he knocked we could hear him and his wife having a furious row. I thought maybe they'd escaped from Mickleover where there was a large mental hospital. He introduced himself and announced loudly that I was to drive his ex-Works car in the "Colmore".

With typical "Rhymney" directness [her South Wales birthplace], Rose was all for chucking them out. I didn't know the recent history of the car and on inspection the engine sounded a bit clapped so wasn't very keen. In the end he persuaded me to go along with his idea. In its early days, AOX 4 had been driven by R.J. (Joe) Richardson, whose family firm Richardsons of Oldbury were contractors to AMCo.'

Bert's nephew Peter Penny takes up the story:-

'I was still a schoolboy when my Uncle Bert asked me "Would I like to passenger him on the first post-war Colmore trial?" Needless to say I was thrilled about this. I knew something of Uncle's achievements of course and not only that, he'd got hold of an Austin "Grasshopper", though it was not one of "his" cars. As I remember it, we were doing very well, in fact in the lead. That's until we reached Leverton Hill near Broadway in Worcestershire. There was a loud clunk from the engine and we stopped! Bert said "That's it Peter, sit tight while I get some help." After that we were eventually towed all the way back to Twyning Road, Stirchley. Afterwards, I remember saying to my mother "Uncle Bert just got out saying 'that's it' – he didn't even open the bonnet – how did he know?" [In fact, the crankshaft had broken.]

Clarkson had got in to some bother over claims for National Health Service work and the Grasshopper was in Herbert's lock-up for weeks awaiting collection. Bert observed he could have probably got AOX 'for a song' but did not take it further.

Eric Findon had persuaded Bert to put pen to paper, resulting in an article which appeared in 'The Light Car' for May 1946. 'To The Day' is an interesting read and recommended to all prospective Shelsley Walsh competitors! Find it in Chapter 10. Meanwhile, Bert's contacts with his pre-war racing chums were beginning to bear fruit. After Murray Jamieson's departure to ERA, TMJ, supported by his chairman, Humphrey Cook (HC) tried to persuade Hadley to join the team at Bourne. However, Bert was not happy with the life style of some of the main players and decided to stay put at Longbridge. By 1939, Cook was in sole control of the company and having relocated to Donington Park had finally persuaded Lord Austin to release Bert to drive for ERA in the forthcoming Donington G.P. which of course in the end did not happen.

After war-time storage in Coalville, the ERAs were now at Dunstable, near Luton. HC was uncertain as to the way forward with the 'E' type cars, which had shown some promise but were somewhat fragile. Cook was not an engineer so turned to Bert for a detailed appraisal of the cars. He respected HLH's knowledge and experience and would pay Bert handsomely for his time and trouble.

Bert was by now firmly established on the Ministerial ladder and was able to take time off from the Coventry office. A vacant runway (now part of Luton Airport!) provided an impromptu test facility and Bert gave the sole running car a good workout. He was not impressed. The cars had been unreliable before the war and there were aspects of the basic design and quality of construction which concerned him. In the end he suggested that Cook should cut his losses and unload the lot. Enter Leslie George Johnson (LGJ) whose family firm were furniture manufacturers based in Walthamstow, East London. He purchased ERA in its entirety. Johnson had achieved some results driving the ex-Fane Frazer Nash-BMW. He would later enter one of the ERAs in several races but without success and the cars and spares were sold off to various people. One of the cars which I encountered on several occasions in the 1950s was converted into a 'hairy' Jaguar-engined sports-racing car, driven to every meeting as was the norm in those days. Johnson saw the future of ERA as a design and development concern. Having purchased an early Jowett Javelin saloon and found it to have competition potential, his company would eventually be involved in a project which resulted in the Jupiter sports car, of which more later.

Hadley later wrote that exercising the ERA on the old airfield was both *very interesting and enjoyable* and revived his interest in motor racing, though at the time he had no idea where that might lead. He was doing well at the Ministry with a secure future – a 'job for life' should he so wish. This did not stop tentative enquiries coming his way – many teams were looking for drivers of proven ability. One approach came from Alfa Romeo no less, though Bert did not fancy working with people who, until recently, had been our enemies. Of course, many of the personnel engaged in the pre-war scene were still active in top level motor sport in the early 1950s.

One Sunday morning his old friend Jack Emmott came over to Ashbourne with Leslie Johnson. LGJ had obtained an early Jaguar XK120 OTS (open two-seater) car along with a provisional entry for the 1950 '24 Heures du Mans'. The sensation of the 1948 Earls Court Motor Show, the XK was something of a stop-gap model to publicise the new twin-cam 6-cylinder engine intended for the forthcoming Mark Seven Saloon which was someway off production. This remarkable power unit had been developed by William Lyons and his colleagues Bill Heynes and Walter Hassan during wartime fire-watching duties, with later technical input from Harry Weslake. Using a chassis and running gear based on the OHV-engined Mark Five, the XK was clothed in an elegant Lyons-penned body, hand-built mainly of ash framing, panelled in aluminium.

Jack Emmott.

In fact only 240 of these two-seaters would be built before a hurriedly-devised production version with steel pressings largely replacing the timber framing and much of the aluminium was tooled-up for, such was the worldwide interest plus actual orders generated. All new cars at this time were scarce with long waiting lists for many of them. Certainly this was the case with the XK. The competition potential was obvious so William Lyons arranged for a handful of these early cars be made available to selected racing drivers who would enter as private individuals. These were mostly registered by the Works using the Coventry 'JWK' series. It would not be company policy to have official entries until the appearance the following year of the 'C' Types, which famously ran with painted-on 'Trade Plate' registrations! The 'JWK' cars were prepared at the Works and had the full backing of the embryonic Competitions Department headed by Frank Raymond Wilton England. 'FRW' always known as 'Lofty' – he was well over six foot – had pre-war experience looking after Bira's cars as part of the 'White Mouse' team and would be known to Hadley. England would eventually rise to become Managing Director of Jaguar before retiring to Austria, from where he regularly corresponded with Bert.

Johnson had already had some success with his car JWK 651 and was looking for a reliable co-driver for Le Mans. Emmott's firm were of course major component suppliers to Jaguar and knowing of Bert's re-kindled interest in a competition drive, he immediately recommended Hadley. After some considerable discussions with Rose and with his employers, Bert accepted Johnson's offer to partner him in the world's greatest sports car race which attracted many top teams and drivers. After taking more time off for a brief test session at Silverstone, Bert got out his pre-war overalls and cloth helmet and with LGJ headed off for the ferry.

24th/25th June 1950. Le Mans 24 hour.
Hadley and Johnson await Scrutineering.
JWK 651 was driven from Coventry with full equipment, this being removed for the event.

As they shared the controls en-route to the circuit, Bert suggested that Leslie might 'go easy' on the clutch as they had a lot of miles to cover. His observation was to later prove his point. HLH was now 40 years old, his colleague a couple of years his junior. The war years seemed to have aged Bert, the long hours and heavy responsibilities having left their mark.

The 1950 race featured a number of newly-introduced cars and this would be the Coventry concern's first appearance at the Sarthe circuit. Of the several XKs entered, the Johnson/Hadley car No.17, following a quick getaway by HLH at the famous Le Mans start, was going well and making steady progress at the head of the field. The circuit was largely unchanged from 1937 when Bert had driven in the Longbridge team, so thirteen years later he was able to put his previous experience to full advantage, lapping at speeds of around 115 mph with great consistency, something he found came naturally to him.

24th/25th June 1950. Le Mans 24 hour.
Bert makes a smart getaway at the Start.

Excellent pit work was also proving beneficial to the team's position and by midday on the Sunday they had moved into 3rd place overall and gaining on the two leading cars. At around 2.30pm with an hour and a half to go before the 4pm finish, the clutch started to slip, requiring careful 'nursing' by the drivers. Although further progress was not possible, they were still holding on to 3rd place when during the final hour, the clutch centre-plate broke up and their valiant drive was over. The race was a home victory for the French Talbot driven by father and son, Louis and Jean-Louis Rosier. The XK's demise enabled Sydney Allard in one of his own cars to clinch 3rd place, another great achievement. After the event Bert received a letter of thanks from William Lyons himself, congratulating him for his contribution to what turned out to be a 'glorious failure'.

24th/25th June 1950. Le Mans 24 hour. A well-known photograph.
'Mr Consistency' circulates at around 115mph in the early hours.

PROGRAMME OFFICIEL
100 francs

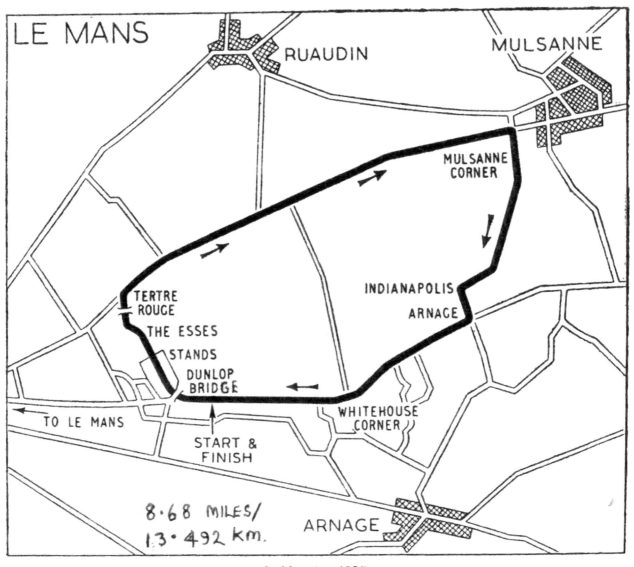

Le Mans (pre-1956).

The Hadleys had by this time been living in Ashbourne for some nine years with Clive attending the local Parents' National Education Union (P.N.E.U.) independent school. Life on North Avenue was in many ways very pleasant but the winters were still a problem, especially when Bert was away. During the particularly heavy snowfalls of 1947 an enforced stay in hospital had been a worrying time for Rose, who missed regular contact with her family. With Clive due to change schools anyway, they decided a move back to the West Midlands would be beneficial for everyone.

Clive Hadley *(Back row, second left)* at the P.N.E.U. School, Ashbourne.

The '47 winter was a bad one nationwide. Rose stands alongside the Hillman Minx backed by an impressive bank of Derbyshire snow.

Through his contacts Bert found a modest semi-detached house on Red Lane at Burton Green on the outskirts of the pleasant Warwickshire town of Kenilworth, just 5½ miles south of Coventry. Known locally as one of the 'new houses', number 78 overlooked open countryside at the rear. It was owned by the Chairman of the Coventry-Eagle Cycle Company and available for rent with a possible option to buy. Brought up to be careful with money, Bert now felt secure enough to become a home owner.

As soon as he could he had a 20ft garage/workshop built at the bottom of the garden. Clive was now growing up into a lanky lad with a mop of fair hair, the clear Derbyshire air having proved beneficial to his well-being.

Phil Groves, who also lived on Red Lane, remembers Clive attending Burton Green Junior School. Their respective fathers were good friends with shared interests. Mr Groves senior worked for Motor Panels (Coventry) who were respected prototype engineers to the Motor Industry. Projects he'd been personally involved with included Donald Campbell's 'Bluebird' land speed record car, the Jaguar XJ13 and the Rover-BRM gas turbine car which Graham Hill drove at Le Mans. After junior school both boys would complete their full-time secondary education at Kenilworth Secondary Modern School.

Clive Hadley c.1948.

121

Encouraged by his showing at Le Mans, Bert was keen to follow this up with further drives and on this score made a direct approach to William Lyons. In surviving correspondence, Lyons assures Hadley he is *'top of their list'* but could not offer anything specific *'at present'*. HLH's patience seems somewhat stretched and later complained (to Leslie Johnson) that he seemed to be passed over for *'inferior and less experienced drivers'*. Johnson, in a long reply, insisted he (LGJ) was doing his best for Bert but suggested he go to Brown's Lane (Jaguar HQ) and treat Lyons and his Engineering Director Bill Heynes to a good lunch! In fact, Heynes had Bert in mind for the following year's Le Mans team but kept quiet about it. There was also talk of Bert joining Jaguar on a full-time basis (he'd have made a superb development engineer) but his secure position with the Ministry decreed otherwise.

Bert later wrote frankly about this period:

> 'Bill Heynes wanted me to partner young Stirling Moss for 1951. I liked the idea but Jaguars didn't seem to know where to go from there. I also asked for a car for the 1000 kilometres race at the Nürburgring. They were keen but Sir William Lyons wanted to keep the thing appearing as if it was a private entry. I heard nothing further and then I had a long-winded letter from Jowetts promising me all sorts of things including rallies. For some unearthly reason, I accepted – what a shower they were! Bill Heynes did come back to me but by then it was too late as I'd given my word to Grandfield [Jowetts' Engineering Manager]. Jack Fairman took my place with Stirling and crashed the car in the Esses. Looking back, I think Moss and I would have won. Must have been something wrong with my head about this time!'

Johnson was looking for project work for his small ERA Company and it was he who suggested to the Jowett management that the mechanical components of their advanced Javelin saloon, wedded to a suitably stiff chassis, would make a good basis for a sports car. The Board eventually agreed to this and ERA was given the go ahead to design and construct a rolling prototype.

Unlike some of his contemporaries Bert was never interviewed in depth which is a great pity. The 'Motor Sport' team of Bill Boddy and Denis Jenkinson did try to arrange a get-together in 1973 but sadly it never happened.

HLH's post-war association with Jowett Cars Ltd of Idle, Bradford, in Yorkshire's West Riding was a brief and bitter-sweet experience. Noted Jowett author Edmund Nankivell spent a day at Kenilworth and has kindly provided an account of conversations he had with Bert.

Edmund writes:

'I first made contact with Bert in 1978. Various letters and phone conversations followed plus a visit to Kenilworth in 1983. He was a mine of information with a pin-sharp memory for people, events and details of his sometimes stormy relations with Jowett. He combined a good engineering background with a strong belief that he could assist the Company's fledgling competition department to greater things. He was also a very quick and consistent driver. Hadley was liked and admired by all the great men of the time from Leslie Johnson to Stirling Moss and the people at Jaguar. A fine man and for Jowett a wasted talent.'

The traditionally–Yorkshire Jowett company had been rejuvenated after the war with a new management team including Charles Grandfield as Engineering Manager. Grandfield had been in the Longbridge drawing office in the late thirties, for a while part of a team known as the 'Foreign Legion', drawing up parts from rival manufacturers and being associated with 'Experimental' matters, and would have known Hadley as a leading Works driver.

(Edmund Nankivell)
Bert sees Jowett author Edmund Nankivell on his way after the interview at Kenilworth. The car is an Adams and Robinson bodied Jupiter Coupé. Photograph probably taken by Rose.

Johnson proposed to engage Dr. Robert Eberan-Eberhorst to head the chassis project. Eberhorst had a proven track record with Auto-Union before the war. However, he was an Austrian national then currently working for the ailing Cisitalia outfit in Turin. At that time he would, as an alien, require a Work Permit to come to England. Bert Hadley, by now holding a secure 'middle management' post in the Ministry of Labour was approached, and knowing of Eberhorst's credentials was instrumental in arranging the necessary paperwork to expedite the Herr Doktor and his family's arrival at Dunstable.

By 1951, Jowetts were looking for team drivers. After the 'successful failure' of the 1950 Le Mans race with the Jaguar XK120, Bert was also on the look-out for further driving opportunities. Grandfield approached Hadley and persuaded him to join the team. Bert had been impressed by the 1949 successes (class wins in the Monte Carlo Rally and the Spa 24 Hours Race with Javelin saloons) and with the prospects of the new sports car, he thought the fledgling team could benefit from his combined driving skills and experience. He could drive for them as and when required on a race-to-race basis. Bert was very impressed with the ERA/Eberhorst-designed Jupiter chassis and regretted that the Austrian was never engaged to design a better engine for the Jupiter.

LES 24 HEURES DU MANS 1951

PROGRAMME OFFICIEL

200 francs

123

These then, were the events in which Bert drove for Jowett Cars Ltd:

1) Silverstone May 5th 1951

BRDC Production sports car race. Hadley immediately took the lead in the 1.5 litre category in the rebuilt 1950 Le Mans Jupiter GKW 111. After 15 of the 26 laps, the Jupiter blew a head gasket and Hadley had to retire. This was in the car that had run 24 hours at Le Mans in June 1950 to win its class.

2) Le Mans June 22nd-23rd 1951

Jowett fielded two lightened 'standard' Jupiters and one R1 model.

Bert rightly thought that as he was fastest of the three drivers, he should have the fastest car (the R1), but Grandfield gave it to Tom Wisdom as he was a motoring journalist and Grandfield thought he could get more publicity for Jowett.

22nd/23rd June 1951. Le Mans 24 hours.

Bert watches the Jowett crew unload Tom Wisdom's R1 Jupiter, apparently into the Mulsanne forest! Bert's car was No.42, a standard production Jupiter.

(Edmund Nankivell)

Bert said of Tom Wisdom:

'He was a good friend who I knew for many years. He was not a quick driver but he never claimed any such distinction. Grandfield thought it was a short cut to publicity for Jowett, which was just one of the mistakes he made. I haven't time to catalogue the remainder!'

Bert said he demonstrated he was faster than Wisdom (in the sole R1) by *'playing ducks and drakes with him.'* Hadley led Wisdom for 10 laps then slowed to let Wisdom through.

Bert's Jupiter in the 1951 Le Mans was the second car to retire (after only 19 laps) with mechanical failure in the engine department. Hadley said that if the right parts had been carried he could have repaired the car and carried on. There was a big bust-up in the Jowett pit between him and Grandfield, and Bert stomped off and was to return to England with his friend Jack Emmott in Jack's 3-litre Alvis. Jowett's Managing Director Arthur Jopling then wrote a grovelling letter to Bert apologising and asking him to stay on in the team for 1952. Bert agreed to continue with Jowett though he would regret it, as Bill Heynes belatedly asked him to partner Stirling Moss in the Jaguar team. Being a man of his word, HLH had to reluctantly decline their offer.

Bert said to Grandfield in 1951 he would have to do something about the engine as it was not competitive. But Grandfield, timid before the war, was arrogant after the war and would shout people down – the war changed him (he'd risen to the rank of Lieut-Colonel) *'Grandfield was alright up to a point, he was a developer but with no original thinking, and an awkward person to deal with'*. Bert said *'Jopling had Grandfield weighed up'* saying about the Jowett Company (I think in 1952) *'this lot won't last another year'*.

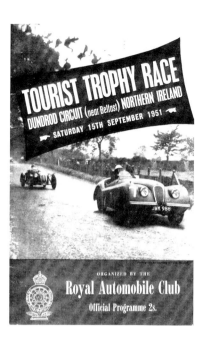

3) RAC-TT Dundrod September 15th 1951

Bert Hadley's Jupiter HAK 366 held together, much to his surprise, so he won the class. Hadley showed he was the faster driver with a best lap of 70.07 mph against Tom Wisdom's 69.52 mph.

15th September 1951. RAC Tourist Trophy Dundrod, Northern Ireland.
Bert hauls Jupiter HAK 366 around another corner on his way to winning the 1500cc Class.

It was Wisdom's turn to have a Jupiter that failed (although he did just crawl to the finish after 4 pit stops for water, so a gasket was going) and he had a blazing row with Grandfield using obscenities that were recalled for me many years later by an appalled eavesdropper (the episode, not the actual words!). So it was impossible for Wisdom to drive for Jowett again!

4) RAC Rally March 31st to April 5th 1952

The Jupiter given to Hadley (with his great friend Bill Butler navigating), was not prepared at all (Roy Lunn the Jowett Chief Designer admitted) it was just the Works hack GKY 107! The brakes failed on the way to the start! Luckily Lunn was in the team in another Jupiter and he managed to sort the brakes out. However, in the driving tests at Castle Combe, reverse gear failed the first time Hadley needed it – and he did not need reverse again until after the final Scrutineering at Scarborough, Bert told me. The box was repaired or changed later during the rally.

5) BRDC Silverstone Production Car race May 10th 1952

Hadley was in a Javelin this time. Very fast, he said, and he led his class but the engine blew up with two laps remaining. Hadley discovered that it was an engine with experimental pistons which had done many hours on a test-bed – a man from Hepolite came over and identified the engine (from memory this could have been George Hepworth).

6) Prescott Hill Climb May 18th 1952

Jowett would not fit the lower final drive ratio Hadley requested, which he thought the car needed to optimise it for Prescott, although they could easily have fitted a Javelin ratio crown wheel and pinion. Hadley engaged Harry Spears to prepare the car as he had no faith in Grandfield. The Jupiter was HAK 366 his Le Mans and Dundrod RAC-TT car. Hadley was 4th in class at 53.77 seconds.

18th May 1952. Prescott Hill Climb.
HLH on the start line in the TT class-winning Jowett.

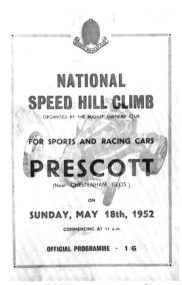

1952 Prescott. Bert keeps a tight line as he exits Pardon. Notice HAK 366 now has its bumper removed.

126

7) Le Mans June 14th-15th 1952

All three Jupiters were the R1 type. Hadley led the other two R1 Jupiters until the Gatsonides R1 failed with a broken crank after 68 laps, but after 149 laps the same fate befell Hadley's Jupiter. Bert said *'The R1 Jupiter was a nice car to drive – a very safe motor car, no vices. Unfortunately it did not have enough power'.*

Bert told me he got Grandfield most of his jobs after he left Jowett. Grandfield held one job for 10 years, passing the end of Bert's road twice a day, but never called in, so Bert said he felt *'used'* by him. Grandfield was ok on production work, seven events, five failures! No wonder Bert was sceptical about him, being clearly more than careless about the car provided in the two events (4) and (5). Also he was not competent to develop the engine to the 70bhp for Le Mans in 1952 when Jowett crankshafts *'were breaking on the test-bed like carrots'* as Bert put it (I have seen 90bhp claimed around that time for other makes of sports racing cars). Bert also said the R1 could have been better streamlined at the front.

If 1951 was the year of blown gaskets (solved for 1952 by the use of Wills Rings top liner seals - not a production solution but fine for racing), 1952 was the year of broken cranks which Jowett (under Grandfield) had foolishly decided to machine and harden themselves to save money. Of all the Jowetts Bert drove for the factory at least one has survived. HAK 366, his most reliable Jupiter, resides reclusively in a restored condition in its native county of Yorkshire.

For Hadley it continued to be a busy year behind the wheel and although he did not get the chance to race a Jaguar in anger again, Bert was approached by the British Racing Drivers' Club (BRDC) to see if he would be available for an extended visit to Montlhéry. This was the banked track just outside Paris where HLH had accompanied Murray Jamieson in the late summer of 1933. Once again HLH had to arrange more time off from the office but this was not a problem and Bert was able to accept the invitation.

6th-12th August 1952. Montlhéry 'Seven Days and Seven Nights'.
A dramatic shot by the official photographer.
The drivers were presented with a souvenir album of the event.

Headed by Leslie Johnson, the plan was to run an XK120 FHC (Fixed Head Coupé) on the banked oval for exactly one week 'non-stop' (apart from pit stop/driver changes) at a minimum speed of 100 mph. Jaguar had only recently brought the closed version of their best selling sports car to the market place and would be providing LWK 707, one of the pre-production examples, plus three mechanics. The whole operation would be overseen by Secretary of the BRDC Desmond Scannell and his deputy Mortimer Morris-Goodall.

The car, resplendent in metallic bronze (a standard colour) with the BRDC logo on the doors, was virtually standard but incorporated catalogued performance extras such as the regulations allowed. Apart from additional instrumentation and lighting, plus the installation of a bulky 'Pye' two-way radio, it was very much as you could order from your local dealer. An interesting driver line-up was recruited. LGJ, Hadley, Fairman and 23 year-old Stirling Moss would share the driving as all apart from Fairman had experience of Montlhéry on previous occasions.

At night the banked oval would be in darkness (apart from the pit area) with the perimeter illuminated merely by flickering hurricane lamps, as had been used since the 1920s. If the weather was favourable, the lights of Paris could be clearly seen but this could be an annoying distraction to the drivers. The run commenced on August 5th and by the seventh day the team's target had been achieved, though not without some late drama. During the final day the constant pounding generated by the aging concrete surface caused a rear spring to fracture. No spare was carried on board in the car so the mechanics had to remove both rear springs and change them over side to side, after lashing the damaged item together using whatever was available (and permissible).

6th-12th August 1952. Montlhéry 'Seven Days and Seven Nights'.
Hadley, Johnson, Moss and Fairman clamber aboard LWK 707 after achieving the target 100mph for the run.

Despite the crew's best efforts the run was delayed by some four hours. In fact, refusing to put his co-drivers at additional risk, Johnson undertook to drive the final nine hours himself, driving near the limit in order to regain the target average despite the broken suspension. In this he was successful and it was an amazing achievement. Along the way five Class 'C' records had been established and '707' actually covered a total of 16,851.73 miles at an average of 100.31 mph!

It was a remarkable team effort and of course wonderful publicity for Jaguar Cars and the British Motor Industry in general. Some years later when re-acquainted with the car, Bert recalled driving at speed on a tightly banked track akin to being whirled around in a bowl but one soon got used to it! He found driving about two feet from the outer edge helped him concentrate (!) and kept the tyre temperatures down. LWK 707 was seen on display from time to time in very original order. Unfortunately only a few years ago a motoring scribe, who shall remain nameless, was careless enough to hit a barrier at a Goodwood Festival meeting, whilst having a 'play'. '707' survived but inevitably some of her original patina has been lost.

In 1951 'C' Type Jaguars had won using drum brakes like everyone else at the time. However, maximum speeds were increasing and showing up the greatest braking problem – severe fade. The erstwhile New Hudson Company, best known for cycle manufacture, had become a leading brake supplier when it took over the classic rod and lever system devised by Captain Girling. It was adopted by many leading vehicle manufacturers including Austins. Girling reluctantly came into the hydraulic arena after the war, even producing hybrid hydro-mechanical systems up to 1951. The Dunlop organisation through its Aviation Division had successfully developed disc brakes for high-speed aircraft applications and by 1952 had produced a system suitable for automobiles. Dunlop subsequently withdrew from the vehicle-braking market and Girling effectively took over, further developing their own disc systems.

It was this Dunlop system that enabled Tony Rolt and Duncan Hamilton (No.18) to win the 1953 Le Mans against more powerful opposition. Famously, they were both (allegedly) nursing huge hangovers at the time, though this was not strictly true – nice story though. Even Ferrari and mighty Mercedes-Benz were struggling with huge multi-finned drums, some even water-cooled. Lockheed's on the other hand had produced reliable hydraulic systems, adopted by the likes of Morris for instance, since the late 1920s but had been slow in developing the disc type. To counteract this situation, Jack Emmott had arranged a production Jaguar 'C' Type to be fitted with a prototype disc set-up of their own. Lockheed's occasionally called upon HLH to do brake tests for them, mainly on the Silverstone Circuit. Bert would usually take a day off for this purpose – after all it was more interesting than 'work' – it certainly was on this occasion, vividly remembered by Bert:-

> 'I was driving a 'C' Type with a low axle ratio which gave a maximum of about 132 mph. Approaching the "old" Woodcote Corner [a fast right hander immediately before the pit straight – of happy memory!] I would normally brake at 200 yards. Having felt something odd at "Becketts" beforehand, I braked at 300 yards. Nothing happened so I tried to spin it out onto the infield. It wouldn't go. I spun into Woodcote at least eight times and stopped so close to some angle iron and wire netting that I couldn't open the driver's door. The front brakes had failed due to the fluid boiling – residual pressure forced the rears to lock on. There used to be a water filled dyke [in front of the grandstand] – I could see it coming at me for days after. Clive [11] witnessed it all and very pleased and excited said "Could you do it again please?" Jack, standing alongside him nearly gave birth! On the way back in the Jaguar there was a thumping sound. On arrival at Leamington where AP [Automotive Products] were based, we found a twelve inch section of a tyre tread had lifted due to the loading on the left hand rear wheel. Had it burst it could have been very serious. Very thankful – perhaps someone was watching over me again……'.

After the excitement of the previous season, Bert was able to relax over the winter and take stock of the situation. His job was going to plan with him increasingly involved with innumerable meetings and visits, mostly concerned with labour relations, throughout industry there was never a shortage of union trouble! Clive had settled in to his new school and was doing well. Meanwhile Rose was in her element, keeping the Hadley 'nest' spick and span.

By the year end he was on the look-out for more driving opportunities. He had a compliant employer who

FÉDÉRATION INTERNATIONALE DE L'AUTOMOBILE

ROYAL AUTOMOBILE CLUB
PALL MALL, LONDON, S.W.I.

No. AC 1684
LICENCE FOR A DRIVER
Valid up to 31st December, 1953.

Should the holder of this Licence be deprived of hi
Driving Licence, he shall return this document to th
Royal Automobile Club.

Issued to ...... Herbert Lewis Hadley
Under the approved assumed name of ......
Born the 18.4.10 at Bimingh
Permanent Address 78 Red Lane, Kennilw

Given at London the 20th day of February 1953.
Chairman of the Royal Automobile Club.

Signature
of Holder:

P.T.O.

H.L.Hadley's International Racing Licence for 1953. Only 43, but looks older…..

would allow him time off and he would (usually) get well paid for his efforts. At times it almost seemed like having two jobs! With his proven ability to concentrate for extended periods whilst safely driving at high speed, he knew his forté lay in long-distance events.

A major event on the international calendar was the Mille Miglia, a road race covering a thousand miles through towns and villages in rural Italy. Started in 1927 and revived twenty years later, the event had a fearsome reputation for breaking cars and serious accidents. Despite this it attracted a huge entry with many British crews attempting to beat the locals who of course had the advantage of intimate knowledge of the route.

So his pal, L.G. Johnson, approached Hadley with an offer he could not refuse – or could he? LGJ was very familiar with the event having driven the Le Mans XK120, LWK 651 into a splendid 5th place three years earlier, largely in pouring rain and at the time the highest placing for an all-British entry. This time Johnson had got his hands on a white 'production' Jaguar 'C' Type, registered by the Works as MHP 825 but now his own car. Suggesting Bert might like to co-drive in the M.M., he had a cunning plan to reduce the number of fuel stops en route. He intended to install a massive 40 gallon fuel tank which would effectively fill the tail of the 'C' Type apart from the necessary spare wheel. As we know, Bert was more than familiar with the 'XKC' and was concerned about Leslie's idea and opined that the extra fuel sloshing about could seriously upset the very neutral handling the 'C' Type was blessed with. Bert considered that the normal 27 gallon tank would be adequate to see them through to the check points, which were compulsory anyway. Additionally there was a great possibility that the light alloy tank would eventually fracture, due to the poor roads they would encounter, with the obvious risk of fire. Johnson however would not be deterred by Bert's views so HLH declined his offer and they parted amicably. In any case, Bert was already in demand elsewhere.

At the 1952 Earls Court Motor Show a new model, the Healey 'Hundred' made its debut. Based on Austin A70/A90 components installed on a light but rigid floor-pan and clothed in Gerry Coker's timeless 2-seat body, the single prototype on display was an instant sensation, much as the XK120 had been four years earlier. Leonard Lord, in charge at Longbridge saw the design and both he and Donald Healey realised the latter's tiny Warwick concern would not have the facilities to cope with the expected demand so promptly did a deal on the spot to take over the project with a royalty to Healey who would be retained as a consultant. By the following year the car was in full production at Longbridge as the BN-1 'Austin-Healey 100'. Before this, 19 pre-production prototypes were hand-assembled at Warwick. Four of these vehicles were designated 'Special Test Cars'. Numbered AHR5 to 8, intended for serious competition work and to be entered by the recently formed British Motor Corporation (BMC) following the Austin-Morris merger.

Three of the cars were prepared for the Mille Miglia, with final assembly in the Longbridge Experimental Department under the direction of Alf Depper no less, who was still there under his 'job for life' agreement! How much he was actually involved in the project is not known but it is just possible that Ral Appleby might have had some input into the engine or gearbox assembly as that is what he specialised in during his later years at the Works. Although looking very much like the catalogued car as was intended, these A-H 100s were special in all aspects, from the 'Birmabright' body panels to up-rated suspension, engine and transmission. It was a mixed team of drivers, No.548 (registered NOJ 392) Hadley paired with Bertie Mercer (who was a serving R.A.F. officer), No.552, two ex-T.T. motorcyclists – Johnny Lockett and Jock Reid and a third car, entry No.604 crewed by Donald Healey himself and his son Geoff. Actual race practice, or lack of it, was one of the problems for many British competitors but the Austin-Healey team did manage practice

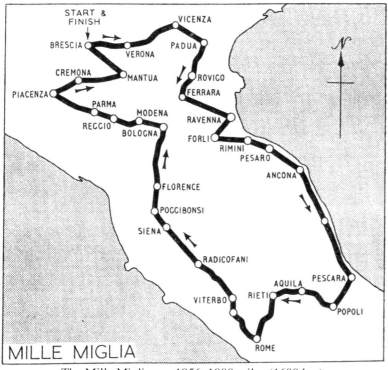

The Mille Miglia pre-1956. 1000 miles (1600 km).

on some of the more difficult sections of the route, including high-speed testing on the Milan-Brescia Autostrada. During their time, the team were entertained, fed and watered at the palatial Villa Mazzotti at Chiari, just outside Brescia. Count Franco Mazzotti had been one of the original founders of the event in 1927 and his son Bindo inherited the title. Most of the British teams stayed here, attended to by some fifty servants. Bert observed the great gap between the very rich few and the poor peasants they saw en route. No doubt a fertile breeding ground for the communists who were very dominant in Italy at that time.

In the race, the A-H team were progressing well with Bert putting 87 miles into the first hour over unfamiliar wet and winding roads. All three cars were experiencing gearbox oil seeping onto the clutches. Hadley and 'Joe' Mercer were to encounter further problems but before they did, they caught up with Johnson's 'C' Type which was running as No.555. It had overtaken them some way previously but now it was slowing down, just as the outsized fuel tank broke away from its brackets. Bert witnessed the Jaguar's final progress in the event, fuel dripping on the ground, just as he had predicted. Having made certain his friend and co-driver were safe, Hadley and Mercer pressed on, only to be thwarted by the throttle linkage falling apart, dropping vital bits onto the road and eventually the clutch failed near Ravenna. Lockett and Reid suffered a similar problem, though managed to lash things together only for their clutch to fail just 16 miles before the finish. The Healeys managed to finish, though somewhat behind. It had been a great effort in largely untried cars, with valuable lessons learnt for the future.

Leaving NOJ 392 to be collected by the BMC support team, Bert and Joe hitched a lift home in a Standard Vanguard which belonged to Laycock Engineering, the Sheffield manufacturers of the overdrive units designed by Captain de Normanville and which were widely used on British vehicles. Their service engineer was following the event to tend to any competitors having overdrive problems. Hadley and Mercer were due to fly home from Le Touquet in France. All was going well and heading towards their destination, when 30 kms from the airport, the car expired in a cloud of steam. The head gasket had gone and a slight panic ensued. They decided to enlist, i.e. bribe an old chap who had an ancient Berliet truck with which he towed the Vanguard and crew to his garage. He told them during the war, he was forced to transport German troops about and he arranged the exhaust system to poison his passengers. They were kindly able to use his facilities which provided them additional tools to lift the cylinder head.

Despite frantic enquiries, no Vanguard head gaskets were available locally, but Bert found several used ones in the boot. He set to work repairing the best gasket of the bunch, using pieces of tinplate and some solder. Between them, the crew threw the whole lot together and leaving more precious francs with their host, sped off to the airport. However, the UK was fog-bound so all cross-channel flights were on hold. So it was flat out to catch the ferry at Boulogne. They had left the Healeys in Arras but in the end they were home before HLH. Some months later, Bert met a Laycock engineer with the same Vanguard who said they'd had constant gasket trouble with it from new, but 'Bert's bodge' had solved the problem.

After all the excitement of the Mille Miglia, it was Le Mans time again. Leslie Johnson admitted Hadley was right to have had doubts about his 'C' Type plans and to renew their friendship offered Bert another drive.

LES 24 HEURES DU MANS 1953
PROGRAMME OFFICIEL
Donnant droit au numéro spécial de « MOTEURS COURSES »
Prix · 200 francs

This time it was for the Nash-Healey team. Leslie had driven for Healey the year before with some success and needing a reliable partner – who else but Hadley? Donald Mitchell Healey (DMH) was born in Perranporth, Cornwall, where the family garage still operated and had started the Donald Healey Motor Company immediately after the war. Prior to the conflict he had been a very successful rally driver. Initially Healeys were Riley-powered but with exports high on the agenda, DMH had done a deal with the Nash-Kelvinator Corporation to supply chassis fitted with the Nash engine and transmission. Farina-styled roadster bodies were fitted in the States. The chassis was based on the Silverstone, an earlier sports two-seater, a model much prized today. Several cars, both left and right hand drive were retained and fitted with lightweight racing bodies. The Nash engine, a big OHV 6-cylinder unit, was progressively worked on and eventually 'stretched' to 4.138 litres capacity.

13th-14th June 1953. Le Mans 24 hour.
HLH enjoys a trouble-free run in the Nash-Healey.
(Right) Following a works C-type Jaguar through the Esses.

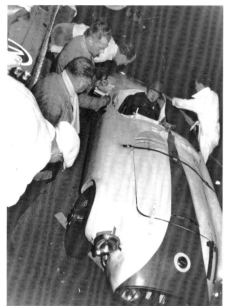

(Left) Bert takes over from Johnson for a further night session behind the wheel.
(Right) A somewhat travel-stained HLH enjoys some refreshment after completing his drive.
With Bert is Bill Butler's friend Alf Briggs from Derby, but who are the gents on the left and the right?.

Nash-Healey was a brand name in its own right and American owned and as such the two cars were painted in the US racing colours of white with a blue stripe. The running of the team and personnel would be the responsibility of the Healey family. It would also be the final outing for the Warwick team as all the competition activities would in future be under the Austin-Healey banner and run by the BMC Competitions Department. The Healeys would be still involved from time to time but actual car production at the Cape Works would eventually end in 1954.

In the race itself, things went largely to plan for Johnson and Hadley though the sister car went out early with oil pressure problems. They entered as No.11 and finished in the same position. The car finishing in twelfth place was none other than NOJ 392, Bert's mount in the Mille Miglia. Happily, and despite a chequered life including time as Geoff and Margot Healey's honeymoon transport and a long sojourn in Australia, '392' has survived in splendid order and in 2013 featured in an upmarket auction at Goodwood. Bert remembered the '53' Le Mans with some satisfaction. Firstly the Nash provided him with a relaxing drive, even at racing speeds, and additionally it was very pleasing to finish the event for a change.

LES 24 HEURES DU MANS 1955
PROGRAMME OFFICIEL
Prix : **200** francs

No. **FIA 5 : 2546**

Fédération Internationale de l'Automobile
Licence for
COMPETITOR (Entrant) DRIVER
issued by the
ROYAL AUTOMOBILE CLUB

Valid throughout the territories of the Fédération Internationale de l'Automobile

Issued to .......H.....L.....HADLEY......

Permanent Address ....78,.....Rod.....Lane,......
.........Kenilworth,.........
.........Warwickshire.........

Born on ...15. 4. 1910......... at ...Birmingham.........

Given at London the ....9th.........day of ...Feb.....1955

Chairman of the Royal Automobile Club.

Signature of holder

Pall Mall, London, S.W.1   P.T.O.

PHOTOGRAPH OF HOLDER MUST BE AFFIXED HERE

All particulars to be written in Block Capitals

For whatever reason, 1954 seems to have been a quiet year for Bert with no record of him taking part in actual competition but he would return for one final race in 1955. Bert was keen to continue racing and considered he still had something to offer. His contacts with the motor industry brought a call from Ken Richardson of Standard-Triumph Ltd. Ken and Bert had known each other since before the war when Richardson worked for Raymond Mays at Bourne. He would later be involved with the BRM project but had joined the Coventry outfit in order to develop the TR sports car. The TR2 had become very popular and whilst it was proving a success in rallying the 1955 Le Mans race would be the factory's first foray into long-distance racing.

Richardson was now Triumph's Competition Manager and he proposed running a team of three cars carefully prepared but close to normal specification. He invited Bert to co-drive with him in car No.28. No.29 would be conducted by veterans 'Mort' Morris-Goodall and Les Brooke, whilst the third and presumably late entry of No.68 would be crewed by Bob Dickson and the up and coming Scottish driver Ninian Sanderson. Bert was given first stint and made his usual 'Le Mans start' (in those days the drivers lined-up on one side of the track with their cars neatly parked in echelon on the other side). At the drop of the Tricolore at precisely 4pm on the Saturday the drivers would sprint across the track, leap into their respective cars, hopefully start up and away! It was an exciting spectacle for the spectators and could be traumatic for some of the drivers, which is probably why they do not do it anymore – more's the pity. Bert was particularly adept at this. Sir William Lyons had observed *'Two bounces and Bert was gone!'* On this occasion Bert's getaway was so rapid he almost took his team mate's wing off and he remembered making a mental note to go for an eye test!

Initially weather conditions were dry and favourable. The Jaguar team headed by Mike Hawthorn and partnered by Ivor Bueb, was anxious to add another victory to their tally and was up against some formidable opposition in the form of a phalanx of Ferraris plus an impressive driver line up in the Mercedes team. After two and a half hours had elapsed, Hawthorn in Jaguar 'D' Type No.6 was leading a Ferrari but was 'pushing it' as he was intending to handover to his co-driver Ivor Bueb. Archive film makes compelling viewing and clearly shows what happens next. Lance Macklin in an Austin-Healey (No.26) is proceeding relatively slowly on his own towards the pit area and slightly over to the left hand side of the track, which is rather narrow at this point.

Hawthorn is seen storming up behind Macklin's right side, squeezes past him and is gone. As if taken by surprise, Macklin instantly twitches over to his left. Meanwhile the 50 year old French veteran Pierre Bouillon, who raced as 'Levegh', on a charge in the Mercedes has clearly intended to take Macklin on the left hand side but now has nowhere to go. The Mercedes hits the back of the Austin-Healey which acts as a ramp, launching Levegh's car into the air and towards the grandstand on the left, packed with spectators. The car somersaults several times, catching fire as it does, the engine and other major parts breaking away and other debris flying in all directions as the car destroys itself. After the initial impact, the badly damaged Austin-Healey careers into the barriers, just allowing Juan Manuel Fangio in his Mercedes enough space to squeeze past at full bore.

It was now exactly 6.26pm and 30 seconds earlier Fangio had passed HLH who was about to hand over to Richardson. Those not in the immediate vicinity of the incident (the Le Mans lap is 8.5 miles long) were not aware of the carnage for some time as the race continued. The organisers had taken (in hindsight) the wise decision to continue the race under yellow flags whilst the debris was cleared. To have stopped it would have prompted a mass exodus by the public, preventing the dozens of ambulance and other emergency vehicles from reaching the circuit. The death toll, which included the unfortunate Levegh, rose to over 80 with hundreds of horrific injuries caused by flying and burning debris.

11th-12th June 1955. Le Mans 24 hour.
HLH keeps a tight line as he hustles the TR2 past the pits.

1955 Le Mans. Bert passes the packed grandstands before the tragic accident occurred.

As it started to rain at daybreak, Mercedes had already withdrawn their team at 2am. Jaguar decided to continue as the rain increased in its intensity. The Browns Lane team won again but it was a somewhat hollow victory. As so often happens at sporting events, the rain eased off after the 4pm finish. Remarkably, Lance Macklin was not badly hurt in the collision but was in deep shock, and would retire from motorsport after two more events. Had he been driving a left hand drive car, he would undoubtedly not have survived the Le Mans accident, so severe was the damage to his Austin-Healey. Surprisingly (or then maybe not!) this self-same car (NOJ 393) has since been resurrected so successfully that it was recently sold at auction for no less than £858,000...... Of the Triumphs, at least one has survived, the Morris-Goodall/Brooke car, but No.28 mysteriously disappeared off the radar during the 1970s without further trace. For the record, all the TRs finished with no major problems apart from when Les Brooke in No.68 beached at Tertré Rouge and had to dig himself out of the sandbank. No.29 (Hadley/Richardson) finished in 14th place, No.29 in 15th and No.68 in 19th position. Of the 21 finishers, 15 were British entries.

After the event, the grandstands and pit areas were completely demolished and rebuilt with a much wider race track, eventually culminating in what is there today. By the time of the 1956 race, further safety measures had also been implemented around the circuit. Despite the trauma of the weekend's racing, Bert felt confident he could compete for a few more seasons, and indeed had received an enquiry from the Aston Martin team regarding his future availability. However, in deference to Rose's increasing concern for his safety as track speeds increased, he decided he'd had a good run, having had some close shaves yet unlike some of his contemporaries escaped serious injury, and at the age of 45 decided to retire from motor racing.

- 10 -
BITS AND PIECES

Acknowledgement is given to the late H.R.H. Prince Birabongse and his book of the same title (a recommended read). Here we have a gathering of some further aspects of Bert's life not already covered in detail in earlier chapters.

Craigantlet Memories

1979 was the 50th Anniversary year of the Craigantlet Hill Climb in Northern Ireland and for the Golden Jubilee event, the Ulster Automobile Club were making a special effort to celebrate the occasion. Bert received an invitation to attend as a guest of honour with the hope that he could also bring an Austin single-seater over for some demonstration runs.

Despite his best efforts, the sole complete car had never run satisfactorily since its rebuild at Tom Wheatcroft's some five years earlier. His own car was still in a neglected state with many important parts missing. The unwarranted aggravation he'd encountered during the engine building saga had sorely tested his initial enthusiasm. He was however very touched by the Ulster Club's invitation but regretfully had to decline. His happy memories of pre-war visits prompted him to submit an extensive article for the Souvenir Handbook outlining his career whilst at 'The Austin', an edited version of which follows.

During the Austin team's visits they usually stayed at the Grand Central Hotel in Belfast whilst the car and equipment was based at the Austin Distributor's garage. 'The Team' usually consisted of the driver, one mechanic and Bill Sewell in charge of admin and general Public Relations. Ral Appleby went over with Bert in 1936 and 1938 but for '37 Bill Rogers looked after things as HLH was driving the 'other' Twin-cam, his regular mount being unavailable owing to an engine blow-up. Despite being without his customised seat, steering wheel and throttle pedal, Hadley bettered the record he'd established the previous year in the Side-valve.

For his final visit Bert had his own car, but rain prevented another record time. As it was, he made FTD anyway, thrilling the sodden spectators with his mastery of the wet conditions. Another entertaining aspect of these meetings was that many of the racing cars taking part were driven to and from the event on public roads, in Hadley's case a double journey of over five miles each way. What an audio-visual treat for the locals!

Bert Hadley looks back:-

> 'I had been looking forward to seeing Craigantlet again and some of the many friends I made during four visits in the thirties. The idea was to show one of the Twin-cam Austin single-seaters: in fact the one mainly driven by my colleague Charles Dodson. A slow demonstration run was envisaged. The existing car does suffer from a few ailments and since there are absolutely no spares available it is important to look after this car. Inexplicably all spares were consigned (by over-active patriotism or design) to the scrap metal drive during the war. So for various reasons beyond my control, the Austin will not be visiting the scene of its pre-war triumphs on the occasions of this 50th Anniversary meeting and I am indeed very sorry about this.
>
> My first visit here was in 1935 when I acted as mechanic for Pat Driscoll who drove one of the Side-valve Austins. The following year, having started driving for the company, I was sent over to Craigantlet again with the Side-valve. I broke the record on my first run, much to my surprise because

I seemed to be pointing the wrong way most of the run. Up to that time the record was held by E.R. Hall and I suppose I expected loads of congratulations from him but he seemed to take less than a fair view. This proved something of a tonic and I think I proved the point by making even better times on subsequent runs.

The prize-giving was a memorable affair, held I think at Newtownards, I have never forgotten the wonderful hospitality of the Ulster Automobile Club, and the help given by the chaps at Harry Ferguson's garage where we made our headquarters. Mr. Harry Ferguson, who was a great follower of motor sport, both before and after the war, gave me lots of useful advice, and I used to think just how much better the Austin Motor Company would be with him in a senior position. I also remember Messrs. Thompson and Reid very well and there were many others – their names have disappeared – but I well remember how they used to meet us off the boat. Nothing was too much trouble.

I took the Twin-cam single-seater over to Craigantlet in 1937 and 1938. I know I improved the time and I think I made fastest time each year. We made considerable modification to the car for 1939 and in addition to improvements in power output; we also got down to correct gear ratios. I was looking forward to Shelsley in 1939. I am sure I had the answer there and also my next visit to Craigantlet where I knew I would be able to make considerable improvement on my time. A pity, because it would have given the chaps who took it off me in 1948, a much more difficult target to aim at.

I drove at a number of hill climb events but Craigantlet gave me most pleasure. Not because of successes, these came elsewhere anyway, but Craigantlet I found long enough to make things interesting. The pull up after the finish line was a bit dicey. Earlier competitors were permitted to park on one side of the road and when I arrived at the end of my first run the place seemed to full of iron and scampering people. I expect this has been sorted out by now.

Well I am sorry I will not be present but may I say all good wishes to the club for a memorable 50th Anniversary meeting. At least one ex-competitor will be thinking about you from over the water.'

Trialling with the Grasshoppers

'I took part in many Reliability Trials as they were called, between 1935 and 1939. The events I covered were mainly in the winter as summer was taken up by racing. As for the cars, I will start with the BOA series as I know the full list has been catalogued elsewhere. The four speciality built two-seaters of the 1935 Le Mans returned to the Works after a somewhat inglorious performance. I was working with Jamieson at that time. He was not involved in their preparation. I remember his remarks before the cars went to France – "Too heavy, no thought given to streamlining and no punch."

There the cars sat until one day, Lord Austin sent for Goodacre and Hadley. He said, "I'm thinking of entering the Le Mans cars in reliability trials. Have you any thoughts on the idea?" Secretly I thought that's about all they are good for. Austin said to us "Do you know anything about these trials?" Charlie said he didn't which was strange coming from him because he usually had some way out subscription to make on any subject, however varied. Charlie didn't have much to say that morning.

Did I know anything about trials? Not much I said but I had acted as sidecar passenger to a Norton rider named Mountford in trials like the Victory Cup and the Colmore etc. He was in a conversational mood that day so he said "Was that interesting?" I said it was, particularly on what was known as Observed Sections, where at times Mountford seemed to go raving mad, sometimes getting away with it, on other special assaults, losing it and pitching me out in the process. I thought the best thing to do would be to take a car to the Cotswolds where I knew of a number of sections of interest. Lord Austin said "Right. Do just that and let me have a report." So off we went the same day with BOA 60 and tried some of the motorcycle sections used in the Colmore Trial. We felt the car lacked the sort of power required to guarantee success. The Le Mans cars were of course un-blown at that time. Ground clearance too was an obvious problem because rock outcrops would foul the front axle. Another awkward situation was the hand brake adjuster and front brake fulcrum which could be folded back permanently, locking on the front brakes. It all added up to picking a suitable path, not easy on these narrow roads. We felt that for the time being we would have to pick and choose our events.

My first success was a Silver award in the London to Exeter Trial in December 1935. It was then decided to enter the Colmore of 1936. Three cars ran and we finished up with what were called Third Class Awards.

The next one could have been the Coventry Cup Trial which started from Bridgewater. My team mates were Buckley, Scriven and Goodacre. I did quite well after some hectic steering. I took the award for the best SUNBAC entry.

14th March 1936. Coventry Cup Trial.
2nd Class Award (best SUNBAC member). Note the terrain!

Hadley and Simpson ready to outfox the opposition if necessary.

My passenger from the outset was Bob Simpson, a mechanic in the Racing Department. Later on, Bob looked after Kay Petre's side-valve Jamieson single-seater. Bob was an excellent man with no nerves. Not apparent ones anyway. My colleague Charlie Goodacre told Bob he was crazy to ride with me as I was completely mad. I told Charlie that he must have forgotten his record and he should look it up. It was all good fun.

In the spring of 1936, all the cars were fitted with Centric superchargers, belt driven and perched on the cylinder head – not a very elegant layout. They gave very low boost at the outset, subsequently increasing to 9lbs on 1:1 engine speed. The downdraught carb protruded through the bonnet so we fitted a cowl over it. At that time of course we ran with locked diffs and competition tyres. Both were banned later on which took a lot of the interest out of it for me as this resulted in lessening the severity of the observed sections. A lot of bureaucratic nonsense I thought. I did the United Hospital Trial in the Cotswolds on the 29th March 1936 and took a premier award. As I recall next, the Lands End and I gained a First, which was all one could win. A Third Class in Edinburgh – got bogged down here and there. Then the MCC Buxton Trial – a First Class Award. In the Roy Feddon Trophy I won the Anthony Cup - best performance up to 1100cc.

27th February 1937. Sunbac Colmore Trial.
Blown but still low chassis. 1st Class Award.

I'm not absolutely sure when we started to use the high chassis, certainly in 1937. It was my idea and I applied it to BOA 60. Charlie Goodacre thought it worthwhile too but I must say we were somewhat shattered at first by the odd appearance of the car. Incidentally, the naming of the cars, "Grasshoppers" emerged when they were running on the low chassis. One day when I was talking with Goodacre and Len Brockas, Bill Sewell rushed into the department saying, "I've got it." Goodacre said, "Good, then go away. We don't want it." "No, you misunderstand" said Sewell, "A name for the cars – Grasshoppers. That's what we will call them." Goodacre looked at him pityingly and said "What's the world coming to?" Adding "Who will be Grasshopper number one?" as if I didn't know. It transpired that Sewell had Dennis Buckley in mind. Didn't worry me, after all, Dennis had done a few trials before we started. What Charlie had in mind was you didn't have to have a father who was Austin sales manager, but it did help and Dennis was assured of a bevy of cheer leaders including, it seemed, our flamboyant team manager Bill Sewell. [BOA 60 became Grasshopper II.]

The behaviour of the Grasshopper cars on normal roads with the locked diff and competition tyres was unusual and fast cornering became fast sliding.

I taught the girl who was to become my wife, Rose, to drive BOA 60. She was at that time an accomplished A7 Ruby driver. In 1937 we had many tearful sessions in the Ruby. She said, if she did anything wrong, which was often, my temper was dreadful.

Well, she became very proficient in Grasshopper BOA 60. She accompanied me on a few trials; one in particular on the army tank testing ground at Camberley in 1938 in COA 119.

I fell asleep on the way home with Rose driving. It was raining hard when I came to. The rain was streaming off her face and by the look of the rev-counter we were doing just over 70 mph. I was sure she had the ability and with more practice I believe she could have competed, but she didn't seem to be particularly interested. A pity, because so many people considered themselves suitable material when in fact they didn't have a clue.

(Ferret Fotographic)
1938. Rose passengers with Bert on a trial held on military ground at Camberley in Surrey.

But I digress as usual. Back to the end of 1936 when I discovered that quite a lot of needle existed among the trials crowd and the atmosphere was different to the racing people. It was the MG Cream Cracker and Musketeer teams who got up my nose. There seemed to be a Gentlemen and Players set-up. You may guess my category. Very toffee-nosed they were and for some reason they regarded me as a "pot-hunter".

As a Works driver, it should have been obvious that it was my job to do the best I could for the Company. Furthermore, unlike some of my colleagues in the Austin team, excepting Charlie Goodacre, I was not very keen on the uncontrolled binges which took place after the events, often with disastrous results. Maybe I was a bit too much of a Spartan but behaving like a pack of bloody fools was not my scene.

I resolved to teach the Abingdon lot a lesson in the forthcoming Vesey Trial run by SUNBAC. I asked Jack Woodhouse, secretary of the club, to place me near the end of the competitors' list, which he did with a knowing smile. Then, after consulting Murray Jamieson on my calculations for increased boost, which he agreed, through my father who'd recently retired from Cadburys, I had a blower driving pulley made outside the Works. In fact it was made in the Machine Department at Bournville. This pulley was identical in every detail except that the diameter was increased by five eights of an inch. This gave a very significant increase in boost over the 9 psi at 1.1 engine speed we were then applying. I had felt for some time that we must have more power, if only for the tests and observed sections. We rebuilt the engine carefully and dropped the compression ratio by fitting a slightly thicker steel gasket as I thought we could run into detonation problems.

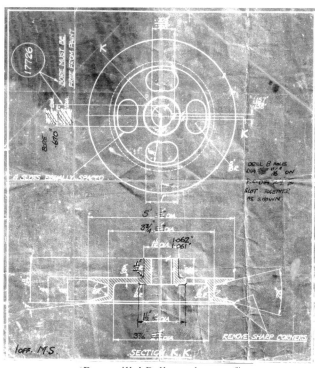

'Bournville' Pulley – the proof!
Original blueprint with inked in alterations.
For the attention of the
Cadbury Bros. Engineering Department!

(Ferret Fotographic)
1st May 1937. MGCC Abingdon Trial.
Hadley and Simpson in confident mood.
Bob is actually smiling!

I recall taking the car out on test. The blower had a much higher note (during an event, should anyone remark on this, we'd put it down to a worn ballrace!). It went up Rose Hill at the Lickey Hills, near the Works, so fast in third gear I had to shut off before the summit.

We felt like a real pair of conspirators, well at least I did. Bob said we don't have to worry, think of all the other fiddles which we know have gone on and forget about it.

We did about 30 miles at high speed with no problems. Any improvements however small are worthwhile and after all there was nothing stopping other interested parties from doing likewise. We decided to fit the pulley on observed sections and if convenient remove afterwards. I made a spring clip to place in front of the holding nut which was barely tightened.

141

(Ferret Fotographic)
1st May 1937. MGCC Abingdon Trial.
This section was known as 'Tin Pan Alley'.

(Ferret Fotographic)
Despite the sticky end, HLH won the Watkinson
Cup (for best visitor).

In the Vesey [6th November 1937], I climbed everything, with Bob of course. I knew I had done well in all the tests, the last and longest one being completed in the dark. We checked in at the pub, I think it was The Talbot at Belbroughton and there was a large room occupied by the competitors, with a board taking up one wall showing results. The chortling of the MG people seemed to indicate that they had done well. My team mates, Buckley, Scriven and maybe Goodacre, I'm not sure, all looked depressed. Then the Secretary called for silence and said "It looks like we were a bit premature with our findings, Bert Hadley has a clean sheet and has won all the driving tests." Dropping a pin would have made a clatter among the MG people. A cheer went up, not from the Austin team, but from Singers, led by my friend Bill Butler. He said "Your car goes well", then saw the look on my face and dried up. I noticed Alf Depper in consultation with Buckley and Scriven and they moved quietly out of the room. Bob Simpson followed and caught them with the bonnet up on BOA 60, peering about with torches. He asked if they had lost something. There was bags of "Just checking" etc. and they moved away. The pulley was in Bob's overcoat pocket but I doubt very much whether there was sufficient technical knowledge about to spot anything if the pulley had been attached. That made me decide not to tell them.

Lord Austin was pleased as a result of the local publicity. Bill Sewell wrote a piece in the Austin magazine, saying how unusual it was for one man to clear the board etc. After the Vesey, I also won the Shell Cup in late 1936. After that I did not use the higher boost until once or twice late in 1937. When we started to use the COA series, ex-1937 Le Mans and Twelve Hour Race cars, mainly to see just how fast the three bearing engines with their Murray Jamieson modifications and blowers would go, the result was impressive. I won many awards and went on competing up to 1939.

'Grasshopper II' casually abandoned
outside 22 Twyning Road.

(Ferret Fotographic)
14th May 1937. MCC London/Edinburgh Trial.
Hadley and Simpson gained a Premier Award.

The Torbay and Totnes English Riviera Trial was interesting. It was, in fact the only time I ever rolled the Grasshopper. The club included a section, a very steep difficult hill by the inelegant name of S.O.B. Both Buckley and Scriven failed low down and I noticed that one had to do a proper S.O.B. to get past the point where they failed. I did that, then came a very tight left hander, followed quickly by a right. I used a large flat slab of rock like a banking. I climbed and would have got away with it but the near side front wheel hit a rock and over we went, completely upside down. I thought – this is bloody silly if you like. The engine was still ticking over, I found the key and switched off. The spectators lifted the car off us and I didn't have a scratch but Bob was badly shaken, having had difficulty breathing. I offered to retire but he was unwilling. We were towed to the top by tractor, then we looked the car over. Filler caps, petrol and water were pushed in but no leaks. Lost some oil but we replaced that. I had to make up time to the next observed section which we managed. I thought it a demonstration of courage on the part of Bob Simpson. I didn't fail on any of the succeeding hills or tests, though the steering was a bit odd which slowed me and lost us some time. We were beaten fractionally by Dennis Buckley. We took the award for best runner-up. All's well that ends well.

Some good natured banter back at the Works from Charlie Goodacre, who reminded Bob that he had warned against riding with me. I didn't roll it again, but in an Abingdon Trial I went flat out at a hill called Tin Pan Alley which nobody climbed. I landed awkwardly in a sea of mud which left the car at a funny angle, the driver's door buried in mud. Stanley Barnes, who became Chairman of the RAC Competition Committee post-war, said quietly "You can get out now Bert." His brother Donald drove Austins, at times competing with the Dutch Clogs in racing and also Grasshoppers.

(Ferret Fotographic)
1939. Bert nearly overdoes it in COA 119 – no wonder he had back trouble!

I wouldn't want any of you to think all this is about me but the trouble is I cannot recall all the exploits by other Grasshopper drivers. There was quite a long list of them when so many got in on the act.

Charlie Goodacre seemed to do more when we started using the COA cars. He drove COA 121 while I had COA 119. One day he said "I'm fitting a Dutch Clog engine to COA 121." I said it was a waste of time if the intention was trials. He wouldn't listen. He arrived at one particular steep section on the Colmore Trial called Leckhampton near Cheltenham. He started well back on the main road and must have been doing at least 65 mph when he hit the hill. Half way up, the revs dropped and he stopped. Afterwards I said 56 bhp at 6000 rpm Charlie, but nothing under 2000 rpm. That engine was soon pulled out. Incidentally, COA 119 flew up the same hill using the high boost pulley, although I had problems with other sections due to lack of adhesion. Sometimes on short muddy observed sections, we removed the tyre valves (we used security bolts). It was quite easy to re-inflate to about 10 psi to get to the next section, even using short stretches of main road.

I was very unlucky not to win the Plymouth Motor Club 200 in May 1939. I made best performance but was disqualified owing to losing time when held up by a road accident. I did well in the Southsea President's Trophy and also the NW London MC Coventry Cup. I took my Big 7, accompanied by Bob in the Exeter Trial of 1939 and gained a Premier Award. It made us wonder why we had endured all that open car and drenching rain nonsense.'

This was to be Bert's last published article (1992) when he was the A7CA President.

Hadley on Dodson

'Losing one's friends at any time is a sad business and for me the year 1983 saw the loss of both Pat Driscoll and Charles Dodson. I cannot recall any mention of C.J.P. Dodson in vintage affairs and so I will provide a picture of him as a person.

Of his death I know he was riding a Sunbeam 90 TT bike, 1929 model, at Brands Hatch in one of the historic bike parades. He crashed but did not regain consciousness. Some doubts were expressed at the time about the advisability of allowing a man his age to ride at all. He was, I believe, 81 years. All I can say is Doddy, as we all knew him at Longbridge, would not have chosen a different way to go than riding one of his beloved Sunbeams.

Doddy won many major races at home and abroad for the Wolverhampton firm including two senior TT races in the Isle of Man. For me, and Charles Goodacre, Doddy was a top flight racing motor cyclist when we were still at school and we used to read of his successes in "Motor Cycle".

I first met Charlie Dodson at Brooklands in 1934 which was about the time when he started to carve a new career for himself on four wheels. I believe his first success was in the Mannin Beg Race in the Isle of Man, driving John Cobb's Monza Alfa Romeo when he finished second. I met him on the day when Murray Jamieson was trying me out in one of his Side-valve single-seaters on the Mountain Circuit. It was clear to me then that Doddy was joining the Austin outfit. He gave me some useful tips and after three exploratory laps I broke the existing Class H record, unofficially of course, frightening myself considerably in the process. I just about regained a reasonable degree of nonchalance before returning to the paddock. Doddy said "Jamie, this bloke is a natural." which I may say did a lot for my confidence.

So what manner of man was Charlie Dodson? In appearance he was small, dark and very good looking. A wiry little man with lots of stamina. He didn't say much about his background but as I recall, he came from Manchester and I feel sure he talked about his brother from time to time. Doddy lived at Henfield, Sussex in the thirties with his first wife. I cannot recall any mention of children. He always drove a large American Dodge car. He brought this car to Longbridge one day and Lord Austin took a dim view when he spotted this alien vehicle parked in the South Works yard. Mind you, he was even more incensed on the day in 1938 when L.P. Lord arrived to take up his new post as Works Director. LP was sufficiently unwise to park his 4.5 litre Bentley right outside Lord Austin's office. This was the spot occupied by the Old Man's Clifton tourer and other cars from the start of the firm. The resultant row was worth seeing. LP was no pushover when words were flying around but he backed down smartly on this occasion.

Charles Dodson was married twice and I met his first wife several times at race meetings. She was an attractive girl and they seemed very happy. Something went wrong around the middle of 1938 which seriously affected Charles' attitude to driving. He was not the type to unburden his feelings.

Before the problems arose, Doddy showed plenty of fire and I think his most noteworthy diversionary exercise was partnering John Cobb at Utah when they set up long distance records with the big Napier Railton. He did very well too, driving Freddie Dixon's Rileys, very quick and often unusual motor cars. Fred Dixon, not a man to be trifled with, was a first class engineer and race driver who also started his career racing motor bikes, being particularly associated with the Douglas. Charlie Dodson was not trained as an engineer and come to think of it, I didn't ask about his experiences in a practical sense. This may sound remote but remember, with the exception of Goodacre and Hadley, it was customary for Austin to recruit race drivers from outside the firm, i.e. people with known reputations. In discussing Charlie Dodson, I can take the view that he was the most talented driver Austins recruited from outside sources. In spite of his excellent record, one never heard him make flamboyant claims, nor did I hear him complain about his car. He did his level best for Murray Jamieson. There was plenty to moan about in terms of team and pit management in the immediate post-Jamieson period and Doddy voiced his opinion on that score on numerous justified occasions.

Doddy drove one of the un-blown Austin two-seaters at Le Mans in 1935. I didn't get a ride in that race as I was busy elsewhere. They did quite well to finish in 28th place. The Le Mans cars of that year, of course, became the first examples of the famous trials cars, subsequently known as the Grasshoppers. The alterative would have been to scrap them, as it was they performed a very useful publicity function.

I shared a car with Doddy for the 1937 Le Mans race. Four new cars were built for this race with lighter, door-less bodies and the three bearing engines were modified by Murray Jamieson, providing a helpful power improvement. He wanted to alter the blunt shape of the car to reduce drag but this was not received with enthusiasm by the Austin top hat clearance design hierarchy of the period. It was at this point, i.e. just before the 1937 race that Jamie left us to join ERA Ltd. He left because he could no longer endure the rotten treatment dished out by the anti everything brigade at Longbridge which had to be seen to be believed! As for the Le Mans engines, Jamieson had specified flexible braided pipes for the internal oil rail but of course, when he had gone they were discarded in favour of the good old solid pipes. I said they would break and they did. All three cars failed almost at the same time, around 2am, when the pipes broke at the unions and knocked out the big end bearing shells. I suggested we should repair our car as we had a good lead over the other team cars and we had all the necessary bits available anyway. This was ignored or overruled in the hail of recriminations flying around. To prove the point and after all we did need the cars for transport to get home, we removed the battery and drained the oil from our car on the Sunday morning. Then we placed the car on its side and changed the big end shells. The centre bearing was still usable and the journals, though a little scored, were also usable. We made up a substitute pipe and the total time to get the car running again was one and a half hours. We drove flat-out to Boulogne and the oil pressure was satisfactory. This was one example of the very poor team management at that time.

Later in 1937, I joined Doddy again in the same car for the 12 Hour Sports Car Race at Donington Park where we did very well. Charlie had his moments. First incident was the disappearance of the nut and bolt which anchored the torque tube to the chassis, causing the torque tube to clout the tunnel disconcertingly. Charlie spotted the trouble and found a tommy bar in the kit which fortunately was longer than standard. By using a box spanner for extra leverage he managed to bend it enough to reach our pit where we found the bar was a reasonable fit so I bent the bar to a complete 'U'. Apart from the occasional clonk, we had no further trouble and there was no wear to be seen after the race.

Doddy had displayed considerable initiative. The second hiatus was more serious as the race was stopped by a dreadful accident in Redgate Wood. Two cars locked together and hurtled into a wall at the exit to the wood. One driver was killed and the road completely blocked by debris. Fred Craner, Clerk of the Course, eventually restarted the race at that point. Charlie was driving the car at that time and after the restart he came into the pit, suggesting that it might be a good idea to re-fuel and change over a little earlier than planned. I remember thinking Doddy looked a bit peaky and I had not even reached top gear before I realised why this was so. The rev-counter had disappeared from view and I knew some modification to the steering had developed, however, the car seemed happy on both locks and it didn't wander so I proceeded on full noise. We were using the short cycle type wings so I had a good view of the side. Then I spotted the trouble. The steering arm from the swivel to the side tube was bent downwards towards the axle beam. I pressed on but kept a wary eye on it. I could see little Charlie peering out our pit. Next time we changed he said "Everything ok Bert?" I said yes Doddy, just the same as you left it. Nothing more was said. We did well and had a good laugh after the race. It appears that the accident happened in front of him, blocking the road and the Austin brakes, normally useless, gave him a bad time and he clouted a lump of wreckage. I suppose he should have said something about it. I didn't see the point of flogging the incident after the race. I changed the arm and checked the alignment etc. and that was the end of it.

I have said that pit and team management was poor in the immediate post-Jamieson period and this was clearly highlighted in the 1937 Empire Trophy Race at Donington when Charlie came close to death as a result of atrocious pit work. When Jamieson left us he was in the process of perfecting a pressurised re-fuelling system which of course was thrown out when he had gone. Back we went to the old fashioned splash and trip churns circa 1928 and all the problems that went with that system. The pit manager of the period considered all pit stops, scheduled or otherwise, as occasions for supplementing oil, water and petrol levels! Thus, when Dodson came in shortly after the start it was all systems go! Doddy kept his engine running as he had obviously lost a cylinder. Len Brockas removed the bonnet and immediately spotted the trouble, a plug lead had jumped off, not having been properly fitted. He pushed the spring loaded terminal on again and Doddy could have been away in seconds. Len saw the re-fuelling pantomime going on at the rear and wisely switched the ignition off. The dead cylinder had caused the engine to run rich leaving un-burnt fuel in the exhaust manifold. Switching off caused a loud plop and a long flame from the tail pipe right against the re-fuelling mechanic who dropped the fuel churn, spraying Doddy on the head and shoulders. The churn was on fire, so was Doddy and the rear of the car. Doddy saw no future in staying there after leaping out as nothing was being done for him. He ran across the track, head and shoulders on fire, where he was grabbed by John Cobb who rolled Doddy in the grass in front of the grandstand, finally extinguishing the flames by lying on him. It was remarkable that Cobb should have been there since, as I have said, John Cobb gave Doddy his first ride on four wheels. People from the neighbouring pits put out the car and churn fire. As often happens, the car was undamaged. I was in the race but saw nothing of the incident.

I had numerous pit stops as a result of all sorts of problems. The obvious solution would have been to give me Doddy's car but this move was quite beyond the imagination of the management of the period. After the race which I finished in a poor frame of mind, I rushed off to Derby Royal Infirmary where I found Doddy propped up in bed with burns to his head, chest and shoulders. He was in considerable pain and very uncomplimentary about a number of people from Longbridge. It was a black day for us, a race we should have won, a driver injured and an absolute fusillade of adverse and justified criticism from the motoring press.

I lost touch with Charlie when the war came in September 1939 and in fact I did not meet him again until May 1951 at Silverstone. This was the "Daily Express" Production Car Race. I drove a Jowett Jupiter and had the 1500cc class sewn up until a head gasket blew with just a few minutes to go. Motor racing can be full of disappointments. When I met Doddy that day in practice at Silverstone he said he was driving an XK 120. I think it was entered by a chap called Harry Broadhurst. Doddy said, "Am all at sea with this car Bert, where am I going wrong?" I went to various points of the circuit and watched him. This was his first race after the war and he was obviously race rusty. I went into detail with him. He was setting the car up all wrong for some corners. Anyway, he trusted me and the car and got down to a good lap time. He finished second to Stirling Moss, also in a Jaguar XK 120. I thought Doddy did very well averaging 84 mph. I thought how nice it would be to share a Jaguar 'C' type with him at Le Mans or Rheims. My participation with Jowetts was not giving me much fun anyway. Suddenly and before I could launch the idea at him, Doddy said "Are you going to carry on with this bloody silly game Bert?" This was about ten minutes after he had done so well in the race. I mentioned that I was hoping he would have a go.

There was a period after the war when I had no interest at all in racing. I had many offers, including from abroad but the lasting prospects didn't seem too good for a chap who had to earn a living. It took the combined efforts of Leslie Johnson and my friend Jack Emmott to persuade me to go to Le Mans with the Jaguar. I suppose this fired the old urge a bit but to return to Doddy – quite surprisingly he said "Well, I have had enough, I am packing it in." Then Doddy pointed out his second wife who was waiting for him on the public side of Woodcote Corner. I didn't meet her but when I think about it I can still see her standing there. I am sure Doddy was very happy and he probably made the right decision. After that I didn't see him again until 1974 when Tom Wheatcroft arranged the Austin get-together party at Donington Park. Those of us who met that day were all agreed on one point, that Tom Wheatcroft had done a marvellous job in refurbishing the Side-valve and one of the Twin-cam single-seaters and also for bringing us together again for a wonderful day.

I had met Tom Wheatcroft before our get-together at the Park. This was at is workshops in Leicester during the Austin car rebuild. He related how he used to cycle to Donington as a boy to watch the practice and races. It seems he became an Austin devotee at that point. He had very little money so his entry to the Park was a surreptitious one and I understand he used to camp out the night before a meeting to make sure of being there. Our start In life must have been on similar modest lines, the difference now being that Tom is a millionaire and I am not! But good luck to him, he has certainly put a lot of effort into the struggle on the way up.

I had a long talk with Charlie Dodson on our get-together day and he talked about his cottage in Tenterden, Kent and how he occupied his time driving a small van for a chap in the village who made wrought iron garden furniture etc. He said he could not understand how a company the size of Austin Motor Co Ltd could have allowed their racing heritage to become so neglected and he was even more uncomplimentary than Hadley about the management responsible for throwing all the spares and ancillary equipment to the four winds. I didn't see Doddy again. It was a day one could never forget.'

Sporting Big Sevens

We have already learnt that DOV 768, the Big Seven Forlite saloon, had been driven with some verve by Bert in both road and trialling events and later he bought it for his own personal use. Bert confirmed to me that he had fitted all the 'Le Mans' performance parts he could lay his hands on, special camshaft, alloy head and better manifold and it was still in this tune when he finally parted with it during the war. He later regretted selling DOV and often wondered what became of it.

HLH's colleague Bill Scriven, who worked with Ral Appleby, bought one of the later Grasshoppers, possibly COA 120, but it was destroyed by a fire at Scriven's parents' home in Alvechurch. After this he too bought a Big Seven, registered DOB 306 which he also trialled. Bert recalled *sticking funny engines in one or two Rubies* including a blown one. *'Obviously it was quite quick but needed careful handling'.* Quite so. 'The Le Mans Sports' is something of a myth though it is believed several prototypes were mocked-up and even a brochure was printed.

Here's the Hadley take on it, as related to Chris Gould in 1986:

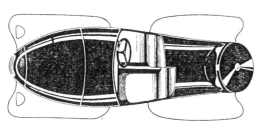

SPECIFICATION

ENGINE.—Bore 2·235in. (56·77 mm.). Stroke 3·5in. (88·9 mm.) ; Cubic capacity 900 c.c. ; R.A.C. rating 7·99 ; Cylinder block and crankcase in one casting. Special features : Detachable aluminium cylinder head ; sports type pistons, connecting rods and valves ; compression ratio 7 to 1.
FUEL.—Mechanical pump feed from rear tank with 12 gallons capacity ; extra large Zenith carburetter with intake silencer and air cleaner.
LUBRICATION.—Pump feed from large capacity oil sump.
COOLING.—Thermo-syphon and fan.
IGNITION.—Coil and 6 volt battery with automatic control.

CHASSIS.—Standard Big Seven with extra low centre of gravity.
GEARBOX.—Four-speed, synchromesh with remote control.
CLUTCH.—New type flexible single-plate, with very smooth engagement.
TRANSMISSION.—Open propeller shaft and torque tube.
FINAL DRIVE.—Three-quarter floating, spiral-bevel rear axle, with a special high performance ratio.
BRAKES.—Powerful and smooth Girling type.
STEERING.—"Hour-glass" worm and sector, with spring steering wheel.

SPECIAL FEATURES SET IN HEAVY TYPE.
For full specification, see main catalogue, pages 8 and 9.

THE AUSTIN MOTOR CO. LTD., G.P.O. Box 41, Longbridge, BIRMINGHAM

(via Robin Taylor)

Publication 1652 jumped the gun in describing
the exciting new 'Le Mans' Big Seven Sports.
Only a couple of prototypes are thought
to have been completed.

'There was one sports car project at Longbridge which may have escaped public attention, but I may be wrong of course. This in fact was the development of the Big Seven for participation at Le Mans and other suitable sports car races. As we know, the Big Seven appeared in 1937 using a 900cc monobloc type engine. It was a pleasant little car and I suppose in general terms its styling was in line with its competitors. However, in 1938 it was decided to consider a scheme for a Big Seven sports but we soon realised that this was to be a half hearted venture with restricted development future. At that time I was heavily engaged with the Twin-cam cars, trying to keep them racing on a shoe string, and so was not involved to any extent on the Big Seven scheme.

Lord Austin did ask me what I thought of a 900cc car's chances at Le Mans, very restricted I thought if adherence to a side-valve engine was unshakeable company policy. I also thought the standard chassis, a sort of stretched Ruby with its inability to take larger brakes, was also a non-starter.

It so happened that we had a prototype of the car which became known as the Austin Eight, also using the 900cc engine with some modifications to produce slightly increased power. This car saw departure from the old chassis. It had cross braced, welded and pressed steel platform type of chassis using semi-elliptic suspension all round. Brakes were by Girling using cone type expanders. Very hard test work on mountain roads in Wales demonstrated the durability of the platform. The engine was up-rated with higher compression than the one fitted to the Big Seven. It also had re-designed tappet gear and a stronger crankshaft. At least two engines were produced on the foregoing basis, destined for use in the Le Mans cars. They had high lift camshafts, alloy cylinder heads and improved porting. If I mentioned bhp I would be guessing as my notes have disappeared. I tried one in the prototype Eight and it certainly pulled well. I also tried one with a Centric supercharger installation using 8 lbs boost. This was quite impressive for the period as it passed Lickey Church at the top of Rose Hill (where the Old Man rests today) at 70 mph in third gear. Schemes were drawn up for both the Big Seven chassis and the Eight pressed platform and Dick Burzi, who was a first class body stylist, an Italian who had previously worked for Alfa Romeo, produced a sports car body of excellent proportions and a conception unlike any previous Austin sports example. This was one area where the Old Man could not blue-pencil Burzi's ideas as he had done so many times with production saloon cars. In the event the 900cc Le Mans cars did not emerge. They became one of the first victims of the political uproar and uncertainty following the Munich crisis.'

Donington Hall in the 1930s

An extensive country estate had been established on the Leicestershire and Derbyshire borders by the Rawdon-Hastings family. In 1790, work started on their new residence, Donington Hall, an imposing stone-built edifice set in acres of rolling parkland.

By the early 20th century, ownership had passed to the Gillies Shields family who rented much of the land for farming. During the Great War, captured German officers were interned in the Hall and its environs. After Fred Craner had persuaded John Gillies Shields to open up the Estate roads, initially for motorcycle, later car racing, the Hall was brought back into use as a hotel, for the convenience of competitors and officials or casual visitors, from 8/6d per day (43p).

Bert recalled the antics of a certain group of high-spirited drivers who, for some reason or other, mostly drove Rileys. Known to many as the 'Crazy Gang' after a well-known troupe of stage comedians, these included Percy Maclure, Charlie Martin, Charles Brackenbury and the redoubtable Freddie Dixon. When the action was at 'The Track' (Brooklands) it was the Hand and Spear at Byfleet or the Duke's Head in Addlestone which bore the brunt of their escapades.

When Donington Hall was opened up commercially, it was already in a run-down state and though it was superficially spruced up, the facilities, even by 1930s standards were somewhat basic. En-suite bathrooms were a rarity, therefore each guest would be provided with a chamber pot. Imagine the surprise – if not the consternation - of the occupants when they awoke to discover most of the 'guzunders' had been spirited from their rooms overnight and placed in neat rows on the front lawn. By any standards, a remarkable piece of organisation on someone's part, but the fact that most of the 'gang' were resident at the time, suspicions were directed in their direction, though hotly denied. Bert and Rose were moderate drinkers and because of this they much preferred the quieter hospitality offered by the Donington Manor Hotel or their good friends the Butler family at Ashbourne on these occasions.

Without an army of servants on hand, the accommodation was almost barrack-like. Kay Petre recalled staying at the Hall with the rest of the Austin team during a particularly cold and miserable week-end. *'Because I was a female, special dispensation was granted for a fire to be lit in my room and over the week-end my quarters looked like a Chinese laundry with everyone's coats and overalls strung up in an effort to dry things out.'* She also recalled that on arrival at the

Hall, Alf Depper assembling his troops, declaring everyone would be present for breakfast at 8am sharp as the egg and bacon would be on the table. *'No excuses'* and pointing a stubby finger at Mrs Petre *'that includes YOU madam!'* Ever the diplomat……

In late 1939, the whole estate was requisitioned by the War Office and later The Hall, like many similar buildings, provided accommodation for service personnel and refugee families. Donington Hall was eventually purchased by the burgeoning British Midlands Airways who refurbished, converted and extended it into their corporate headquarters in 1982, eventually employing some 800 people there. However, with the Company's recent sell-off, the future of Donington Hall was uncertain. Just as this narrative was being completed, it was announced that local firm Norton Motorcycles (UK) Ltd had purchased the Hall as its new Design and Production Centre.

(Author)

The impressive main entrance
to Donington Hall.

Le Mans

'For those who have not visited the Le Mans 24 hour race, they should know it is quite unlike any other event, except possibly Indianapolis which also has its own charisma. The competing teams locate themselves in the many villages surrounding Le Mans and up to 20 miles distance. Every year fresh hideaways are discovered. I drove five times at Le Mans, between 1937 – 1955, and stayed at the Hotel Continental in the town with Austins, Hotel Ricardeau Loume with Jaguar and Hotel Sanson in Le Mans itself with the Jowett team. I also stayed at a large chateau when driving a Nash-Healey and the Auberge Three Musketeers at Torce-en-Vallec with Triumph. The last named was a delightful place run by a Londoner named Dan Bona, who'd given up a restaurant in the West End to live in France.

Le Mans 24 is not just a race – it's a carnival. The vast infield at the rear of the pits is covered by fairs and restaurants. It's possible to see religious services taking place in daylight on the Sunday morning. Seeing these happenings from a fast car after a long stint in the darkness, I found very impressive. At least 250,000 people foregather to cover the 8.5 mile circuit. The atmosphere at the start was electric. Each time I drove, I was the first driver of the two. The cars were lined-up in echelon, the drivers stood on little numbered discs on the other side of the road. When the flag fell, one had to sprint to the car. I drove a Jaguar XK 120 in 1950 and Bill [later Sir William] Lyons had grave doubts about my ability to even reach the car. Much to his astonishment, and mine too, I was first away. He said afterwards "You bounced twice and were gone." Of course, they don't use that method now.

The competition throughout the race is terrific. Drivers have to like the challenge of long stints at the wheel. Maybe I was lucky in this respect as I found I could retain my concentration for a long time. The trick is to find a part of the circuit where one can "rest" which sounds unlikely, I know, but curiously I found this was possible on the long Mulsanne straight.'

(Written in late 1991.)

149

Raleigh Appleby

With a workforce approaching 20,000, Austins employed people from a myriad of backgrounds, irrespective of their role within the Company, including a number of foreign-born nationals. Those employed on the 'shop floor' by and large came from the 'working classes' of society. However, there were exceptions, for instance Raleigh Appleby (RA) one of Bert's colleagues in the Longbridge racing team. 'Ral' as he was popularly known started his time at 'The Austin' in 1915, so was one of the earliest to take advantage of the newly-introduced Apprenticeship Scheme.

He was the younger son of a family who had a substantial business in the Worcestershire town of Bromsgrove, an easy commute south of Longbridge. Thomas Appleby had taken over an existing hardware business at 69 and 70 High Street and by the time Raleigh arrived in 1899, Applebys were well established as General and Horticultural Ironmongers. Their activities would encompass many ancillary trades including 'tin making and brazing' and in 1918 Thomas Appleby marketed a new type of cheese-making vat which was quite probably made on the premises. The firm occupied a prime corner site and operated from a remarkably ornate half-timbered property which incorporated three separate shop fronts.

The impressive and substantial Appleby Ironmongers property in Bromsgrove c.1910.

With the Great War having started in August 1914 and despite Ral now being into his indentured period, by the time he reached the age of 18 he would have been liable for conscription into military service. He had already registered with the Royal Navy Volunteer Reserve (RNVR). In the spring of 1918, despite the belated entry of the United States into the conflict, Allied losses had been on such an horrific scale that the country needed every able bodied man available. MB 2701 Ordinary Seaman Appleby R. reported for duty and after training was seconded to HMS Hermione based at Southampton.

Raleigh Appleby (in cap) with older brother Tom with a smart side-car outfit.. Probably c.1914.

This elderly cruiser was now the HQ ship for the Coastal Motor Boats, more popularly known as Motor Torpedo Boats (MTBs). These craft were usually built by the famous firm of John I. Thornycroft and the hulls were based on their racing designs with a length of 55 feet or more and typically capable of over 40 knots. They carried a crew of five, two junior officers, a wireless operator and not one but two mechanics to maintain the 375hp V-12 power units. Having been promoted to Chief Mechanic, Ral's naval service ended in September 1919 after an interesting and at times exciting sixteen months. It was then back to the comparative calm and safety of Longbridge to complete his allotted time which ended in 1921.

With his natural engineering ability and additional naval experience, Ral was soon moved into the Experimental Department under the beady eye of foreman Alf Depper. In due course, Len Brockas, himself a veteran of the Western Front, would be appointed Chief Mechanic. Before arrival of Tom Murray Jamieson in 1932, Appleby, being unmarried was for a time seconded to the London Service Depot working with Stan Yeal, attending to the needs of the Dutch Clog/Rubber Duck single-seaters when they performed at the Brooklands Track.

As far as the family business was concerned, after their father died in 1927, RA's older brother Tom took over and successfully ran it until his death in 1961. Soon after, Applebys ceased trading and the property was somewhat redeveloped, though part of the ornate frontage has survived.

When Charles Goodacre joined 'Experimental' he was seconded to work with Ral from the outset and learnt a great deal from him. As we know, the young Hadley was under the wing of Brockas, and after Jamie's arrival, they would all work together closely as key members of the racing team. HLH was very impressed with Ral's all-round ability and always maintained he should have been in charge of the racing activities. Appleby had other talents, for instance he was an expert wood carver and designed and constructed animated wooden toys for his brother's children. He was also fond of sketching local scenes, one of which was on the wall at Red Lane. Throughout the Second World War Ral worked on vital war work including a spell at 'The Aero'. Returning to 'Experimental' he had plenty to do as Austins were working flat-out with a new range of vehicles, all designed with exports in mind. Alan Hess, a journalist and racing driver before the war, was AMCo's Publicity Officer and embarked on a series of ambitious events to bring the Austin marque to the fore, particularly in the United States, a market which held great export potential. On two occasions, Ral Appleby was selected as part of the back-up team, travelling with the drivers and cars on the Queen Elizabeth in 1949 and 1950, on both occasions the venue being the famous 'Brickyard' oval track at Indianapolis Speedway.

The Austin A90 'Atlantic' had been styled specifically for the American market though eventually sales were disappointing. However, the team's combined endeavours did capture a clutch of 'Stock Car' records (i.e. 'standard') which created much useful publicity.

At least the mechanical components of the A90 would eventually spawn the creation of the Healey 'Hundred', which, as the Austin-Healey, would become a major success.

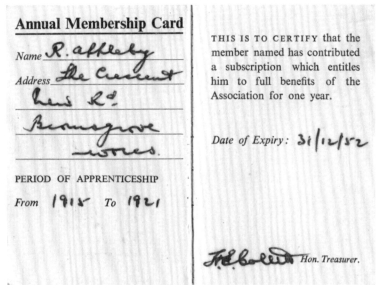

Ral Appleby's Austin Ex-Apprentices Association membership card.

Although Ral was quite a handsome chap, he took his time in settling down and he was nearly 48 when he married a local girl, Phyllis Merriman. He continued to work at Longbridge until he retired in 1964 after 49 years of loyal service. During that time he never sought the promotion which would have seen him take on administration duties, being content to get on with what he was so good at – 'fettling of the highest order'. RA died in early 1980 and Bert naturally attended his funeral. He was surprised to see so few family members present. Phyllis had pre-deceased him and they had no children.

Appleby left the proceeds of his estate to the Royal National Lifeboat Institution. His relatives offered HLH the tools Ral had accumulated over the years. These Bert declined but he did keep an exquisite Twin-cam valve spring compressor made by Ral. He also salvaged some family photographs, a few animal sketches and three of Ral's pocket-books, with entries dated from the 1930s up to his retirement. The notes make fascinating reading with all manner of information ranging from valve timing diagrams, supercharger ratios and power outputs for specific engines. Other diverse items include fuel consumption calculations for the Jamieson Side-valve cars and catering costs incurred at Brooklands! Entries covering the 1959-61 period refer to various 'Porsche' gearboxes detailing much trouble with tolerances, gear selection and synchro baulking rings. Could these be early Minis? Later notes refer to modified 'Sprite' gearboxes for 'Abingdon and Italy'. The final entry is dated April 10th 1964 *'[Reference] SPL 940-H Production ADO 17 [Austin 1800] stripped by me and fitted with new crank and flywheel and latest rear plate and seal.'*

They're Better Blown Y'know!

Whenever Bert's long-time pal Bill Butler phoned, he usually made the above statement in a sonorous voice, as a means of introduction. As we have heard, Bert and Rose owed a lot to Bill and his wife Ann not least for finding them a place to live in 1941. Since Bill and Bert's first meeting in 1935, they enjoyed a friendship which would last some 58 years. William Cornelius Butler (WCB) had an interesting career. Born in Derby in 1903, his first job was building 'crystal sets', an early form of radio, plus loud-speaker equipment. Whilst still in his early twenties, WCB was involved in a bad motorcycle accident which nearly cost him his eyesight. Luckily for Bill, a brilliant surgeon came to his rescue and additionally he also received a handsome pay-out by way of compensation. This capital enabled him to start a small business, 'Harcourt Motors', a brave move considering his lack of experience. By hard work and good business sense, he made a success of this and by the mid-thirties was able to enjoy the 'luxury' of getting cold and wet in trials events. At the outbreak of war, he held several agencies, including Triumph motorcycles and Fiat cars. As we learnt in Chapter Eight, his premises were requisitioned for Merlin aero-engine component production and Bill's son Brian clearly remembers the showroom full of capstan lathes and other machine tools during the war. Because of fuel shortages, the enterprising Butler converted a Fiat 'Topolino' to battery electric power, which enabled him to commute between Ashbourne and Derby with impunity.

In 1947, looking for a new challenge and thoroughly fed up with tighter food rationing and other restrictions imposed by a Labour government, Bill teamed up with fellow motorcycle trader Alfred George Briggs, who'd been a very successful works competition rider. Their idea was to go over to Canada to seek a suitable location for their respective families and a proposed joint business venture. They sailed to New York, taking with them a brand-new Ford Anglia (RC 9355). This they drove towards their intended destination, London, Ontario, over the border into Canada. They attracted quite a lot of publicity en route, their tiny 933cc 'English auto' averaging 40 mpg and capable of 'at least' 50 mph, though possibly not at the same time. They even managed to visit Frank L. Zimmerman, president of the Harley-Davidson Corporation. Eventually Butler and Briggs returned to the U.K. but the venture did not materialize. Instead, the Butlers emigrated to South Africa, but Ann Butler could not settle, so within a year the family came back.

They eventually settled in Leamington Spa where Bill re-started 'Harcourt Motors' and carried on until his retirement in 1963. They spent 18 years at Box in Wiltshire and finally settled in Bradford-on-Avon. Ann Butler died in 1987, two years before Rose. However, Bill was able to attend HLH's funeral where, afterwards in the confines of the Clarendon Hotel Kenilworth, Neville Barr enjoyed a long 'chinwag' with him about 'life in Derby' before, during and after the war. Bill Butler died fourteen months later at the age of 91.

Sixty years wed . . . Mr and Mrs Bill Butler

60 years race by for rally pair

RETIRED rally driver Mr Bill Butler, 85, and his wife Anne, 81, of 9 Sandy Leaze, Bradford on Avon, are celebrating their diamond wedding today.

The couple were both born in Derby and spent most of their married life in the Midlands, moving to Wiltshire when Mr Butler retired from mechanical engineering in 1963.

They spent about 18 years at Box Hill, moving to their present home six years ago.

Mr and Mrs Butler have happy memories of the 1937 RAC rally at Blackpool in which they both took part and won a prize. Mr Butler was a keen trials and rally driver in those days.

They have two sons Brian, who lives at Rudloe, and Douglas, who lives at Warwick.

A small party for family and friends will be held at Brian's home.

The couple compete in the Blackpool Rally in 1937

Hadley's Haul of Achievements

Before his retirement, Bert thoughtfully asked his secretary to annotate his competition results in neat order. It makes impressive reading and he did not only enter national events, particularly in trials, 1936 – 39 were four <u>very</u> busy seasons!

i) Reliability Trials

December 27-28th 1935	**M.C.C. London - Exeter Trial** 2nd Class Award
February 22nd 1936	**SUNBAC Colmore Trophy (Cotswolds)** 7hp - 3rd Class Award
March 14th 1936	**N.W. London Motor Club 'Coventry' Cup Trial** 7hp - 2nd Class Award. Special Award for best performance by SUNBAC member
March 29th 1936	**United Hospitals Trial (Cotswolds)** 7hp – Premier Award & Team Award with Buckley & Scriven
April 10-11th 1936	**M.C.C. London - Lands End Trial** 1st Class Award
May 28-30th 1936	**M.C.C. Edinburgh Trial** 1st Class Award
November 7th 1936	**M.C.C. Buxton Trial** 1st Class Award
November 14th 1936	**Bristol MC&LCC Roy Feddon Trophy Trial** Clean sheet. Anthony Cup. Best supercharged 1100cc performance
November 21st 1936	**SUNBAC Vesey Cup Trial** Vesey Cup - Best performance of the day
January 1-2nd 1937	**M.C.C London - Exeter Trial** Premier Award.
February 27th 1937	**SUNBAC Colmore Trophy Trial** 750cc Award – Best performance
May 1st 1937	**M.G. Car Club Abingdon Trial** Watkinson Trophy for best performance by a member from a visiting club
May 14th 1937	**M.C.C. London - Edinburgh Trial** Premier Award
July 16-17th 1937	**M.C.C. Torquay Rally** Bronze Award
November 6th 1937	**SUNBAC Vesey Cup Trial** 2nd Class Award
November 20th 1937	**Torbay & Totnes M. C. English Riviera Trial** Eric Perry Cup – 2nd best performance
December 4th 1937	**N.W. London M.C. London - Gloucester Trial** 2nd Class Award

January 7th 1938	**M.C.C. Exeter Trial**
	Premier Award
November 12th 1938	**Bristol M.C. & L.C.C. Roy Fedden Trophy Trial**
	2nd Class Award
November 20th 1938	**Hagley & District Motor Club**
	2nd Class Award
December 27th 1938	**Ford Enthusiasts Trial**
	Best performance up to 1100cc
January 6-7 1939	**M.C.C. London – Exeter Trial**
	Premier Award & Simms Hill Award
	(Big Seven DOV 768)
February 11th 1939	**N.W. London M.C. Coventry Cup Trial**
	Runner-up for Whittingham Trophy
	(best performance under 1100cc)
February 25th 1939	**SUNBAC Colmore Trophy Trial**
	2nd Class Award
February 26th 1939	**Southsea M.C. President's Trophy Trial**
	1500cc Cup
May 29th 1939	**Plymouth Motor Club '200' Reliability Trial**
	Best performance in Trial but disqualified owing to late arrival (held up owing to an accident)

ii) Speed Trials

July 18th 1936	**M.A.C. Madresfield – Side-valve**
	3rd in Class 1
August 8th 1936	**West Hants L.C.C. Southsea – Side-valve**
	1st in 1100/850
	1st in 1500/1100
	3rd in 3000/1500
August 22nd 1936	**Lewes – Side-valve**
	2nd Unlimited Class
	3rd 1100cc Class
September 26th 1936	**Brighton (Madeira Drive) – Side-valve**
	1st 850cc Class
	3rd 1100cc Class
	4th 1500cc Class
May 22nd 1937	**Bristol (Aerodrome) – Twin-cam**
	1st in all Classes and fastest time of day.
	(Classes D.E.F.G.)
September 25th 1937	**Brighton (Madeira Drive) – Twin-cam**
	1st 1100cc Class
	2nd 850cc Class
	3rd 1500cc Class

iii) Hill Climbs

July 25th 1936 **Bristol M.C. & L.C.C. Backwell – Side-valve**
2nd racing cars up to 850cc

August 29th 1936 **Ulster Automobile Club Craigantlet – Side-valve**
Dunlop Trophy - Fastest time of the day (new record for the hill)
1st up to 850cc
Clanrye Cup - 1st 1100cc
Newsletter Trophy - 1st Unlimited Class

September 12th 1936 **Shelsley Walsh – Side-valve**
3rd. (46.91)

June 5th 1937 **Shelsley Walsh – Twin-cam**
1st in Class.
M.A.C. Challenge Trophy & £25.
Team Prize with Goodacre & Bäumer

August 28th 1937 **Ulster Automobile club Craigantlet – Twin-cam**
Fastest time in Unlimited Racing Class
Dunlop Trophy
Fastest time of the day
Newsletter Trophy
New Record – 1 minute 21.4 secs

September 11th 1937 **Shelsley Walsh – Twin-cam**
5th Team Prize with Goodacre & Mrs Petre.
40.74 secs.

May 28th 1938 **Shelsley Walsh – Twin-cam**
2nd – 40.09 secs (new record for class)

August 27th 1938 **Ulster Automobile Club Craignantlet – Twin-cam**
Fastest time of the day – Dunlop Trophy.
Fastest time up to 1100cc – Clanrye Trophy.
Fastest time Unlimited – Newsletter Trophy.
Fastest time Handicap – Nobel Trophy.
1 minute 23.8 secs (wet)

September 10th 1938 **Shelsley Walsh – Twin-cam**
2nd fastest time of the day – 40.05 (Challenge Trophy)
Team Prize with Buckley & Dodson

June 3rd 1939 **Shelsley Walsh – Twin-cam**
1st in class – 40.56 secs.
4th fastest time of the day – M.A.C. Trophy.

July 30th 1939 **Bugatti Owners Club Prescott – Twin-cam**
1st in 750 Class – 47.40 secs.
5th in general placing.

September 9th 1939 **Shelsley Walsh**
Cancelled owing to the outbreak of W.W.2.

iv) Racing

April 10th 1937 — **British Empire Trophy Donington Park**
Completed course – finished 12th

May 12th 1937 — **Donington Park Coronation Races**
2nd in Event 4

June 12th 1937 — **Nuffield Trophy Donington Park**
1st (Junior Handicap)

June 26th 1937 — **L.C.C. International Relay Race (Brooklands)**
1st (put in a lap of 121.68 mph)

July 10th 1937 — **Brooklands Campbell Circuit Races**
1st in National Race

July 24th 1937 — **Derby & D.M.C. Donington 12 Hour Sports Race**
2nd – Hadley & Dodson (in COA 121)

August 14th 1937 — **Crystal Palace Cup**
1st

April 2nd 1938 — **Coronation Trophy Race Crystal Palace**
3rd in Heat 1 & 4th in Final

April 9th 1938 — **B.R.D.C. Empire Trophy Race Donington**
6th

May 14th 1938 — **Coronation Trophy Race Donington**
1st in Handicap up to 850cc
1st in Handicap up to 1500cc

July 9th 1938 — **Nuffield Trophy Race Donington**
2nd

September 24th 1938 — **Dunlop Jubilee Meeting Brooklands**
1st in Seventh race – The first Dunlop Jubilee Trophy Race (Road Circuit) – Scratch
2nd in Ninth Race – The Fourth Dunlop Road Handicap.

April 1st 1939 — **British Empire Trophy Race Donington**
2nd (69.57 mph)

June 10th 1939 — **Nuffield Trophy Donington**
8th in general placing
(Scratch race for cars up to 1500cc)

July 1st 1939 — **Crystal Palace Cup**
1st in Heat 2
2nd in Final

August 26th 1939 — **Imperial Trophy Crystal Palace**
1st in Heat 2
1st in Final – Imperial Trophy

England declared war on Germany September 3rd.

To the Day!

Bert wrote this article for the May 1946 issue of 'The Light Car' for his pal the Editor, Eric Findon. With 'Hadley approval', the magazine of the Austin Seven Clubs' Association (A7CA) featured it some 45 years later. After some five years with the Ministry, Bert had developed an eloquent and easy writing style and we make no apologies for reproducing it here once more.

'A few days ago I met the Editor and we fell to talking of those potent little motorcars, the "camshaft" single-seater Austins. The mantle of years seemed to fall away and once again I could hear that fierce staccato bark and feel the thrill of sheer power. The Editor was talking but I could hear him only subconsciously, for I was back at Donington Park winding my Austin round that wonderful circuit.

My first recollection was of rounding Coppice Corner and shooting past Fred Craner's house, clipping the verges along that snaky bit, then on to that awkward turn over the hill where one seemed to need all the road. I suddenly remembered a race when the dynamic little Charlie Dodson, my team mate, passed me on the outside of the bend, going like a train, with his arms working like pistons. That really shook me! Down the straight we went, only inches apart, where the Austins on a favourable day would reach nearly 120 mph. There was that horrible lifting feeling again where the cross wind at Red Gate crossing seemed to be trying to pluck our little projectiles from the road. Then we were at the summit of Melbourne Hill with its overwhelming temptation to lift ones foot. It could be taken flat in the Austin but only with absolutely correct placing. I felt again the thrilling leap over the brow of the hill and saw the sea of faces and parked motorcars coming up with a rush to meet me.

Dodson's brakes were smoking and there was a puff of smoke each time he made a crisp gear change. He was so small in the cockpit that one could not see him at all from directly behind. Round the turn we slid and fought for the advantage of the inside on the pull up Melbourne Hill. Yes, I know this will be regarded as a fratricidal struggle but we did not pull our punches in irksome team procession. Next we were shrieking past the pits and bouncing into the Red Gate Corner. The mixture was dead right and the pick-up almost bomb-like as we nipped through the Gate and into the semi-darkness under the trees beyond. I can see my mind's eye that floating offside front wheel as we rushed downhill in third gear to the Hairpin (which is not a hairpin anyway). Down to second gear, a jump, and we were diving for the stone bridge where one must cut out promptly to see the other side of the ensuing left-hand bend in one piece. Up to McLean's Corner, a cream-coloured car had dived into the inside ditch and the tail was sticking out unpleasantly. Full bore again up the hill beyond………

"Are you with me in this old man?" Gosh! I am still with the Editor. "What do you think of the Austins' chances, if any, at Shelsley in future, and if you feel like dreaming will you commit your dreams to paper for the benefit of thousands of other dreamers?"

Shelsley. Since 1939 I have thought many times of that thousand yards of twisting road. With my pal Bill Butler, the Derby trials wizard, I have plotted every corner and undulation (all from a fireside chair!) and let me tell you dear readers, we broke the record many times – at least that was the only logical conclusion the way we figured it. I have often been asked "Is it possible to break Mays' existing record with a '750' Austin?" Yes, I think it could be done and in saying so, I am not necessarily suggesting that I am the chap to do it. Any youngish subject with a flair for small motor cars and a little imagination about the future would be suitable material, at least to train.

Without a trace of conceit, I believe I had reached the maximum, or perhaps we had better say minimum, time possible in the Austin in the guise it appeared at Shelsley up to June 1939, but modestly I venture to suggest that if the September climb of that fateful year had been held, the Austin, with the slight modifications we had made, would have bettered 40 seconds.

A word about Specials

Road circuits and speed hill climb courses vary a good deal in their reactions to structural alterations on any particular vehicle. Shelsley, Prescott and the rest are not a question of fantastic power-weight ratio, but of requisite power combined with qualities of adhesion, accurate steering born of effective suspension and really safe braking. I believe a "Special" could be built to shake the two-litre ERA but not on the lines adopted by the majority of "Special" builders before the war. I know very well it is all a question of expense, but it seems to me that a good deal of money was spent ineffectively.

The line usually taken was to plant a motorcycle engine or a pretty lusty car engine in a frame, tack on four wheels, plus some retarding arrangements, place oneself in a strategic position to pilot the "heap" and hope for the best. No, I am not taking a superior view as I am only a poor man myself, but I do say to you chaps who are the enthusiasts likely to get the sport cracking in the near future, please plan your job on a drawing board. Start with your chassis (tubular ones can be built up quite cheaply these days), make up your own suspension or adopt something on the "independent" plan from a good, light, but no longer wanted, standard motor car.

The engine problem is taken care of by the existence of the ever-popular V8 (which can be blown), or if you are building lighter, the high-speed motorcycle engine of the multi-cylinder type. What I want to impress on you is the importance of starting with your basic principle correct, with the idea of ultimately turning corners quickly in addition to rushing up straight roads. Reverting to the Austins, I think the cars could be modified to the extent of putting up an amazing show both at Shelsley and Prescott, but whether this will happen or not I haven't the faintest idea.

Advice to drivers

Many people have asked me about the physical side of a quick run at Shelsley and how I reacted. Well, for those of you who are new to the game and are going to run at the first meeting in June, I would say you will soon find out then whether you are potential speed hill climb drivers, long-distance road drivers or not suited at all. Successful men in both spheres are few and far between. I have seen first-class road and track racing drivers who were "slow" at Shelsley. My advice is keep fit and turn away from alcohol (it is permitted in your tank!), particularly immediately before the climb, get plenty of sleep and remember, a good motor car representing hours of toil, can be wasted on a jittery driver. The greatest self control is needed a few seconds before you make a start, pick your place carefully on the line, give yourself plenty of room for the first hump and the ensuing Kennel Bend. It is all a matter of "line".

Remember Euclid's* Definition

I have taken the little Austin through the Kennel Bend flat in second gear by keeping a good line on the run in and drifting wide as I came out. Use all the road up to the Esses by attempting to strike the straightest line possible and whatever else you may do wrong, do fix a cut-off point in practice for the first left-hand bend of the Esses. A yard or so too far and you have "had it", probably in more ways than one.

I found it best to keep well off the side for the approach, and to make a rather late cut across, so as to avoid a disconcerting lump on the inside. The tail was then set dead correct for the right-hand bend through the tunnel. Watch out for the rather acute camber as you pull into the straight and try to keep in the centre of the road to the finish, and oh, yes, just imagine it is Sunday afternoon without a soul in sight – just you and the motor bursting to get to the top in the shortest possible time.

The best of luck to all you chaps who run at Shelsley. Good hill climbing!'

* An Ancient Greek mathematician, and noted Handling Guru.

Correspondence Corner

Both before and after his retirement, Bert was a prolific letter writer, of necessity and by choice. A number of letters addressed to HLH have survived within the archives. Here's a selection in chronological order, which makes interesting 'period' reading.

T. MURRAY JAMIESON
B.SC. (ENG.), A.M.I.A.E., M.S.A.E.

10 RUTLAND TERRACE
STAMFORD LINCS
TELEPHONE 2314

23rd May 1937.

My Dear Bert,

I am so sorry that it is now over a month since I had your letter. As you may have perceived, I tried to get you alone after the Coronation meeting at Donington, but owing to the shortage of Austin transport it was impossible.

I was very disappointed to see your car let you down in the last big race, particularly in view of the fact that Charles' car stayed together. I was in the woods on the first lap and saw smoke coming from your cockpit, and Charles get by. I knew something was wrong because Charles and Kay Petre were so close on your tail. After seeing the smoke I was rather surprised to see you round again at all. What was wrong with your car? Who put Charles' car together?

Now, turning back to your letter, I will reply to it step by step, and no doubt you will recognise what I am talking about although by now you will have forgotten all detail of what you said.

S.C.H.D's report on the Empire Trophy. Nobody could take any exception to what he said. I have sent a copy to the Old Man, just in case. I think he oversteps the mark in wanting two men standing by with extinguishers at the ready and blankets and so on in every pit. There would not be enough room for all the men, and no brassards left over. We have been pressing the R.A.C. for nose refuelling apparatus to be permitted and I think it will come off. I have NO DOUBT however, that my apparatus will be shown to be completely wrong, and you will have a plain tank on the roof and a hundred gallons of fuel on the road in a second, with a cook that sticks open. You will see. I told someone or other on the Thursday that you would have trouble and soak the driver with fuel when I saw that the old drip-and-splash fillers had been resurrected, but I did not actually expect a fire. I wrote and told Charles that he did the sensible thing in crossing the road, and not leaving the Austin pits to put him out - they would only have poured more petrol over him.

I have no doubt that the race would have been just money for jam for you if nothing had gone wrong. I can't understand your first item of what was wrong, you say "slow running ????? in carb gradually opening throttle" and one word looks like "join". What is it? Shock absorbers - these

- 2 -

should have been all right if you adjusted them in practice with a full tank. Did they get soaked with oil? Do you think they were tampered with? Did the water get on them? Plugs - I left the plugs all sorted, and there were quite a number of other grades available. We did not use 500 even for the 120 mph records I think. 480 You should have been running on 440 if high boost. 360 if low.

Your fuel feed troubles were due no doubt to the valve now that you have thrown it out. It must have been because the valve was the cause of every one of our numerous failures over the past four years, including all Baumer's failures, the records and obviously was the cause of broken valves, magnetos and oil pipes - it also accounts for the fact the E.R.A. have never won a race, being fitted with such a valve. This must be right, because the Motor and Light car say so, and no doubt they got their information for the Austin Motor Co. (Of course, if the valve was incorrectly piped up, this is quite a detail, and obviously so because everyone would expect a conrod to work just as well upside down, and if it didn't it would clearly be quite useless.)

The only possible way in which the air gauge could read pressure that wasn't in the tank would be for the valve unit to be wrongly connected. Even if the valve itself seized, these symptoms could only arise if there were a wrongly connected air gauge as well as another wrong connection. With a seized valve and correct connections the pressure follows the boost, giving too much on full throttle, and possibly suction on the over-run. The valve cannot cause fuel wastage.

Van Keit lost his South African race through a seized hand pump.

The old float chamber was NBG I know, but there was a brand new one, properly designed with all sorts of refinements to make it operate with greater efficiency (anti-rolling orange in level &etc) and reliability (brazed steel float and arm - &c). However, since I designed this it could obviously be off &c no possible use. Instead the two standard float chambers are just twice as UN reliable as the other one. To be perfectly frank your chances of failure due to any sort of trouble with the new float chambers only are increased about five to six times. I know just all the weak points of both types. In addition you will probably find you use a little more fuel on a course like Donington - and possibly a bad pick-up after braking. (Stanley & Sophie in particular for instance).

Fuel can only get into the leak-away pipe if the tank

160

T. MURRAY JAMIESON
B.SC.(ENG.) A.M.I.A.E. M.R.A.E.

10 RUTLAND TERRACE
STAMFORD LINCS
TELEPHONE 2314

- 3 -

is filled to above the air pipe junction, the filler cap
shut, and the car left to stand. The slight pressure which
builds up in the stationary tank (fuel vapour pressure) will
push fuel slowly down the air pipe. If any fuel thus gets
into the valve and is left, corrosion may cause sticking, but
if the valve is started in a race quite clean, it cannot
possibly give trouble. The trouble in the I.O.M. was due
to the excessively dusty course. Dust got in through the carb
and blower to the induction pipe, hence up the boost pipe to
the valve and stuck it. After this I had three small felt pad
air filters made, and these are either in the stores or Podmore
has the pieces. I did not fit them because we did not again
run into such dirty conditions, and quite frankly I did not
went to add a single union that someone might bodge - and my
design get blamed.

I suppose you are still using my design of engine,
chassis, brakes, axles, steering, gearbox, and such unimportant
details? I was very disappointed when I had a talk with
Appleby (D.O. variety) to find that he has had the wool
successfully drawn over his eyes. He told me that the valve
had been a continuous source of trouble, and that since it had
been thrown out the consumption had been decreased no end. As
I had used the valve two years before he came to Austins, and
since nobody knew what the consumption was before the valve was
thrown out there is some doubt about the statements.

Which car is which? Presumably you have Wizard's car
that Charles had last year, while Charles has Dodson's old car,
and I noticed he has the synchro gearbox. Dear dear, and he
was always so keen on a crash box, saying that since the
Continental Stars did not use a synchro box, obviously such
a thing was a waste of time. However I suppose we can all
change our mind - but having done so it is a little funny to see
how VERY sure some people are of themselves.

Have you the carburettor needle that came out of
Dodson's car after the records? This is the best needle ever,
and as I told you, if you get hold of it and a blank, I will
make you a copy. and moreover, if you like, and can get me
a few old thick ones, I will make a short series very close to
it, that you can slip in your carb on your own, and get down to
some really accurate tuning.

I thought the side tank filler caps were pitiful.
Surely the Old Men is not
taken in.
Just a face-saving move I suppose.

You know where we live. All the best. Let's have
your news. Steam up! Murray Jamieson

P.F.O.

I am running in my E.R.A. on
my "Austin" fuel - shell variety,
with a very slight modification.
It is called "4JUS X".

Have Nuffield entries
this morning. See your name.

Give my best wishes to all the crowd.

Chaps in the shop often like.

Don't I often prefer not to get.

Him is know often are in touch with
me.

What's meryn with no Stephen?

Doesn't seem to like me.

Letter 1

T. MURRAY JAMIESON
B.SC. (ENG.). A.M.I.A.E. M.S.A.E.

10 RUTLAND TERRACE
STAMFORD LINCS
TELEPHONE 2314

Thursday night,
30th Sept 1937.

My Dear Bert,

This is a bad business about Kay. I heard yesterday from Tommy Wisdom that she is partly coming to, and is talking 11 years ago. There have been just sensational stories in the Sunday papers that I hardly know what to believe, but I rather gather she is pretty sure to climb out. It was rather funny that we should have mentioned Parnell last time we had time to talk. Hope to see you on Saturday at Donington and hear some reliable news about her.

And what about Goodacre in the 500. Bloody disgraceful after your do at Shelsley. I decided the other day that for your sake and any other driver I had better give the Old Man a shove before the cars collapsed on the floor in a heap. I said among other things, mentioning no names - "You had far better not run the cars if you are not prepared to keep them in a safe condition of repair and adequately insure the drivers." The last is a dig for Pat. I hope they have you covered a little better. I presume that Goodacre's "broken track rod" really was a broken track rod, or was it some part that would have the same effect?

What happened to your piston? Would you have done any good? Dodson seems to have gone well. He's had a rotten season.

Went over to Donington yesterday. The cars are simply grand, and Rosemeyer is a first class driver. Hasse and Muller are just plain third rate. I think you and in fact almost any of the accepted good English drivers could leave them cold on the same cars. Rosemeyer is careless and will come badly unstuck one day. I did not see any of the Mercedes running, only the Onions.

See you Saturday I hope. I shall avoid the pits and am trying for a very special super pass to get me everywhere.

Yours sincerely,

Letter 2

T. MURRAY JAMIESON
B.SC. (ENG.). A.M.I.A.E. M.S.A.E.

10 RUTLAND TERRACE
STAMFORD LINCS
TELEPHONE 2314

26th October 1937.

My dear Bert,

I was very sorry indeed to see and hear you blow up in the Siam race. Piston I suppose. Never mind, I am about as disgusted as you yourself I should think. I have insulted everyone at Longbridge by now out nothing seems to make any difference. I see and hear that Earl's Court was unlucky for Longbridge. Long delayed effects of long existing causes are long lived and long to stop. Epigram. Trite. No, not Tripe.

Will you be at Grande Vitesse's talk before the M.&.C. next Wednesday the 3rd November? If you will let me know that you will be there I will be more likely to come.

How did your Woolworth steering arms behave? I would like to know whether you found the steering a little less definite? Did you find the car more inclined to wander as you braked for the Fork? Did it kick as you went up the Banking at the Top Corner?

Mays is almost certain to go to S.A. in which case let us hope the Start remains in the West this year. E.R.A. tourer going on well. All engine castings and forgings and many bits machined already in.

All the best, and kindest wishes to you Mother and Father. See you next Wednesday?

Yours sincerely,

14th March, 1938.

H. L. Hadley, Esq.

I did not go to Brooklands on Saturday so cannot give you any news of Pat Driscoll or anybody like that.

With kindest regards to your [illegible]

Yours sincerely,

[signature]

See Kayume here from todays paper

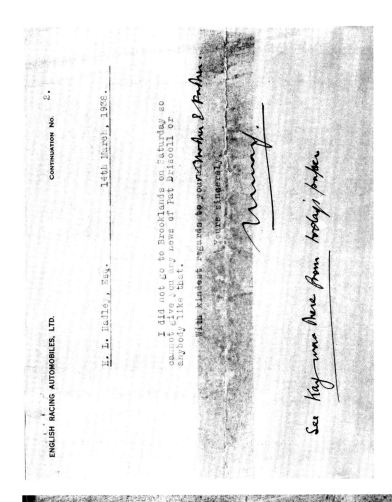

ENGLISH RACING AUTOMOBILES L⸆ᴰ
BOURNE LINCS
TELEPHONE BOURNE 121

DIRECTORS
H.W. COOK RAYMOND MAYS
PETER BERTHON

OUR REF TMJ/JB.
YOUR REF
DATE 14th March, 1938.

MANUFACTURERS OF

"E.R.A." RACING CARS

MURRAY JAMIESON SUPERCHARGERS

AUTOMOBILE RESEARCH ENGINEERS

H. L. Hadley, Esq.,
22 Twining Road,
Stirchley,
BIRMINGHAM.

My dear Bert,

I was rather wondering why I had not heard from you recently and noticed that you did not appear in one or two Trials recently, notably Colmore. Arising out of this I see that Dennis Buckley won the Shell Cup.

It was not until Friday when I saw you mentioned in the "Light Car" that I knew anything was wrong with you at all, and whatever it is, you may assume that nobody wishes you a quicker recovery than I do.

I suppose it was because of your internal difficulties that I heard nothing from you about the miller. However, we are now on the look out for a really skilled tin-basher and I am wondering whether you could give Rubin the tip. I don't think that Redditch Ned would be quite the man for us, but I think Rubin would, that is of course, always assuming he has not gone up to the Shadow Factory.

We are now building up the first two passenger car engines and hope to get them running in a few weeks time.

Do let us have your latest news and let me know how you are.

I hear that Charly Goodacre has left the works again and now joined up with Ethyl Export.

AND AT BROOKLANDS TRACK, WEYBRIDGE, SURREY

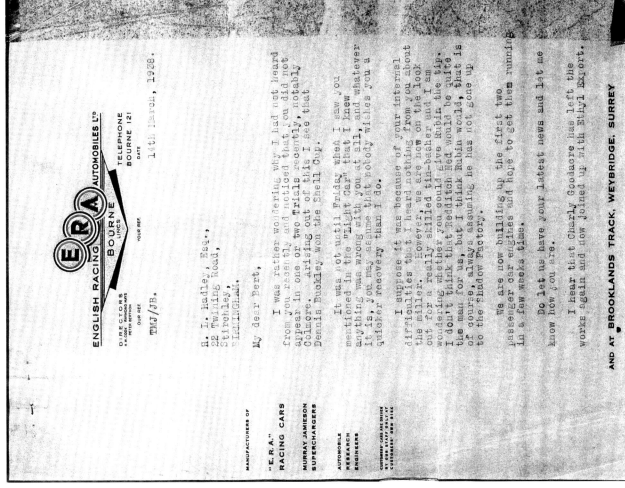

T. MURRAY JAMIESON
B.SC. (ENG.). A.M.I.A.E. M.S.A.E.

10 RUTLAND TERRACE
STAMFORD LINCS
TELEPHONE 2314

25th April 1938.

My dear Bert,

Now at last I have time to reply to your letter of the 16th March, for which many thanks. As you will gather, I have been busy - now being a fully fledged FATHER now. The SON and his MOTHER are both doing 100% well. Was glad to hear your operation was successful - had no idea it was coming off until I read something in the Autocar about it. Nasty, but I feel sure you will be better for it. Having a new start, take my tip and watch yourself carefully - keep down smoking, don't take any alcohol but what is necessary to be polite, and then in your particular position not during race week - don't overeat and drink only between meals - never with meals, don't eat after three hours before bed, not a scrap - not much breakfast, no chocolate between meals. Excuse me. Try it all the same. Getting as bad as Sammy.

Now, I am very glad the old cars did some of their stuff on Empire Trophy day at Donington. Also the very deepest regrets for what happened to your car before the start. It just goes to show that you can't be too careful - never mind people thinking you are finicky. Strange too that Lord should have done something I had been trying to do for four years, and the cars immediately won the race. One version is that how Alf Depper is unable to spare any time for the cars, Bill Sewell is wholly responsible for the win, in fact he would have driven as well, but for his feet. How did you manage to tune the cars without assistance from Ethyl?

Regarding your paragraph about Reuben, I can only say that I sometimes think everything is a leg-pull.

The touring car goes on a (slightly) pace. Two first engines just finishing assembly. Clutches finished. Gearboxes partly machined. Axles and so on partly in hand. I built the first two engines for £1000, over half being in tools, patterns, dies and so on. All work done out, so includes overheads and all.

Racing cars are progressing with much telephoning, telegraphing, tremendous efforts, night shift, boloney, at exclusive and enormous expense. Cars appear in 1939.

Let's have your news from time to time. And MUCH better luck next time. International Trophy? Or nothing?

Yours ever,

Best wishes to your
Father & Mother

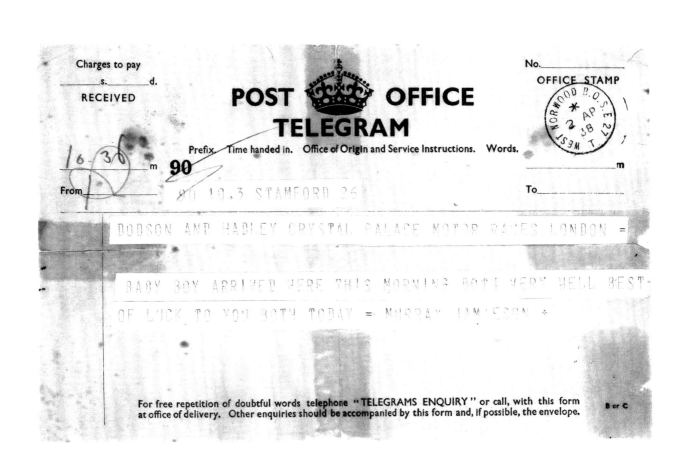

FILE COPY OBTAINED BY H.L.H. FROM AUSTIN'S SECRETARY!

PERSONAL.

June 21st, 1939.

Humphrey Cook, Esq.,
Messrs E.R.A. Limited,
Castle Donington,
near Derby.

Dear Mr. Cook,

I have been thinking over the matter
mentioned in your letter of the 16th in connection
with the services of our driver Mr. Hadley, and I
hope you will not mind my coming to the conclusion
that I could not agree to his driving one of your
cars.

I should like to have helped, but I feel
that this is something that we could not do as a
matter of principle.

I hope however that you will be able to
get someone equally as good as Hadley.

Yours sincerely,

The British Racing Drivers' Club

LTD.

President: THE RT. HON. EARL HOWE, P.C., C.B.E., V.D.

Vice-Presidents
Capt. WOOLF BARNATO, Dr. J. D. BENJAFIELD, Sir MALCOLM CAMPBELL, M.B.E., J. R. COBB, CECIL KIMBER.

Hon. Treasurer: H. W. COOK
Hon. Solicitor: KEITH ERSKINE

Committee
R. J. W. APPLETON   K. D. EVANS
DR. J. D. BENJAFIELD W. G. EVERITT
O. H. J. BERTRAM   H. P. MCCONNELL
SIR MALCOLM CAMPBELL T. B. ROSE-RICHARDS
A. C. DOBSON   C. S. STANILAND
H. N. EDWARDS   R. J. B. SEAMAN

Secretary
D. J. SCANNELL

12 QUEEN'S GATE TERRACE,
LONDON, S.W.7

Telephones: Western 0092-3
Telegrams: Speedmen, Southkens, London
Cables: Speedmen, London

Fifteenth,
February,
1939. DJS/LM.

H. L. Hadley, Esq.,
22, Twyning Road,
Stirchley,
BIRMINGHAM.

Dear Mr. Hadley,

As requested in your letter of the
13th inst., I have much pleasure in in sending you
herewith a form of application for Membership of
this Club.

Yours sincerely,

Secretary,
The British Racing Drivers' Club.

Encl.

From: Lord Austin, KBE, LLD.

Telegrams: "Speedily" Telex Northfield.

Telephone: Priory 2101.

Longbridge Works,
Birmingham.

11th October, 1939.

Mr. H.L.Hadley,
22, Twyning Road,
STIRCHLEY.

Dear Sir,

I have pleasure in handing you herewith a cheque for £150: 0: 0d and congratulate you on the efforts you made and the successes you obtained during the year.

It is unfortunate that we cannot continue the Trials and Races for the time being.

Yours faithfully,

Austin

ENC/

NEW ADDRESS

E.R.A. LTD.
CASTLE DONINGTON
NR. DERBY

TELEPHONE
CASTLE DONINGTON 260

RAIL
L M S CASTLE DONINGTON

BOURNE 121

YOUR REF.

OUR REF.

DATE

RWC/NH/JB.   HLH.   30th August, 1939.

H. L. Hadley, Esq.,
The Austin Motor Co.Ltd.,
Longbridge Works,
BIRMINGHAM.

Dear Mr. Hadley,

Thanks very much for your letter of yesterday in connection with the forthcoming Donington Grand Prix. As you say, it is our intention to enter two cars, one of which will, of course, be driven by Arthur Dobson.

I should very much like to have given you an opportunity of driving the second car in this race, but owing to the refusal of Lord Austin to entertain your driving for us when I approached him earlier on in the summer, I had to look round elsewhere, and have tentatively fixed up another driver for this event, should he prove suitable in practice.

I am sure you will appreciate that, in these circumstances, I cannot alter the present arrangements for the remainder of this season.

If you are at any time near here I should be very pleased if you could call in and see me, when perhaps we can discuss the possibilities of coming to some arrangement with Lord Austin next year, should he feel inclined to change his decision.

In the meantime, I am afraid I am unable to do anything further in view of the circumstances.

Yours sincerely,

AND AT BROOKLANDS TRACK, WEYBRIDGE, SURREY.

MANUFACTURERS OF

"E.R.A."
RACING CARS

AUTOMOBILE
RESEARCH
ENGINEERS

From - Lord Austin, K.B.E.LL.D. Longbridge Works, Birmingham.
Telegrams: Speedily, Telex, Northfield.
Telephone: Priory 2101.

June 13th. 1940.

TO WHOM IT MAY CONCERN.

HERBERT LEWIS HADLEY.

The above is, I understand, applying for a position with the Ministry of Aircraft Production, and has asked me to furnish a reference, which I have pleasure in giving.

I have known Mr. Hadley for the past fourteen years. He served a five-years apprenticeship with the Austin Motor Company from 1926 to 1931, during which period he passed through all Departments connected with Automobile Engineering.

He was then engaged in the Research Department at Longbridge Works, which included the development and testing of all new models of vehicles. This Department was also responsible for the firm's participation in racing and hill-climbing events, and in this connection Mr. Hadley was an eminently successful driver.

During the period in which he has been employed at Longbridge Works he carried out his duties to my entire satisfaction, his personal conduct has been exemplary, and I have pleasure in recommending him to anyone requiring his services.

Austin

From - Lord Austin, K.B.E.LL.D. Longbridge Works, Birmingham.
Telegrams: Speedily, Telex, Northfield.
Telephone: Priory 2101.

June 10th. 1940

TO WHOM IT MAY CONCERN

HERBERT LEWIS HADLEY.

The above is, I understand, applying for a position with the Ministry of Supply, and has asked me to furnish a reference, which I have pleasure in giving.

I have known Mr. Hadley for the past fourteen years. He served a five-years apprenticeship with the Austin Motor Company from 1926 to 1931, during which period he passed through all Departments connected with Automobile Engineering.

He was then engaged in the Research Department at Longbridge Works, which included the development and testing of all new models of vehicles. This Department was also responsible for the firm's participation in racing and hill-climbing events, and in this connection Mr. Hadley was an eminently successful driver.

During the period in which he has been employed at Longbridge Works he carried out his duties to my entire satisfaction, his personal conduct has been exemplary, and I have pleasure in recommending him to anyone requiring his services.

Austin

to me. As I saw, the matter is still
open and if anything is done you will be
one of the first to be told. As a
matter of fact I will talk to our people
about it during the next few weeks and
come to a decision one way or the other.

Yours sincerely,

THE AUSTIN MOTOR CO. LTD
LONGBRIDGE
BIRMINGHAM
BOX 41 GPO

The Thurlestone Hotel,
Thurlestone,
South Devon.

H. L. Hadley, Esq.,
Beechcroft,
North Avenue,
Ashbourne,
Derbyshire.

15th
October,
1946.

PERSONAL.

Dear Mr. Hadley,

I am forced to spend a few
weeks down here so your letter of the 10th.
October has been sent on to me.

The position with regard to
Racing Austins is still very much as it was
when Mr. Buckley replied to you. Quite
frankly I have not made up my mind about it.
I would like to do it from the prestige angle
but from the practical angle I am afraid we
have no men and no time in our Experimental
Shops for Depper and his gang to do justice
to the cars. It is no good sending them
out unless we put up a good show, and this
means spending a good many hours both on the
cars themselves and on the consideration and
correction of the few faults which they
showed in the early days, and then again, still
further thought as to the modifications which
may be made to pep them up still more.

I do appreciate your writing

-1-

From
L P LORD

168

JAGUAR CARS LTD
COVENTRY

MANAGING DIRECTOR'S OFFICE

TELEPHONE: 88681 (10 LINES)
TELEGRAMS: JAGUAR. COVENTRY

18th July, 1950.

Bert Hadley, Esq.,
Ministry of Labour & National Service,
CHEYLESMORE,
C O V E N T R Y.

Dear Hadley,

Thank you for your letter on the question of participation in the Silverstone Production Car Race.

I do not know whether we shall have a car, but I will have a word with Mr. England immediately he returns from holiday next week.

Perhaps some time when you are up at the works we can have a discussion as you suggest, although I must again repeat that in general principle, at the present time at any rate, we do not propose to participate officially in racing.

Yours sincerely,
[signature]

JAGUAR CARS LTD
COVENTRY

MANAGING DIRECTOR'S OFFICE

TELEPHONE: 88681 (10 LINES)
TELEGRAMS: JAGUAR, COVENTRY

28th June, 1950.

My dear Hadley,

I would like again to congratulate you on your magnificent driving in the Le Mans Race, and to say how very sorry I am that the car failed to complete the Course, after you and Johnson had made such an untiring effort.

Kindest regards.

Yours sincerely,
[signature]

Bert Hadley, Esq.,
District Office,
Ministry of Labour,
COVENTRY.

169

JOWETT CARS LIMITED

H. WOODHEAD, O.B.E., J.P. (CHAIRMAN); A. F. JOPLING (MANAGING)
H. HOBSON; W. J. SAINSBURY, M.ShELL (SECRETARY)

LONDON OFFICE & SHOWROOMS
48 ALBEMARLE ST., PICCADILLY. W.1
TEL. REGENT 0721-2-3 & 5568

IDLE   BRADFORD   YORKSHIRE

TELEPHONE IDLE 341   TELEGRAMS: JOWCARS, BRADFORD
CABLES: JOWCARS, BRADFORD, YORKS.   CODES: BENTLEY'S SECOND PHASE

5th March, 1952.

Ref. CBG/MH/102:

H.L. Hadley Esq.,
78, Red Lane,
Kenilworth.

Dear Bert,

Thank you for your letter of the 3rd instant and
the copy of the B.A.R.C. Regulations, these will be very useful.

I am sorry - cannot send you any Regulations for the
R.A.C. Rally, since I have only one copy, so you will have to
bother the R.A.C. for them.

I am enclosing some correspondence which has arrived
from the R.A.C., concerning the matter of Insurance we shall
look after that both for the car and you personally so there
will be no need for you to take action with Muir Beddall.

Tom Wise's address is :- "Whitestacks", Scotton,
Nr. Knaresborough, Yorks. and you had certainly better give
some very close attention to the methods of manipulating the
motor car, since we shall be relying very much on the Hadley
effort to keep the good name flying, especially as the 3 seems
to be every possibility that Marcel Becquart will cancel his
entry in view of the R.A.C. refusing to accept his Farina Bodied
vehicle. Marcel's reaction is, my vehicle is build on a Chassis
on which more than 250 have been made, it is heavier than the
normal vehicle, it was accepted in the Monte Carlo Rally, so he is
definitely of the impression that the R.A.C. are victimising him,
anyway at the moment there is a brisk interchange of cables between
here and Annecy and I hope to get his entry finalised one way or
the other within the next day or so.

Kind regards,   Yours sincerely,

P.S. Regarding your Caravan Hinge,
would you please send a telegram to
Jowett Cars at Albemarle Street saying
whether it is a L.H. or a R.H. Hinge
looking at the Bed-settee. The London
Agents cannot supply but the Works probably
can, it would be advisable also if you could send
the broken Hinge to Albemarle Street which would
prevent any confusion.

DIRECTORS
WILLIAM LYONS
CHAIRMAN &
MANAGING DIRECTOR
E. W. RANKIN
A. WHITTAKER
W. M. HEYNES GENERAL
MANAGER

JAGUAR CARS LTD
COVENTRY

TELEPHONES
HEAD OFFICE & WORKS
COVENTRY 66681 (10 Lines)
TELEGRAMS
"JAGUAR" COVENTRY
CODE: BENTLEY'S 2nd.

WMH/MC.7060.

3rd January, 1951.

B. Hadley, Esq.,
78, Red Lane,
Kenilworth.

Dear Mr. Hadley,

Mr. England has passed your letter
forward to me. I have already got you on the list
of probables for next season.

We are very pleased with the
performance you put up in Le Mans last year. As you
know our system of having private owners to drive
makes this settling of a racing programme a very
tricky business, especially regarding second drivers.
Please rest assured we have not forgotten you and
if we can possibly arrange it we should very much
like you to drive for us again, but I will write you
again when I see how the matter stands, which will
probably be in another week or fortnight's time.

Yours sincerely,

W. M. HEYNES.

JOWETT CARS LIMITED

Directors
H. WOODHEAD, O.B.E., J.P. (CHAIRMAN)   A. F. JOPLING (MANAGING)
H. HOBSON, W. J. SAINSBURY, N. SNELL (SECRETARY)

LONDON OFFICE & SHOWROOMS
48 ALBEMARLE ST., PICCADILLY, W.1
TEL. REGENT 0721-2-3 & 3598

IDLE   BRADFORD   YORKSHIRE

TELEPHONE IDLE 341   TELEGRAMS, JOWCARS, BRADFORD
CABLES, JOWCARS, BRADFORD, YORKS.   CODES BENTLEY'S SECOND PHASE

Ref. CBG/MH/102.

11th March, 1952.

H.L. Hadley Esq.,
78, Red Lane,
Kenilworth.

Dear Bert,

Thank you for your letter of the 8th instant. I am very glad to know that Bill Butler has decided to drive with you, I am sure it will be a very strong crew.

Regarding the date when you pick up the car, we are not going to let you have it too early otherwise you may wear it out and probably break it, and I would suggest that you and Bill might come up to the Works here on Saturday the 29th, when you could leave your private cars here picking up the Jupiter and proceeding to Scarborough sometime on Sunday the 30th where accommodation has been booked for you at The Grand Hotel for the Sunday night, when you then start the Rally on Monday.

Regarding the question of Bench versus Bucket Seats, I wonder if you really appreciate the comfortable nature of Bucket Seats fitted to 107, these were the ones which were fitted to the car when it was in the Monte Carlo Rally and were said to be extremely comfortable by Messrs. Wilkins and Baxter. They are certainly very well padded and the passenger's Seat gives side support so that he is not violently thrown about when asleep. If, however, you still think that the Bench Seat would be more suitable let me know and we will change, but since there is a little difference in leg length and overall height between you and Butler I think it would probably be best if you each had a Bucket Seat with an individual adjustment.

Regarding the big Pedals we will have these fitted to your car, I am quite sure you will find room for two small suitcases without under-lining the word small too much.

I am enclosing a letter which has been received from the Esso Petroleum Co., would you please disregard this, since we have a definite arrangement with Shell and they will be supplying special fuel at certain points which I will acquaint you with after having attended a Meeting with Shell tomorrow. Regarding the Bonuses we will see that you are not out of pocket in this respect if a good performance occurs.

Kind regards,
Yours sincerely,

78, Red Lane,
KENILWORTH

14th March, 1952.

Dear Charles,

Many thanks for your letter of the 11th instant.

It will be necessary for us to arrive at Bradford during the afternoon of the 29th - I have to attend a Meeting in the morning. I trust this will be in order.

I am quite agreeable to the bucket seats as you suggest. Thanks for the pedal alterations. According to "Motor" report on 106 the luggage accommodation equals 2 suitcases of 24" x 14" x 8" dimension so I think we shall manage. Perhaps you will let me know if this is not so - don't bother to write if my assumptions are fairly correct.

I note the Esso letter and your remarks.

Tell Tommy Wise that I will try to find out about the Singer Le Mans job. I have better contacts for this purpose than Bill these days. Incidentally, the Singer could be a very potent entry - the 1½ litre power unit as fitted to the S.M.1500 has plenty of scope for boosting. The Company have plenty of problems however at the moment with 850 export cars idle for whom no overseas buyers can be found. They have discharged over 300 people. Under such circumstances they may not run.

Frankly, I welcome plenty of opposition. It is much better I think from our point of view. Walk-overs are a dead loss anyway from a publicity point of view.

I trust my Goodwood aspirations are receiving the Grandfield touch.
Kind regards,
Yours sincerely,

C.B. Grandfield, Esq.,
Idle, BRADFORD.

THE BRITISH RACING DRIVERS' CLUB
LTD.

PRESIDENT: THE RT. HON. EARL HOWE, P.C., C.B.E. V.D.

SECRETARY:
D. J. SCANNELL,
2A, BRICK STREET,
MAYFAIR, W.1
TEL: GROSVENOR 4624.

9th June 1952.

CONFIDENTIAL.

H.L.Hadley Esq.
78 Red Lane,
Kenilworth.
Warwickshire.

Dear Hadley,

There is a project on foot to take a Jaguar XK 120 Coupe to Montlhery for an endurance run of up to seven days duration.

The drivers so far engaged are Leslie Johnson, Stirling Moss and Jack Fairman. Leslie, who is responsible for the project has suggested that you might be willing to share the driving and I should be much obliged if you would let me know by return whether or not you would be interested.

The date tentatively fixed for the commencement of the run is July 23rd next and the car and party would travel over to Montlhery most probably on the night ferry of Monday, 21st July. Thus you would be away from then until about 31st July.

Will you please treat this information as confidential.

Yours sincerely,

Howard Howard
p.p. D.J.Scannell.

JOWETT CARS LIMITED

DIRECTORS:
H. WOODHEAD O.B.E., J.P. (CHAIRMAN)   A.F. JOPLING (MANAGING)
H. HOBSON, W. J. SAINSBURY, N. SNELL (SECRETARY)

LONDON OFFICE & SHOWROOMS
48 ALBEMARLE ST., PICCADILLY, W.1
TEL. REGENT 0721-2-3 & 5568

IDLE   BRADFORD   YORKSHIRE

TELEPHONE IDLE 341   TELEGRAMS: JOWCARS, BRADFORD
CABLES: JOWCARS, BRADFORD, YORKS.   CODES: BENTLEY'S SECOND PHASE

17th March, 1952.

Ref. CBG/MH/102.

H.L. Hadley Esq.,
78, Red Lane,
Kenilworth.

Dear Bert,

Thank you for your letters of the 12th and 14th instant, I do not think we can do anything for the Easter Monday Meeting at Goodwood, although we shall try to do something for the later events.

I am enclosing herewith a letter from C.C. Wakefields again offering you hundreds of pounds of bonus, and I am also enclosing an Agreement from Shell which I would like you to sign and send back to me, this then puts us in the clear with Shell.

There is also enclosed a letter from the Yorkshire Observer and they apparently need your photograph for some low-down publicity purpose.

Regarding the Luggage Compartment on 107, it is smaller than the Motor suggests, since this car is fitted with an extra Petrol Tank, giving you 18 Gallons Tank capacity, we do not want to take the Tank out because it is such an awkward job to get it out, but the size of the Luggage Compartment is 2ft.7ins. x 9 ins. x 12 ins., can you make this do for your small kit during the Rally, regarding the other stuff which you may need at the weekend, you can leave this with me and I will get it over to Scarborough in time for your return.

Thanks for the possibility of getting information about the Singer, we should be very interested to know more about it.

Kind regards,

Yours sincerely,

[signature]

JAGUAR CARS LTD
COVENTRY

MANAGING DIRECTOR'S OFFICE

TELEPHONE : 8868: (10 LINES)
TELEGRAMS : JAGUAR, COVENTRY

Fifteenth
August,
1952

H. Hadley, Esq.,
54, Red Lane,
KENILWORTH.

Dear Hadley,

Although I have personally congratulated you, I feel I must write and do so on behalf of my Company, and also thank you for the part you played in the great achievement at Montlhery.

I feel sure you must feel as proud as we do, at having contributed to an achievement which reflects the greatest credit on British motor cars.

With kind regards,

Yours sincerely,

THE BRITISH RACING DRIVERS' CLUB
LTD.

PRESIDENT : THE RT. HON. EARL HOWE, P.C. C.B.E. V.D.

SECRETARY:
D. J. SCANNELL.
2A, BRICK STREET,
MAYFAIR, W.1
TEL. GROSVENOR 4624

19th June 1952.

B.Hadley, Esq.,
78, Red Lane,
Kenilworth.

Dear Hadley,

Thank you for your letter of the 19th June. I am very pleased to learn that you will be free to join us at Montlhery.

I will let you have details of the arrangements at an early date.

Yours sincerely,

D.J.Scannell.

173

Transcription !

THE BRITISH BROADCASTING CORPORATION
Broadcasting House, London, W.1

TELEPHONE : LANGHAM 4468.   TELEGRAMS : BROADCASTS, TELEX, LONDON

Our Reference : 01/PC/KMK.

21st August ...., 19........ 52.

DEAR Sir,

We invite you to prepare and deliver a talk(s) in the language as detailed below, so that it may be recorded for the BBC Transcription Service upon the conditions printed overleaf. If you accept, kindly sign and return the attached confirmation sheet, or reply otherwise, as soon as possible. (See condition I overleaf.)

B.B.C. TRANSCRIPTION SERVICE.

Title .... THIS IS BRITAIN. - Interview with Stirling Moss and Jack Fairman and Raymond Baxter.

Date of Recording........ Monday 18th August 1952.

Time of Recording...... 3.30 - 4.30 p.m.

Place of Recording...... London.

Fee............................ 2 guineas (inclusive of all expenses.)

Letters addressed to speakers c/o the BBC will be forwarded, but for statistical purposes the letters may be opened before being forwarded unless we are notified of any objection. Letters marked " Personal " are forwarded unopened.

Yours faithfully,

THE BRITISH BROADCASTING CORPORATION,

Programme Contracts Department.

Bert Hadley Esq.,
78 Red Lane,
Kenilworth,
Warwickshire.

F/815/P   30-3-50   1000   PDD

174

THE BRITISH RACING DRIVERS' CLUB LTD.

PRESIDENT-IN-CHIEF: H.R.H. THE DUKE OF EDINBURGH, K.G. K.T.

9 DOWN STREET, LONDON. W.1

PRESIDENT
THE Rt. HON. THE EARL HOWE.
P.C., C.B.E., V.R.D.

SECRETARY
D. J. SCANNELL.

TELEPHONES
GROSVENOR 8737/8

TELEGRAMS
(INLAND) SPEEDMEN, AUDLEY, LON
(OVERSEAS) SPEEDMEN, LONDON

12th December 1955

H.L.Hadley Esq.,
78 Red Lane,
Kenilworth.
Warwickshire.

Dear Bert,

Thank you for your letter of the 4th December and my apologies for not having replied to it sooner.

Your comments about Leslie are only too accurate. For example John Eason Gibson who, as far as I know, is one of his closest friends has not seen him for nearly/year and has had your experience of writing numerous letters and receiving no reply.

I note your interest in Borg Warner Automatic Transmissions and as soon as any literature is available I will see that copies are sent to you. Meanwhile if you refer to the current issue of the Autocar you will find a brief reference to this transmission.

With kindest regards,
Yours sincerely,

THE AUSTIN MOTOR CO. LTD.

LONGBRIDGE
BIRMINGHAM
BOX 41 G.P.O.

18th
September,
1953.

H. L. Hadley, Esq.,
78 Red Lane,
KENILWORTH,
Warwickshire.

Dear Mr. Hadley,

Many thanks for your letter of the 15th. September with regard to the Austin Healey.

The future of this car Competition-wise is really in the hands of Donald Healey, so the best thing you can do is to get in touch with him and I will have a word with him when he gets back from America. Would you leave it at that for the present.

With kind regards and again thanks for writing,

Yours sincerely,

From
L. P. LORD

175

'Jenks' and 'The Bod'

For many years Denis Sargent Jenkinson was the Continental Correspondent of Motor Sport Magazine which was edited by one William Charles Boddy. They had met during the war at the Ministry of Aircraft Production, based in Farnborough, where they worked on producing technical manuals for the Air Ministry. Any article in Motor Sport and signed by 'D.S.J.' was guaranteed to be informative and technically accurate.

Over the years 'Jenks', as he was informally known, regularly wrote to Bert and even dropped in on the Hadleys at Kenilworth on more than one occasion. HLH was fascinated by his unusual lifestyle, living as he did at a remote lodge situated in a wood at Crondall, near Farnham in Surrey, when he was not following the Grand Prix circus. For over a decade DSJ would send a resume of his motoring adventures, particularly during the Formula One close season. Some were typed on varying notepaper, occasionally they would be hand written in Jenks' incredibly tiny but quite legible script.

'Jenks.'

'The Bod.'

William Boddy ('W.B.') was a prolific writer, editing Motor Sport for a remarkable fifty five years and continued to contribute a monthly Veteran to Classic feature almost up to his death. He also authored a number of books, particularly about Brooklands - the motor course he visited as a schoolboy. In later years he 'modernised' his image by becoming popularly known as 'Bill Boddy'.

As early as 1973, W.B. had been trying to organise a visit to Kenilworth. He had already interviewed Pat Driscoll and Charles Goodacre and Jenks had suggested it was time he got 'the facts' from HLH himself. Unfortunately this never came about – it would have made interesting reading to hear what Hadley really thought about his erstwhile racing colleagues (who all remained life-long friends) – assuming Boddy could have printed it!

Here are some extracts from letters from DSJ (Crondall) and WB (Nantmell) in chronological order.

Crondall
24th December 1977

'Dear Bert. Thought you might like to see the internals of the AC engine [1921 4-cylinder 1.5L OHC racing engine] as shown in the enclosed photographs. [Bert had arranged for new pistons to be reproduced at the Skill Centre.] Jenks continues – I've found cracks in the crankshaft front bearing housing which needs welding, but the whole world has stopped for two weeks!'

Crondall
4th January 1982

'Thanks for your Christmas card – sorry about the winter silence but when the ice-age comes I put the shutters up and stay in the workshop (working on my BMW 328 – ready for next summer). Ventured out on my trials bike to play fun and games in the snow and ice in the woods – keeps me fit and healthy.'

Crondall
18th December 1983

'Sadly we lost poor old Charlie Dodson a little while ago, the whole affair seems to have been very irresponsible of someone. I was there and it was very wet. So much happening, I did not know about Charlie's accident until later. I was riding my 650 Triumph-engined sprint bike in a demonstration. Recently bought another machine, a Yamaha RD LC, two-stroke twin – goes like a rocket and we will see most cars off. Rode it in the Weston-Super-Mare sprint – 97mph through the trap.
In the summer, I did a standing kilometre on the blown 1000cc AJS of 1929/30 which Joe Wright rode in a World Record Attempt at about 145mph. Not been ridden since 1946 so I took it pretty easy – trundled through at 92mph.
Have not done much exciting motoring lately – it's all been on bikes – much easier, less road space needed. On my 63rd birthday I rode five of my bikes – great fun! An hour in the woods on my 125 Honda. Then took the sprint bike for a couple of squirts up the lane. A 25 mile tour on the 750 BMW, followed by another 25 miles on the Yamaha, my 'pocket rocket' – goes from 6500 to 9500 [rpm] faster than you can change gear and you need to hang on! Best wishes Bert, and to Rose and Clive.'

Crondall
23rd December 1985

'Your card an letter arrived dead on time. I was sixty five on December 11th when they came. You are right about me joining two clubs this year, only one has a club tie, which I wear with a feeling of satisfaction, not only for the club but for the chap who gave it to me. When I asked you for your autograph in 1938 at Brooklands, I never thought...
I was studying engineering and the college thought I was going to design bridges, or cranes, or something but even then I knew I was happiest amongst racing engines. I always used to say 'If you wanted something bad enough, you'll get it'. I bet you wanted to drive a Works Racer when you first went to The Austin...
Spent the Birthday morning on the trials bike in the woods – only fell off twice. You

were right about 1938 prices – how much was petrol then? ROP [Russian Oil Products] was 1/6d a gallon – I had one shilling a week at college but increased it by walking eight miles instead of the train and missed out on lunch to save more. How else could I afford the 2/6d to go to the Crystal Palace? Used to cycle from London to Lewes for the speed trials – H.L.Hadley in the Works SV Austin – great stuff – but needed 6d for a programme to write all the times down. Good formative years...'

Crondall
1st December 1987

'Always nice to hear from you even if it means you want something! I know the photo you want but Motor Sport's archives stop at 1938 – the shady character who helped The Bod at the magazine scarpered and took all the 1939 stuff with him!
I recently found a work folder entitled School of Engineering: D.Jenkinson, Engineering Laboratory 1939/40, 2nd year. Full of notes on dynamometers, injector nozzles and a report by me on proving the critical speeds of shafts! Good technical stuff but on the cover is a drawing of a Grand Prix car, cross between a Maserati, 308 Alfa and a Merc plus wheels, fuel churns and a portable electric starter. All through the notes are sketches of HRG, MG, Lea Francis, Riley, Frazer Nash, Bugatti etc. – my mind wasn't really on becoming an engineer! Regards to all.'

Crondall
5th April 1988

'No, you didn't see me road-testing a Porsche Motor/Autocar or whatever. I do occasionally drive them but not for publication in the 'comics'. Yesterday went out on the 1935 International 'Cammi' Norton I used to race in 1947. Not ridden it since then but it was always my standard of how a bike should steer and still is – interesting.'

Crondall
5th October 1988

'When I tell people I went to Weston-Super-Mare for my summer hols, they don't believe me! Speed Trials weekend, clocked 98mph on my home-made Tribsa, and 93mph in the HWM-Jaguar I shared with George Abecassis in the 1954 Mille Miglia. Sort of 'golden oldies' celebration. Roy Lane borrowed his old Techcraft single seater and clocked 137mph! Much more fun than the Spanish GP at Jerez which I gave a miss.
Look after yourself Bert, there's not many of us 'good little'uns' left.'

Crondall
24th November 1989

'I was just getting round to writing an end of season letter when yours arrived with the sad news [of Rose's death]. I am indeed most sorry – she was just a sweet, gentle lady. "Stand tall" as they say to us little fellas and keep the old chin up.'

The Hall
Nantmell, LLandrindod Wells
16th March 1990

'Dear Bert. Delighted to hear from you. I read all you write with much interest and pleasure. You flatter me when you say you stood next to me at Silverstone, but did not have the temerity to speak. If only you knew how much I wish I had been less of a duffer at working on cars, let alone racing them! I can assure you the boot is on the other foot. What I have never really talked about is how the cars were taken to the circuits or drivers chosen.
I too spent the war in the Civil Service (Min of A.P.) on handbooks – a joke as I can only just about de-coke an Austin Seven, so have no delusions there! I hope to get to VSCC Silverstone but am now seventy seven….[Bert would be nearly eighty].'

The Hall
Nantmell
25th July 1990

'Sorry to hear about Kay Petre [possibly recently unwell]. I was once invited to some publishing 'do' with my wife and were asked to take a racing driver along. I invited Kay. When introduced the 'top brass' said 'nice to see you – pity you couldn't bring a racing driver' – thinking I'd gate-crashed a third party. Had to explain Kay was one of the bravest of drivers (the big Delage!).
Jenks always had a eye for the ladies, especially motorcyclists' wives who had been recently widowed after a crash. We were all set up to put him in the cottage here and looked forward to him working on my old cars. Then he met Robbie Hewitt coming home on a ship from a Grand Prix and that was the end of it. She had something I hadn't! If Jenks had lived here we could have put all his machine tools in the barn and who knows…'

Crondall
14th August 1990

'Hope this finds you ticking over smoothly. I know how Shelsley has always been dear to you – I must tell you, after ten years or more of trying I've finally done a sub 40 secs, 39.75 secs to be exact on the bike I've ridden all that time. I shall be seventy at the end of the year and just hope the ACU/RAC let me go on for another five years.
I was interested that you said Jamieson went to London [Battersea] Polytechnic for his B.Sc. in engineering. I went there in 1938-41 but no degree! I wish I'd known because by 1937 Jamieson was one of my racing design heroes, along with Reid Railton. Best wishes, Jenks.'

Crondall
18th December 1990

'Always nice to hear from you. Last week I celebrated my 70th in a purely private and selfish way. At 65 I borrowed a 928 Porsche with the express purpose of doing 130mph across Salisbury Plain before everyone woke up. On the way back I got nicked for doing 85! Some birthday treat – cost me fifty quid.
This year I went out in my own 924s to touch 100mph somewhere, not using motorways or main roads. A superb morning and about 80 miles around the byways of

179

Hampshire, saw the 'ton' on eight occasions. Then I went out on my 125cc Honda racer aiming to do at least 80 on two wheels. After that it was shopping on my 400/4 Honda complete with panniers at a sedate 60mph. On return I went out in the woods for an hour on the trials bike. Then it was time for tea – and a rest. Finally it was down to the pub for a meal with a mate in the Ford Escort diesel van at a sedate 40mph. I slept well that night.'

Crondall
11th February 1991

'Regarding your famous August 1939 win at Crystal Palace, I believe the result was a foregone conclusion after practice – there was no way the 1500/2000 class was going to catch up. That was the only meeting at which I had enough money to buy a seat on the Grandstand over-looking the start line (2/6 extra I believe). There was obviously a friend of yours in the stand because while you were standing beside the Austin on the grid, you looked across, opened the breast pocket on your white overalls and indicated the result was in the bag by pointing into your pocket with your right fore-finger.
I was excited as seeing Britain's mini Grand Prix car running away from everyone, but I was mortified to see it whistle past my favourite my favourite GP car, the 2.9 Monoposto Alfa-Romeo.'

The Hall
Nantmell
27th April 1991

'Have just read your piece in the A7CA mag 1991B. Most interesting. I have always believed Pat's Bakewell [sic] crash was due to a broken ball-joint and I was there. Shows how important to history it is to get proper accounts from those on the spot and behind the scenes.
Lots of errors in Motor Sport this time. Perhaps a bit of a Jamieson situation – no one in control and at 78 I am not there to try and exert it. Sad in a way and Jenks will go sky high at Moss driving for VAUXHALL!
And I do like accuracy. Bill.
P.S. Sorry about this oddly designed paper [a Motor Sport compliments slip] – perhaps has some bearing on last para!'

The Hall
Nantmell
8th May 1991

'Thanks for your letter about your friend and Coventry-Eagle, I would like to meet him. Went to a cold Curborough on Sunday, some interesting cars. Am hoping to get the 1931 A7 Saloon up and running again and use the 'Gould' Ulster during the summer. Saw 'Titch' [Allen – founder of the VMCC and another 'Gould' owner] at Curborough. Some more A7s there – an odd repro of a works single seater, that Peter Moores' clone of Kay Petre's car with whining blower and a nice spectating Chummy.
Jenks is off to Monaco GP today. Once shared an aeroplane with him and just as we were about to take off, who should get on but Charles Brackenbury – he tried to set fire to Jenks' beard with his lighter – terrifying!
Excuse this paper – it got wet when the water pipes burst!'

Bod 'all
Nantmell
15th July 1991

'Thanks for yours. I got to Brooklands – a smell of money about the place. Sir Peter Masefield conducted me round – I forgot to duck in time! Shelsley the following weekend – hospitality from a new oil company, which my wife enjoys, whereas I've never been one for junketing or social gatherings. The old legs survived. On the Sunday – off to VSCC Mallory Park, a long haul but not too bad using chunks of the A5. Issued with a signed Track Pass. I tried standing well <u>inside</u> the Armco by the start line. A fat RAC Steward rudely told me to quit. I rather lost my temper and it ruined the day. Got an apology later from the VSCC (have discovered this Steward is a Rolls-Royce owner…).
Glad you still enjoy 'M.S.' despite what the younger chaps do to it, despite my endless telephone calls and letters… Best wishes, The Bod.

The Hall
Nantmell
23rd August 1991

'Have had a bit of Austin-ing, out in Titch Allen's 'Gould' Ulster and also a flip in the ex-Laird Morgan. Fortunately it kept the right way up. Prefer my own 'Gould' replica except for its fixed screen. Short run as had a sort of flu bug and as I don't walk far these days am always fearful of the SU pump or something may pack in, so prefer to have a 'tender car' with me. Do you know, when I came back, I was cured – fresh air I suppose. I took my very old Royal Flying Corps leather helmet to wear in Titch's Ulster. He had a black RAF one but doesn't like to wear it as he feels a fool. Felt he preferred I didn't put mine on! Wish I'd worn my old ex-Brooklands domed crash hat inscribed 'ACU'. Think it was a BMCRC spare for riders who forgot them. One of my many motor oddments that fill too many bedrooms in this not small house.'

Bod 'all
Nantmell
26th November 1992

'It's a long time since I have heard from you and trust you are fit, or as fit as we oldies can be. Have drained both A7s for the winter but no doubt will have the Gould Ulster out for New Year's Day at Ledbury. All good wishes, Bill (W.B.)'

Denis Jenkinson died on 29th November 1996 aged 76.

William Boddy died on 7th July 2011 aged 98.

Registration List

In 1988 Bert compiled a list of pre-war Austins which he, his family or work colleagues, owned or used. He had a good memory for registration numbers and hoped that the odd one or two cars might have survived. At the time none had turned up but in the hope that the situation may have changed, here's that list again.

OM7826	1925	AC Tourer	HCH's first car
OP677	1926	AC Tourer	Len Brockas
UE6244	1928	Swallow 2-seat	HLH (Cream & Green)
YX847	1928	AD Tourer	HCH (London reg) 2nd hand
OF1014	1929	RK Saloon	HCH
OG7449	1931	Windsor 12/6	Ex road-test car (?)
OV1159	1931	Swallow 2-seat	HLH
OV1537	1931	RN Saloon	HCH
OJ9386	1931	Ulster s/c	HLH (1933 reg)
OJ3846	1932	RP Saloon	HCH
OJ3975	1932	RP Saloon	Nurse E. Stallard
OJ8056	1933	RP Saloon	HCH
AOM504	1935	RQ Ruby	Nurse E. Stallard
BOC436	1935	RQ Ruby	HCH
COJ130	1936	RR Ruby	HLH (Ex Goodacre)
DOV768	1937	Big 7 Fourlite	HLH (Ex AMCo Rally car)
EOG67	1938	RR Ruby	Nurse E. Stallard

182   Bert used his trusty 'Box Brownie' to snap his friend Jimmy with the newly acquired Swallow.

(Left) Bert Hadley 'Sporting Motorist'. *(Right)* Herbert's later Saloon – an Austin Seven RP De Luxe.

After the outbreak of the Second World War, Bert continued to use the ex-Works Big 7 and this hard-worked vehicle served him well until about 1943 when he changed it for a Morris Series M Ten. This he continued to run until he was able to purchase a new car, a 1946 Hillman Minx, Bendix brakes notwithstanding! After this came a Singer Super Twelve.

(Left) 1947. The Derby registered Singer 'Super 12'. *(Right)* 1952. Standard Vanguard – a later 'spatted' version..

Along with his continuing climb up the Ministerial ladder, Hadley's cars also went up-market with an early 'Cyclops' P4 Rover, a Standard Vanguard and even a Ford Zodiac. However, reflecting Hadley's status as a recently retired racing driver, his life-long chum Jack Emmott persuaded Bert to become the new owner of Jack's Aston Martin DB 2-4. Emmott had had a vast amount of work put into this expensive vehicle, only some of it under warranty (pistons and cylinder liners replaced at 4,000 miles!). Hadley did not fare much better either, encountering water pump problems, its drive shaft shearing through frost, water in the sump etc. Finally the gearbox (a David Brown product of course!) ruined all its bearings. Bert recalled having to part-exchange the DB2-4 for an early MGB because no-one wanted old Astons at that time.

183

Eventually the market <u>did</u> pick up and he saw his DB2-4 later advertised in Motor Sport for £8,500! After a very chequered career, which saw the car go to America and at one time run with an Oldsmobile engine, amazingly the 2-4 has survived and is now in Holland in excellent condition. The owner is fully aware of its connections with Emmott and Hadley.

(Left) 1954. The Warwickshire registered ex-Emmott Aston Martin DB 2-4.
(Right) 1965. The 'Q' car, an up-rated yet standard looking Minor 1000, also ex-Emmott.

Bert had several more ex-Emmott or Automotive Products Ltd cars over the years, including an early Minor 1000 with oversize engine, servo brakes etc (a real 'Q' car), a left-hand drive BMW 2002 automatic and his final car a Saab 900 Turbo – a delight to drive but expensive to maintain. During the 60s–70s period he mainly favoured Fords – considering them streets ahead of what came out of Longbridge at the time.

(Left) The BMW 2002 Automatic 'left-hooker'.
An ex-Automotive Products vehicle which somehow ended up in Cropwell Bishop…
(Right) Bert's last car, the Saab 900 Turbo. A splendid drive, but expensive when it broke.

LIFE IN A LOWER GEAR (1956-75)

After hanging up his helmet and goggles for the last time, Bert took stock of his life. At 45 and in reasonable health, he could now look forward to a further twenty years in a secure job which he enjoyed and had made steady progress. His loving wife Rose kept an immaculate and comfortable home and their son, Clive was doing well at Kenilworth School. Always careful with money, the Hadleys were 'comfortable'. Holidays often consisted of a week or two in a modest caravan, although they did try camping in Wales – just the once. The weather was so bad that young Clive, for a treat, in his own little tent was almost washed away as the campsite became flooded.

Though still based at the Cheylesmore (Coventry) office, the Department of Employment (as the Ministry was now called) did second him to other areas where his expertise, particularly in Labour Relations, was required. Periods in Cardiff and London come to mind.

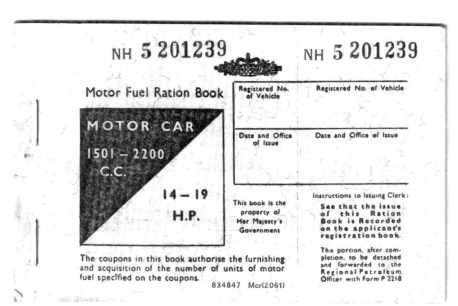 

The Suez Crisis. Petrol coupons 1956/57.

As a life-long socialist, Bert was sympathetic to the cause of the working man or woman, but the sixties and beyond were a time of constant industrial unrest and the impromptu 'walk-outs' made regular and depressing news. HLH was in despair of the blinkered and stubborn attitude shown by many of the (very well paid) union officials who seemed to be living in *cloud cuckoo land'* and also had little or no control of the *'wild-cat'* antics of militant hot-heads. Longbridge was a typical snap-shot of British industry where there seemed to be at least one dispute ongoing every week. But Bert was equally scathing of weak and ineffective management for allowing these situations to escalate whilst our overseas competitors continued to take full advantage of our collective woes.

Though he'd stopped racing, his previous exploits were not entirely forgotten. Bert recalled visiting a family-run engineering business in about 1957. Having introduced himself and preparing to discuss the matter he'd come to sort out, his host suddenly interrupted the flow by exclaiming *'Mr Hadley - Oh Bert Hadley – why didn't you race for ****** a year or two ago?'* Bert confirmed that indeed he had. *'We did a special rush job for that event and I'm sure we never got paid! Do you think you could possibly have a word with Mr ****** for us?'*

1960 was a sad year for the Hadleys when on 9th May Grandma Lydia passed away aged 89 years.

Though not particularly academically gifted, Clive had acquired sufficient 'O' levels to be considered for an engineering apprenticeship. He also had good practical skills inherited from his father and grandfather. At the time, Bert thought the aircraft industry might offer good prospects for his son's future, so in 1957, at the age of 16, Clive started his five year training with Armstrong-Whitworth Aircraft (AWA) as an airframe fitter. A contemporary of Herbert Austin, John Davenport Siddeley had gathered a number of major British companies together, including Armstrong-Siddeley Motors, A.V. Roe & Co (Avro – from Crossleys) and High Duty Alloys. In 1935, further expansion took place with the Hawker and Gloster companies joining what would eventually be known as Hawker Siddeley Aircraft (HSA), though the constituent concerns would retain their individual identities. Siddeley himself, followed Austin into the peerage – as Lord Kenilworth – in 1937.

A huge factory and airfield was established at Baginton (now Coventry Airport) with further assembly and test flight facilities at Bitteswell in neighbouring Leicestershire. The HSA group was a major player in the industry and by the time Clive started with AWA, these two sites alone were employing around 11,500 people. AWA had its own design team which pioneered many innovative aircraft, including studies into 'flying wing' technology and early research into ultra-short and vertical take-off aircraft, pre-dating the 'Harrier' concept.

AWA built Sea Hawks, Hunter and Javelin fighters and the Argosy transports during Clive's training period. A number of Hawk training aircraft, still used by the Red Arrows, were also produced. Clive would have been involved in the manufacturing processes of many of these iconic aeroplanes, together with later upgrading of Shackletons and Vulcans. After he qualified as a Certified Technician, Clive became part of a select team carrying out priority work on military aircraft at R.A.F. bases throughout the UK and Europe, earning him the accolade of *'The Flying Spanner'*.

It was during this busy period that Clive had met Jeanette Welch and they married at Rugby in 1967. The following year, their daughter Jane was born, much to the delight of Bert and Rose.

Clive Hadley is presented with an award during his apprenticeship at Armstrong-Whitworth. Behind his smiling workmates is a Vulcan B2.

Bert continued to work for the Department but a change of scene had taken place. During the 1960s, the government of the day decided to set up a national chain of training facilities, known as Skill Centres.

Millions were pumped into the project, with the best equipment available and time-served instructors to provide proper training for a variety of vocational occupations. These centres were administered by the Training Services Agency as part of the Department of Employment.

As might be expected, Birmingham's Skill Centre, situated on Holyhead Road, Handsworth, was one of the

1962. HLH looks somewhat bemused at a gathering at Bingley Hall, Birmingham. Amongst the 'suits' A.J.Depper explains all. The Goodacre/Dodson car bears the number 26, Dennis Buckley's entry – 30th July 1939 Prescott Hill Climb..

largest but by 1965 the facility was in some disarray. Bert was approached by the 'top brass' and he accepted the challenge of sorting the situation out. Thanks to his down to earth and commonsense approach, he succeeded in re-motivating a previously dispirited workforce and turned the Centre around into becoming a very effective educational unit. He was a popular Manager to work for, not least for his ability and willingness to listen to his staff should they have any problems, including those of a personal or domestic nature. Bert assured me that these were many and varied, particularly on Monday mornings!

Training Services Agency   **SKILLCENTRE**   255 Holyhead Road
                                                     Handsworth
                                                     Birmingham B21 0BT
                                                     telephone 021-554 5222

HLH with his staff outside the Handsworth Skill Centre.

This period was probably the most enjoyable for the Hadleys as Bert continued to improve the Skill Centre and its reputation. With Clive apparently in a secure job which he enjoyed and settled down with his own family, Bert and Rose were able to stretch their wings for the first time and they enjoyed a cruise to Norway with friends in 1968. In subsequent years they made several visits to Malta which they particularly liked.

The British Motor Industry Heritage Trust (BMIHT) had been formed with responsibility for the numerous historic vehicles acquired through various company merges which eventually became British Leyland. With very limited funding available, the Trust had to beg services from all and sundry for the accommodation and restoration of these artefacts. Through his good offices, HLH was able to get several cars refurbished through the Training Programmes – these vehicles are still exhibited at the Heritage Motor Centre at Gaydon.

During the early 1970s Bert had been introduced to Frederick Bernard Wheatcroft (TW), an immensely successful self-made builder, who having purchased the moribund Donington Park estate in Leicestershire, was battling against the planners and other opposition to re-establish the Park to its pre-war glory days as the country's premier road racing circuit. He'd already established the 'Donington Collection' in brand-new buildings to house his ever increasing number of racing cars. The BMIHT eventually took advantage of his offer of spare museum space and so 'Leyland Historic Vehicles' were able to display some of their acquisitions to the general public for the first time.

By a complicated sequence of events, Wheatcroft, or 'Tom' as he was universally known, had obtained possession of three surviving Austin Works single-seater race cars. As has been mentioned, the cars had been moved around since emerging from the damp Longbridge tunnels post 1947. The Goodacre/Dodson car was complete but not running, though it had been cosmetically spruced up for occasional display. The Hadley car was as it was in August 1939, but further dismantling of engine parts had taken place in the 1960s, compounding the sorry situation of the absence of major components which had gone 'missing'. They were joined by the surviving

Jamieson-designed Side-valve single-seater. This was complete and had been a runner. In the late 1950s this car, previously driven by Hadley, Walter Bäumer and Dennis Buckley amongst others, was spruced up and repainted in powder blue as a gesture to Kay Petre who was able to 'gently' drive the car at an early Brooklands get-together and demonstrate it during the 1961 VSCC Oulton Park race meeting. KP never drove this car in period, but at around this time she had been retained by AMCo as a 'feminine' colour consultant.

(Ferret Fotographic)
Kay Petre demonstrates the smartened up Side-valve at an early Brooklands Reunion event in 1960.

Some time later, the cars ended up at what was then the Montagu Motor Museum at Beaulieu, Hampshire. During a visit, Pat Driscoll saw the cars and informed HLH of their current condition. In due course, Bert himself went down to Beaulieu and what he found *made his blood boil*. 'His' Twin-cam, already partially dismantled at the outbreak of war, lay in a state of further disarray, with *'bits strewn all over the place'*. Hadley made his views known to the Beaulieu management in no uncertain terms, but got nowhere with them.

As his race car collection was growing, Tom Wheatcroft had set up a small team of mechanics to get them running and presentable for exhibition to the public. They were based in one of his yards at Wigston, south of Leicester. As mentioned TW had acquired the Austins and proposed to re-activate all three of them. The team had got the Side-valve running again and it received a further coat of blue paint, with a race No.1 identity. Hadley was eventually 'found' by Wheatcroft and asked if he would act as an 'honorary consultant'. Bert was still managing the Skill Centre at Handsworth but agreed to assist. His interest re-awakened, he offered to have a go at the gearboxes and superchargers, all of which were in a seized condition. He proposed to carry out the work at Red Lane in his spare time. As for the Twin-cam engines, Bert suggested these be handed over to someone with the necessary expertise and facilities.

The Skill Centre had some capabilities, in fact it had produced a set of connecting rods for the rare 1920s AC single-seater, then owned jointly by Mrs. Robbie Hewitt and Denis Jenkinson ('DSJ/Jenks' – the Continental Correspondent of 'Motor Sport' magazine). Bert also arranged the casting and machining of new pistons for the same project.

In his search for a Twin-cam engine 'fettler', Bert had heard of a recently-retired engineer of some repute who had a comprehensive machine shop to hand and was based in the West Midlands. In addition, this person was well-known in 'Vintage' circles. Having introduced himself over the phone, HLH went to meet the engineer at his rather smart house and even grander machine shop. Bert was very impressed with the facilities available plus there were a couple of vintage cars present which the owner himself had personally refurbished. Bert outlined what TW's requirements were and after further discussions he suggested to Tom that he could proceed with Mr ****** subject to costs being agreed between Wheatcroft and the engineer. Bert was not involved in any of the financial negotiations.

In the meantime, Bert set to work on dismantling the two gearboxes, both based on the standard 4-speed Austin Seven production gearbox. The one from Bert's car also had the later synchromesh option. Virtually everything was in a seized state and the two Murray Jamieson superchargers were in a particularly parlous condition, mainly the bores of the blower bodies where un-purged fuel, the Shell 'witches' brew, had lain causing considerable corrosion. At the time, the solution chosen was to bore out the affected areas, spray with an epoxy resin, fortified with powdered aluminium and finally carefully re-machine back to size. Bert recalled using some very thin tapered drifts made by his father Herbert, these proving invaluable for splitting open bearing housings and the like.

Bert managed to put both the gearboxes and superchargers in to operational order once more, but there were problems and delays with the engine work. TW was being presented with bigger and bigger invoices with the work far from completed. In the end the units were returned to a disgruntled Wheatcroft and some of the resultant 'flak' reached Bert, TW blaming him for recommending Mr ****** in the first place. Bert refuted this, reminding Wheatcroft he'd only suggested the engineer as a <u>possible</u> person to do the work. He also felt he'd been used, particularly after all the work he'd carried out in his own time and for next to nothing. One can but imagine the conversations between these two formidable personalities – blunt speaking at its finest!

With that, Bert backed out of the project and heard no more until 'out of the blue' Tom Wheatcroft gave him a ring and after a considerable amount of 'soft-soaping' on TW's part Bert was persuaded to visit the Wheatcroft workshop at Wigston to see what progress had been made with the Austins. Pre-War Austin Seven Club member Michael Shearer was, at the time, a young member of the Wheatcroft restoration team and recalls his first meeting with Bert Hadley:-

> 'One day the Austin Side-valve and Twin-cam racing cars arrived. I was fortunate to be given the [Goodacre/Dodson] Twin-cam to dismantle and rebuild. In order to assist the work, further information was required and arrangements were made for one of the original drivers to visit. My first memory of Bert Hadley was when he arrived in the workshop one day, smartly dressed in a suit and white mackintosh, his formal appearance belied his down-to-earth and friendly helpful character. He took a great interest in the project and made several further visits.'

Eventually the Goodacre/Dodson Twin-cam and the Side-valve cars were considered ready to run at Donington Park. The revised circuit was still in the construction stage but the original Melbourne Loop extension, now isolated by Rolls-Royce occupied buildings, provided sufficient space to operate the cars on newly-laid tarmac.

With the help of Longbridge's P.R.O. Jim Bramley, a reunion of pre-war personnel was arranged and those able to be present were Pat Driscoll, Charles Goodacre, Charlie Dodson, Kay Petre and Raleigh Appleby, who had retired from Longbridge only a few years previously. Others approached either declined or were not available. Several had sadly died including Len Brockas (in 1962). At 64, and nearing retirement, Bert was the 'baby' of the group. A number of other well-known racing personalities were present including 'Autosport' journalist and ex-racer, John Bolster. Tom Wheatcroft obviously revelled in all the publicity generated and his son, Kevin, who now owns the circuit, remembers as a schoolboy meeting all the drivers and has particularly fond memories of HLH. Michael Shearer recalls the occasion:-

> 'It was in 1974 when Bert and his team-mates came to Donington for the test-runs. As it had been many years since he had last driven it, I refreshed his memory as to starting and running procedures – I felt honoured to have taught Bert how to drive the Twin-cam – albeit the second time round! Unlike some other drivers who would race off with lots of revs and wheel-spin, as an engineer, he had respect for the engine's original internals and drove cautiously. He obviously enjoyed the day and subsequently we kept in touch.'

Bert was right to be circumspect when trying out both the Austins. The Side-valve was running tolerably well but the Twin-cam seemed to have incorrect castor angle, very poor brakes and he found several short comings in the engine department which needed immediate attention as there was a great possibility of terminal damage being caused. He even put his fears down on paper and provided TW with a written report of his findings and suggestions for rectifying the problems. Despite all his criticisms, Bert did concede that the Wheatcroft team had been working largely 'in the dark' and thanks to TW's interest (and money) the Works cars had been saved from an uncertain future.

Michael Shearer and Bert got on very well but HLH did not 'suffer fools gladly' and was forceful in expressing his opinions, a fact heartily endorsed by the author! Michael continues:-

> 'Occasionally he would write to me, in one letter he enquired about the reproduction "Ulster" I was building and about the body material. I replied with the details to which he promptly responded

correcting a spelling mistake I'd made – too many "L"s In aluminium – I felt I was back at school! Bert obviously had a lot of engineering knowledge and became something of a mentor to me, even to the point of suggesting I leave my job and become an instructor at an engineering college, an offer I chose not to pursue. He didn't seem too offended and continued to take an interest in my pursuits away from work. When he heard I had a racing Mini Cooper, a set of "Minifin" alloy brake drums were delivered to my house, completely without charge – all thanks to Bert.'

Joe Murcott and his wife, sweethearts since schooldays, had built a die-casting business from scratch to become one of the largest privately owned operations of its kind in the UK. Completely self-made and 'Brummie' to the core, Joseph Victor Murcott and Herbert Lewis Hadley had known each other for many years. The Minifins were a Murcott product and when Joe retired his family carried on the business of J.V. Murcott and Sons in the Aston

district of the city and also at Tamworth. Joe had a 17 acre 'bolt hole' in Wales where he indulged in his passion for miniature outdoor railways. Bert and Rose stayed with the Murcotts on several occasions, when Bert learnt to drive a steam locomotive.

April 1975. HLH's retirement cake – well a few more calories won't hurt will they?

1975 arrived and it meant that Bert had to retire from the Department of Employment after a career spanning some 34 years. His staff at the Handsworth Skill Centre were sorry to see him go but by all accounts gave him a splendid send off which included a large cake! HLH was also given a custom-made toolbox suitably inscribed and an 'autograph' book, not only signed by all the staff but by a number of former trainees who had successfully forged new careers for themselves thanks to Bert and his team. Some of the comments were quite touching and heartfelt.

- 12 -

RETIREMENT AND BEYOND (1976-2012)

Part 1 (1976-93)

After finishing at the Skill Centre in 1975, Bert was naturally unaccustomed to his enforced leisure time and greatly missed the 'buzz' of being involved with people and their problems on a daily basis. He would have liked to have continued for a year or two but 65 was the mandatory retirement age in all branches of the Civil Service.

However, it did give Bert and Rose the opportunity to visit friends and family often staying over for a few days. The Hadleys went down to Pat and Peggy Driscoll's place at Hayling Island in Hampshire where Pat had a boat moored on the River Hamble. They also spent time in Wiltshire to where Bill and Ann Butler had retired, firstly at Box and later to Bradford-on-Avon.

During the post-war period, there were times when Bert had been 'loaned out' to the Ministry's Cardiff office when he was required to negotiate with the South Wales steel industry, 'Labour Relations' being one of Hadley's areas of expertise. Requiring suitable accommodation during the week, HLH was recommended to the establishment run by two ladies on Colum Road in Cardiff. One of the partners was Phyllis Spencer, whose brother Eric farmed down at Bryngwyn, not far from the impressive ruins of Raglan Castle. Such was the quality of service provided, Bert always stayed at Colum Road whenever he was in the area.

Phyllis Spencer and Rose enjoy a relaxing moment together.

Eventually, Phyllis sold the Bed and Breakfast and moved into a bungalow near to her brother's farm. Over the following years the Hadleys, as a family, paid many visits to Raglan for short breaks or even longer. Eric Spencer's son Michael was about three years younger than Clive but they became very good friends and would remain so till Clive's death in 2007. Both Bert and Clive often commented on the wonderful hospitality Phyllis gave them, particularly on the culinary front! Mike Spencer still runs the family farm in 2013, though sadly, his 'Aunty Phyl' passed away just a few years earlier.

It was about this time that interest in the 'heritage' movement began to move up a gear. The Brooklands Society had been formed to preserve and maintain what was left of the World's first purpose-built motor racing circuit. A number of reunions took place and naturally the Hadleys were often invited. Bert recalled a particularly enjoyable lunch with Tom Delaney and his wife. Delaney's family firm was a major supplier to the motor and aviation industries and had been the UK concessionaires for the French 'Cozette' superchargers as used by Austins. Delaney himself later achieved some fame as Britain's oldest active racing driver, still competing in VSCC events well into his nineties! Whilst the Hadleys were in the Brooklands area, they were able to locate the Hand and Spear at Byfleet, scene of near-riots when the Freddie Dixon crowd were in residence and the Duke's Head at Addlestone where Bert had occasionally stayed when racing at the track, bringing back more pre-war memories.

In 1976, Leyland Historic Vehicles officially opened at Donington Park and the then 'head honcho' at Longbridge, Alex Park, invited HLH to the opening. By all accounts it was quite a lavish 'do' with many Leyland/Longbridge people present. Having just sold his 2-litre Cortina Mark 3 ('utterly reliable'), he and Rose attended in a newly-acquired BMW 2002, an ex-Automotive Products development car and being left hand drive, used for European road testing of a prototype AP automatic gearbox.

1976. Donington Park reunion. *(Left to right)* Ral Appleby, Pat Driscoll, HLH, Kay Petre, Tom Wheatcroft, Charles Goodacre, Jim Bramley (Public Relations Officer for British Leyland) and Charlie Dodson in the Twin-cam.

Denis Jenkinson, 'Motor Sport's' Continental Correspondent, had been a life-long fan of Hadley since schooldays and corresponded with Bert over many years, usually around Christmas time. However, DSJ also developed a habit of turning up at Red Lane with little or no warning.

The Hadleys always welcomed their surprise visitor, but it did sometimes upset their established routine. One October, the neighbours were aroused by the dulcet tones of a Ferrari 308, which 'Jenks' happened to be road-testing for 'Motor Sport'. Soon Bert was behind the wheel, giving it an extended airing around rural Warwickshire, later describing the experience as *'fantastic'*.

1976. Donington. A wind-swept Hadley looks pleased after re-acquainting himself with Jamie's masterpiece. He is in what will become the pit lane of the as-yet uncompleted circuit. Red Gate Corner is in the distance with the famous Lodge on the left. Sadly this 18th century edifice has had to give way to 21st century circuit 'improvements'.

All this motoring activity took up most of the day but 'Jenks' was prepared, having thoughtfully brought his sleeping bag with him! Thus he happily spent the night on the Hadleys' lounge carpet to awake to a nice breakfast dutifully prepared by Rose. DSJ was a small chap and his spectacles and long grey beard gave him the appearance of a genial gnome. His lifestyle was somewhat Bohemian, always on the move during the Grand Prix season, then returning to his remote lodge in a Hampshire wood with electricity provided courtesy of a Fiat-driven generator. His many bookshelves were equally basic, merely planks of wood, each separated by three or four bricks, as required. The Hadleys always felt they needed a rest after a Jenkinson visit but Bert was highly amused by DSJ's busy if eccentric existence. 'Jenks' was universally regarded as the top motor racing writer of his day and his highly detailed and factual accounts of what was really happening 'at the sharp end' were required reading for enthusiasts of the sport.

During this period, Clive Hadley's marriage had run into difficulties, probably not helped by his absences due to the nature of his job with Hawker-Siddeley, frequently entailing extended visits to RAF bases around the country to carry out up-dates and modifications on front-line military aircraft. Sadly the marriage ended in some acrimony resulting in Jeanette moving away from the Midlands, together with their daughter, thus depriving Clive and the Grandparents regular contact with Jane, especially during her formative years. Clive returned to live at Red Lane once more.

An emerging teenager. Clive and Jeanette's daughter Jane.

In 1977 Bert joined Pat Driscoll at a Mercedes-Benz Press Day at Donington. The Side-valve single-seater was still runable and both of them had a trundle around the Melbourne Loop, Bert noting that the performance was just about adequate but driver space wasn't. He was able to re-acquaint himself with Hermann Lang who had driven for Mercedes in 1938. Both Hadley and Lang came through as apprentices with their respective employers, eventually racing for them albeit at slightly different levels.

Meanwhile, BL Heritage was celebrating 75 years of Austin production and wanted loan of the Goodacre/Dodson car from Tom Wheatcroft. This didn't happen nor was it possible to take up the Ulster Automobile Club's invitation for Bert to bring the car over for the 50th anniversary of Craigantlet Hill Climb in 1979. They still wanted HLH to come over as a Guest of Honour but he regretfully declined, 'not wanting to impose'. However he did provide an excellent contribution to the event's souvenir programme.

March 24th 1977 saw several years of endeavour come to fruition when a small team of Austin Seven enthusiasts gathered at the then disused Goodwood race circuit in West Sussex.

The object of the exercise was to set the class H (up to 750cc Category) International Record for 10,000 Miles. This had never been established and the next shortest distance, 10,000 Km was beyond their reach. British records had not been considered as it was assumed that they would have been out of reach too. The project was headed by Chris Gould, a long time Worthing A7 enthusiast using a car based around one of his excellent glass-fibre Ulster type body shells. Run under the aegis of The Pre-War Austin Seven Club, the project was overseen by the Royal Automobile Club who provided Official Observers, Timekeepers and Scrutineers. Additional support and personnel were gathered from amongst other Austin enthusiasts. In the end, mechanical problems brought the run to a premature halt. However all was not lost, as they had inadvertently set a number of British Records:

Class H 1,000 Miles   (53.89 mph),
Class H 24hrs   (54.50 mph)
Class H & outright 5,000Km (54.02 mph).

The drivers were Paul Bonewell, Chris Gould, Roy Hil, Tony Hutchings, Vince Leek, Stan Marsh, Paul Mullen and Andy Storer.

Bert Hadley was not present for these runs, but later in the year Pat Driscoll introduced him to Chris Gould. Bert advised Chris that he must use a stronger Works type cylinder block if he was to try again. His advice was taken, and with the help of Jim Fumigalli, a colleague of Chris, a new one was produced. Other improvements were incorporated and the whole team was in confident mood for a further attempt.

In 1978 the team re-formed for another record attempt. The same driver line-up was retained, with the addition of Stirling Moss who drove the first 10 laps. During this run, two further records were established:

5,000 Miles   (50.90 mph)
10,000 Km   (49.20 mph).

At the time of writing, all the above records still stand.

Bert wrote an overview of the 1978 record attempt:

'It was approximately 1pm on Wednesday 27th September 1978 and I had just arrived at the Goodwood Circuit with my friend and Austin team mate Pat Driscoll. Within a few minutes we observed the Chris Gould Austin 7 Ulster motoring slowly to the pits. The driver had signalled an unidentified mechanical defect on his radio and the ominous smoke from the exhaust pointed to piston trouble. Rapid removal of the cylinder head by the pit crew revealed number 2 piston to be in a state of progressive break up and as if to accentuate the

PRE-WAR AUSTIN SEVEN CLUB
10,000 Mile Record Attempt

COMMEMERATIVE BROCHURE
PRODUCED BY THE 750 MOTOR CLUB
Sales in Aid of Record Attempt

1978. The fund-raising brochure produced for the record attempt. A great example of Austin Seven enthusiasts joining together with a common aim.

problem there was a primary score on the bore of number 3 cylinder. Spares carried on the car did not include pistons and so a gallant attempt to set a record for 10,000 miles in Class H ended. It was a bitter moment and we who had watched and admired the efforts of pit crews and drivers alike felt the same pangs of despair.

(Ken Cooke)
1978. Goodwood. Apprehension all round. HLH, Vince Leek, Chris Gould *(in glasses)* look worried….

But was it really time for sorrow when one looks at the achievements? Running night and day this little car had set up records for 5,000 miles and 10,000 kilometres. The Austin had covered a total of 8,068 miles before the metal fatigue of some 47 summers took its toll. A wonderful effort never attempted by the Austin Motor Co. Ltd. or others in the early days. By now I am sure Chris Gould will have overcome his natural disappointment. He looked so bleak at the time I thought my wife and Peggy Driscoll were about to mother him.

Hindsight will point to all sorts of things which should or could have been done but all record-breaking is like that and in actual practice it is impossible to cover all contingencies.

As Pat said to me we were privileged to be at Goodwood on every day of this attempt and to witness the last lap.

Some months ago Ken Cooke, that doyen of low cost motoring, invited us to attend the Goodwood party and in due course my wife and I received our official invitation from Sponsorship Manager, Vince Leek. Pat Driscoll had spent a lot of time at Goodwood for the earlier attempt in 1977 and we were invited by Pat and Peggy Driscoll to stay at their lovely home on Hayling Island. We were taken for daily walks by Bonzo the most intelligent Labrador I have seen. This included two laps of the local boatyard where Bonzo has innumerable friends.

Came the day, the 20th September 1978, and we arrived at Goodwood to be met by quiet, thoughtful Chris Gould and arch enthusiast Vince Leek. A smart piece of public relations work by Ken Warren had encouraged Stirling Moss to be there. It was very good of Stirling to give some time to the attempt and he gave the team some useful tips. I enjoyed meeting him again too.

The Goodwood proceedings started with a miscellany of Austin 7s covering two laps of the circuit and I was invited to drive Ken Cooke's "chummy" which is in daily use. It was a strange experience after so many years. Ken told me to "let her have her head" or words to that effect. 52 mph seemed very quick indeed and Pat sitting alongside looked very unhappy in the corners. It was good fun and I thanked Ken for a nostalgic experience.

Stirling started the Austin attempt and did the first ten laps after the official flag had been dropped by Colonel Arthur Waite. Stirling said he was happy with the smoothness and general handling of the car and handed over to Chris Gould for his first stint. There was an air of confidence in the pit and the pit crews were resplendent in their Spring Grove overalls. We thought the equipment was good with everything laid out to hand. Crew orders were posted up in a manner reminiscent of the military which was not surprising when one considered the presence of pit manager Miles Shepherd and Peter Hornby, both serving officers. With so many people involved it is impossible to refer to everybody by name and I hope I will be forgiven for that. Drivers and mechanics alike were a splendid bunch and it was a privilege to get to know them. The attempt got under way and settled to a pre-arranged plan. Pit stops, refuelling and driver changes came and went as part of a smooth pattern. The starter had been removed to save weight. We wondered whether this was wise as the winding by starting handle proved time consuming and we wondered what would happen if the driver 'lost' the car and engine on the circuit. Mind you it all happened when Pat Kent, the ex-marine, was on the handle. I thought he could if necessary wind the whole car with it. A good chap to have on your side.

We came to Sunday and 4,476 miles were behind the gallant Ulster. The car had run without falter when early that morning a half shaft sheared at the hub end, then, of course, we all realised we should have been using the later, stronger shafts. The driver pushed the car to the pits, no mean feat in itself. One sound shaft was being carried as spares and this was quickly fitted, no easy task as the differential must be dis-assembled. The broken shaft was welded while the car was standing as it had to be returned to carried spares to qualify. This I believe was done by the father of young Paul Mullen, a welding expert from Worthing who offered his services because it was obvious that a broken half shaft battle was about to start. He really kept things going. Five times the car rolled or was pushed to the pits. The pit crews were magnificent. The time for welding and axle assembly decreased until it was less than one hour, an incredible achievement. Graham Beckett seemed to live under the car and Paul Bonewell, who had earned his right to be one of the drivers by machining a set of con rods, came up with an ingenious welding fixture. The welder constantly improved penetration by new tactics. Pat and I felt he was on the way to a permanent repair.

The foregoing activities saw the passing of the 10,000 kilometres mark. Average speed had dropped inevitably but everybody felt optimistic that the 10,000 miles target would be reached but this was not to be as I described at the outset.

We were asked for our impressions. Pat's view was that the whole attempt had been an outstanding success and I agreed. The team, pit crews and drivers had become hardened campaigners. The ability to work together without the slightest sign of friction was tremendous. Everybody did their job and we who had taken part on many similar undertakings certainly had not witnessed better comradeship.'

(Ken Cooke)

1978. Goodwood record attempt.
VIPs! Arthur Waite *(seated)*, Pat Driscoll and son Micky, Peggy Driscoll, Rose, Mrs Norwood,
Ron Norwood (ex AMCo sales) and Bert.

Chris Gould has fond memories of Bert *'A friendly character, a bit rough and ready perhaps, but very helpful'*. He recalls he and Bert were standing in front of the car, whilst the half-shaft was yet again being removed for re-welding. The two RAC observers were crouching down at the back, carefully monitoring proceedings. Bert said *'You're going to keep having trouble with those shafts. Get one of your mates to be on the far side of the track with a new one and swap it with the repaired spare shaft* [carried on board as "equipment"] *on the way round. You can explain the long lap time by saying you spun off. That's what the professionals*

Bert presents a bottle of something to A.R.Storer, thought to have Austin Seven racing connotations….

would do. You can pull the wool over the eyes of these RAC chaps. By the way, who are they?' Without thinking, I immediately replied *'The two with bald heads and glasses'*. In unison, the observers looked up at me and gave me a very hard look. Bert's suggestion, whilst 'interesting', was not proceeded with.

Vince Leek recalls: *'I got the impression he could have been an awkward chap to work with, one of those people who were usually right, knew they were right and resented anyone who disputed them. He also seemed to have no time for "upper class twits". However, he was an interesting bloke to talk to and if asked, very helpful indeed'*.

Entrepreneur Martin Hone had an ambitious plan for a 'Birmingham Grand Prix' and even got as far as some race cars being demonstrated along temporarily closed streets in the city centre to assess public opinion. Wheatcroft had released the Twin-cam for this event but its stuttering progress ended ignominiously on the end of a tow-rope. Bert was not pleased on hearing about the fiasco.

As the years went by, a number of HLH's colleagues and friends passed on. Leslie Johnson had already died back in 1959 at the age of only 47. One of Hadley's mentors, Len Brockas died three years later. As Chief Mechanic, LB had presented a somewhat stern image but there was a softer side to him. During Bert's early time in 'Experimental', if the previous week had ended on an 'edgy' note, Len would often call in at Twyning Road on the pretext of passing the time of day with Herbert and Lydia, with whom he had become friendly. In reality, Brockas was ensuring that come the Monday morning, the following week would start off in a pleasant atmosphere.

1980 was a mixed year for the Hadleys. As we have heard, Ral Appleby had died and both of Bert's parents had passed on. 'Jenks' got Bert and Rose out of bed at 8am on a Monday morning. He was on his way back to Farnham after competing at a Curborough sprint meeting near Lichfield, Staffordshire with his 'Tribsa' motorcycle, with which he shared a VW crew bus as overnight accommodation. Despite this intrusion Bert considered 'DSJ' as a *great little bloke*. It was also the Midland Automobile Club's (MAC) 75th anniversary – would a Twin-cam be available? Once again the answer was in the negative – it would be another twenty-five years before the Worcestershire hill echoed to the rasp of Jamie's masterpiece again.

The Hadleys enjoyed their day out at the Syon Park opening of the Heritage Collection [as did the author] but they were shocked and dismayed to hear that just a few days later, thieves had targeted the solid silver trophies and cleared out the display cabinets, without touching anything else. It turned out the premises had minimal security protection installed. Bert was particularly annoyed because amongst the items taken was the magnificent Imperial Trophy he'd won at that final Crystal Palace race in 1939.

August 1980. Syon Park.
Bert and Rose alongside the Jaguar Montlhéry Coupé.

August 1980. Syon Park.
A poignant picture showing Bert with the Imperial Trophy he won in 1939.
Rose's reflection can be seen in the glass.
Thieves cleared the silverware within a week of the opening.

After that event, Lord Austin had promised Hadley a trophy of HLH's choice to keep as a reward for the success he'd achieved for the company. The War intervened of course and the offer was never fulfilled. During the 'BL Cars' era Bert had written a personal letter to Sir Michael Edwardes (appointed by Margaret Thatcher to re-organise the now Government-controlled conglomerate) reminding Sir Michael of Austin's promise. Eventually Bert received a missive from BL's Legal Department outlining his obligations regarding insurance cover whilst the trophy was in Hadley's custody. Bert got the message and dropped the matter. What had really upset him about the thefts from Brentford was that, in his words, *'These trophies had been kicking about at Longbridge for years.'* before being publicly on show for the first time.

The Austin Ex–Apprentices Association had held a reception at the National Exhibition Centre (NEC) attended by the BL 'top brass' and many friends and colleagues HLH had not seen in years, which cheered him up no-end. However this was tempered by the sudden death of his great friend Ron Beach, after suffering an embolism whilst travelling on a Midland Red bus. Beach, who lived near the Longbridge Works, had been Austins' official photographer for 42 years. Even after his retirement he had scoured the archives for missing items and made prints available to Bert, many of which appear within these pages.

The year concluded with The Pre-War Austin Seven Club's Christmas Dinner at the Donington Manor Hotel with the Hadleys as Guests of Honour. Making the trip 'Up North' were Vince Leek and his wife and the 'unattached' Chris Gould. Bert was persuaded to make a short speech in which he likened the quiet, academic-looking Chris to the young Tom Murray Jamieson he remembered coming to Longbridge in 1932. 'Young Mr Gould' had yet to meet Morris Minor enthusiast Angela Simpson so HLH suggested Chris might be 'available' on the matrimonial front. The highlight of the evening was the first 'provincial' showing of the 1978 Goodwood Record Run film. Vince and Chris were of course heavily involved with this event as were several other PWA7C members amongst those present. Bert later admitted he sometimes found it a little difficult talking to small groups of enthusiasts whereas during his time at the Department he would address large meetings with complete confidence.

Bert was now getting regular invitations to various motoring events and reunions but both he and Rose seemed to be dogged by medical problems which often precluded them attending. For instance, an extremely painful sebaceous cyst on his neck required two hospital visits.

Winter colds and influenza regularly affected both of them. A bout of sciatica and a vertigo or inner ear problem also intruded, the latter condition also being experienced by his friend Alec Issigonis. A serious nose bleed which meant yet another week in Warwick Hospital was diagnosed as being due to very high blood pressure. Meanwhile Rose experienced back-pains and later shoulder problems which defied medical explanation. However, they were able to enjoy visits to Wollaton Park for the PWA7C's Autokarna '82 and the Longbridge Rally celebrating 60 years of the Austin Seven.

A wintery view from the Hadley's lounge. This one-legged blackbird apparently came to be hand-fed by Bert for a remarkable *seven* seasons!

The author had been carrying out a lengthy reconstruction of another car for Barrie Foster, who had provided his SS 100 for the Syon Park opening of the Heritage Collection. This was a Jaguar XK 120 Fixed Head Coupé (FHC) which Barrie had originally received for his 21st birthday when it was about four years old. Decades later he discovered 'ECH 505' (in many pieces) and bought it back. After three aborted attempts to get it restored elsewhere, it finally came to me and I completed the project, though not without some problems. Along the way the roof had been sawn off (to facilitate storage!) and some parts had been transferred from another Coupé. I actually took measurements off the Montlhéry car JWK707 whilst it was on display at Donington. Although it was a pre-production prototype, at least it confirmed the true positions of the headlights – on all the 'restored' XKs I'd seen, every one was different!

In 1983, I took the opportunity to visit Red Lane in the Coupé to give it a shake-down. Bert was most interested in it and I was relieved to receive HLH's approval after his 'road test' around Kenilworth. Bert recalled using the Montlhéry car for three months on a daily basis. Through 'Lofty' England, William Lyons had offered the car to him for *a nominal sum'*. As part of the deal, Bert 'opened' Shelsley Walsh and Prescott hill climbs in 'JWK'. In the end, the car was returned to Browns Lane and today it belongs to the Jaguar-Daimler Heritage Trust. As used at Montlhéry, the 2.8:1 final drive employed required two full laps of the banked circuit before the required cruising speed was reached.

BRITISH RACING
DRIVERS' CLUB

LIFE
MEMBER

1983

BRITISH RACING DRIVERS' CLUB
SILVERSTONE CIRCUIT
SILVERSTONE, nr. TOWCESTER
NORTHANTS   0327 - 857271

FULL MEMBERS ONLY

This card must be produced
by a member when signing
on for testing his
car at Silverstone to
obtain members discount

PIERRE AUMONIER
Secretary, B.R.D.C.

MEMBERSHIP CARD
1983

MEMBER'S NAME
H.L.Hadley

SIGNATURE

EXPIRY DATE
31.12.1983

The British Racing Drivers' Club (BRDC) were approaching their 50th anniversary and having checked their list of old members, invited Bert to become a Life Member (for £20!) This of course allowed him free access to Silverstone and the BRDC hospitality facility overlooking the famous Woodcote Corner. Over the following decade, Bert attended a number of major race meetings, usually accompanied by Clive, even braving a couple of British Grands Prix. Bert was always pleased to meet up with old friends but the increasing commercialisation of 'the sport' with its army of hangers-on did not impress Hadley one jot. In fact he had a particular aversion to the 'PR' crowd or *'bull-shit wallahs'* as he called them. The constant hype over driver performance also irritated him greatly. The Hadley view was 10% driver 80% car and 10% luck – simple as that! However, he considered Nuvolari, Rosemeyer and Fangio all won on sheer ability. One wonders what Hadley would have to say about the 'body art' and 'diamond piercings' displayed by some of today's drivers. Probably speechless….

On the industrial front, Britain was going through a painful period of change and Bert was most concerned how many skilled people were losing employment. He fully realised changes were inevitable but was frustrated by the antics of *'thick-headed trade union followers still hanging onto doomed jobs'*. The aviation industry was also undergoing a major re-organisation and was now virtually all under the control of the British Aircraft Corporation (BAC) later to become British Aerospace (BAe). With the closing of Bitteswell, Clive had no option but to relocate to Hatfield in

This is the prototype BAe 146 airliner at Hatfield.
Clive Hadley is in the dark overalls on the left.

Hertfordshire, the site of the former de Havilland Company. Apart from the weekly commute, Clive didn't particularly enjoy his time there, considering it a second-rate outfit. Eventually he was offered a transfer to BAe Manchester but declined and was persuaded to accept a redundancy package after 25 years in the industry.

Luckily he found a new position with Birmingham Executive Airways (BEA), who were operating scheduled services to Scandinavia, Germany and elsewhere in Europe and were handily based at Elmdon (Birmingham Airport), an easy commute from Red Lane. Later on, BEA would be absorbed in to the giant Maersk organisation. Clive became part of a small team tasked with the preparation and checking out of aircraft before take-off and although it involved shift working, he enjoyed being able to put his accumulated technical skills to good use.

Health problems continued to intrude. Bert suffered sciatic pains down the back of the legs *'agony'* and had more problems with balance. He was already quite deaf in his left ear plus some tinnitus then got an infection in his 'good' ear. For millions of the population, premature hearing loss was a common affliction. Bert blamed driving the Twin-cam on *'full noise'*, recalling that he used to protect his ears by *'stuffing in wads of cotton wool'* during the 1930s and even later.

Meanwhile Rose had lost both her parents and was still suffering pains in her back and shoulders and eventually her legs, whilst feeling generally 'down'. Ann Butler had died from heart problems and later Bill Butler would spend a day with the Hadleys *'re-living every trial section since 1935'.*

(Edmund Nankivell)
1983. Rose and Bert enjoying retirement. Bert holds the replica awarded for his Class win in the 1952 Dundrod TT in Jupiter HAK 366.

1985. Edward Way and équipe pay a call at Red Lane en-route for Shelsley. Clive's Montego is behind the Austin truck which carries the ex-Peter Moores Side-valve re-creation, kids bikes, tents etc!

In 1985, Bert was the Guest of Honour for the MAC's 80th Anniversary at Shelsley Walsh and during the lunch break he was interviewed for a full thirty minutes by John Roberts. This was apparently very well received by the attentive spectators but neither the MAC's archive cassette of the interview or Bert's own copy have surfaced which is a great pity.

After two years of on-going tests at Warwick Hospital, Rose was finally confirmed as having lymphocytic leukaemia from which she eventually died of on October 15th 1989, aged 77. Bert was at her bedside till the end and, as he later wrote, a piece of him died with her. They had been married 48 years but had been close for a total of 60 years. Her passing hit Bert very hard, not helped by the deaths of both Charles Goodacre and his wife Ursula a few months previously and of long-time friends Pat Driscoll and Alec Issigonis. Luckily Clive was at home to comfort him but, when Clive was working nights, Bert found Number 78 a very lonely place indeed.

1990. The Montlhéry Jaguar Reunion for the signing of Keith Woodcock's painting. *(Left to right)* Jack Fairman, Stirling Moss, Mortimer Morris-Goodall and HLH.

As a result of this, Bert returned to writing about some more of his racing memories. In 1990 Keith Woodcock had been commissioned to produce a painting depicting JWK 707 at Montlhéry 1952 entitled 'Seven Days and Seven Nights' and at Syon Park Bert joined Stirling Moss, Jack Fairman, Mort Morris-Goodhall together with the artist to collectively sign 450 individual prints of the original painting. It is reproduced on the front cover.

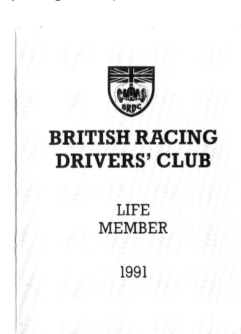

BRITISH RACING DRIVERS' CLUB

LIFE
MEMBER

1991

Despite not feeling too well, Bert accepted an invitation from 'Lofty' England to be Guest of Honour at a Jaguar Rally and Race Meeting at Donington Park during which HLH enjoyed a circuit drive in a Le Mans 'C' Type. England, a year younger than Bert, would himself pass away in 1995. The author was in the process of another major reconstruction project, an Austin-Healey BJ8, and this required several visits to AH Spares at Southam in Warwickshire. I mentioned this to Bert and he said he wouldn't mind coming with me. It was a very hot day when I collected him and as a result he was suffering a bit. However, when we arrived I introduced him to Gordon Barton, an AH director, and after a cooling drink I left them to talk and went looking for parts. Gordon was aware who Bert was and he was delighted to meet him. He'd served his apprenticeship at The Cape works in Warwick so of course knew the Healey family very well. Gordon recalled he fitted seat belts to virtually all the export-specification Austin-Healeys sold to US servicemen serving throughout Europe. At the time 'safety belts' were not a legal requirement in the UK. The astute Mr Healey had secured sole rights to all these 'military' sales which amounted to several thousand vehicles. Bert and Gordon were still having a good natter when I'd completed my purchases and was ready to leave. He told me afterwards that he'd greatly enjoyed his chat with Gordon and before leaving had been presented with a copy of one of the 'Healey' books as a memento of his visit. He also signed their Visitors Book. I eventually completed the BJ8 project but sadly not until after Bert's passing in 1993. He had been looking forward to trying out the finished vehicle.

Bert continued to write to me but the last letter I received from him was in October 1992. He obviously wasn't at all well and had lost weight. I went over to Kenilworth the following month and by chance Clive was at home on this occasion. A compilation of pre-war Austin films had recently been released in VHS format. I took a copy with me on the off-chance Bert might like to comment as he watched it. Clive put the cassette in the recorder and Bert (to Clive's visible discomfort!) cranked up the sound and started to watch. Surprisingly much of the content was new to him but it was a delight to see him taking it all in with a smile on his face as he recalled his time going through various Longbridge Departments. This is where the anecdote about Bert meeting his mate on the footbridge with the road springs under his rain coat emanated from. Subsequently we spoke on the telephone several times but it was to be my last visit to Red Lane.

Bert with Arthur Waite. 'The Skipper' died in 1991 aged 96.

BRITISH RACING DRIVERS' CLUB LTD.
SILVERSTONE CIRCUIT
nr. TOWCESTER
NORTHANTS. NN12 8TN
Tel: 0327 857271
Fax: 0327 857296

CLUB SECRETARY: Peter E. Warr
MEMBERSHIP SECRETARY: Adrienne Watson

BRITISH RACING DRIVERS' CLUB

LIFE
MEMBER

1992

As Bert's health problems escalated, he too would be eventually diagnosed of having a form of leukaemia, which had an effect on the relationship between father and son with HLH experiencing some dark moods through periods of depression. He was still driving locally but for any distance he would rely on Clive to do the chauffeuring. However he did have a final thrash in the Saab 900 Turbo just to see if he could still 'top the ton'. He could, and he did!

Sensing that time was running out, Bert asked Clive to drive him once more around the South Birmingham area he'd known so well. The houses he grew up in and the local schools were still there and still in use. Venturing northwards into the city was a bit of an eye opener for him – the Handsworth Junior Day School had survived as an educational establishment but the Holyhead Road area shocked him, it 'looking like a battlefield'. The Skill Centre where he'd spent a happy decade was now closed and appeared to be abandoned and it left him in a sad frame of mind. Today all of that part of Handsworth has been completely re-developed and the Centre is now somewhere under a Morrisons car park.

Rather late in the evening of the 30th July 1993, Clive Hadley rang me, explaining he was calling from a hospice in Leamington Spa. Bert was with him and he wished to speak to me. As the call came 'out of the blue' I was a bit confused. 'Allo Jiff' came a familiar 'Brummie' voice. He explained that he was lying on the floor 'as it was the most comfortable place to be'. We didn't speak for long and he sounded tired. He handed the phone back to Clive who, obviously upset, said he'd ring me the following day.

204

Afterwards, it suddenly hit me. Yes, Bert *was* in a hospice but I couldn't believe we wouldn't talk again. Clive did call back as promised, only to tell me that his father had slipped away overnight. As a result I'd missed the opportunity to say 'thank you' to Bert, something I regret to this day. The funeral took place a week later at Oakley Crematorium, not far from Gaydon.

I travelled over with Neville Barr to formally represent the PWA7C, though other members were present, along with the family, a whole host of friends and former colleagues from the Civil Service, Industry and Motor Sport. There were also three Austin Sevens in the car park, two of which were due to compete at Prescott the following day. An appropriate touch. Amongst the many floral tributes was one from 'Lofty' England, still domiciled in Austria. Later Bert's ashes were placed alongside those of his beloved Rose in St. Nicholas' Churchyard, Kenilworth.

1993. An appropriate Longbridge presence at Bert's funeral.

August 1993. HLH's funeral. Some of the many floral tributes.

Part 2 (1994-2012)

After Bert's death Clive and I kept in regular touch and I well remember him coming over to Nottinghamshire and together paying a visit to the Newark Air Museum where he gave me a very knowledgeable tour around the splendid aircraft collection. Feeling it was high time his father's name be recognised in some way, I suggested that a suitable trophy could be presented on an annual basis. Around this time, thanks to the late Dave MacCurrie, I'd been 'eased' into the position as the PWA7C's first Competition Secretary. The club was again promoting Austin Seven Production Car Trials and also obtaining some invitations to sprints & hill climbs organised by other clubs. Clive was immediately in favour of the proposal and offered to fund such an award. Thus the splendid 'Bert Hadley Memorial Cup' came into being in 1994, to be presented for 'Sporting Excellence' to the individual who, whilst entered as a PWA7C member, had achieved the greatest success over the past year either in Trials and/or Speed Events.

Kay Petre sent this to Bert after she finished active racing. Her much older husband died in 1962 and with no family her later days were spent in some reclusion in the same St.Johns Wood mansion block as the Goodacres. Kay died in 1994 aged 91.

By now sufficient invitations were being received for the Austins to run together in their own class which gave the increasing number of members participating something to aim for and the decision was made to create an officially-recognised championship, which again met with Clive's enthusiastic approval. Actually, the idea of Sprints for Austin Sevens was first aired in a pub in down-town Moseley. This would have been in the late-eighties during the author's time as Club Chairman. We were on something of a goodwill mission to 'foreign parts' that evening, i.e. the West Midlands, but then (as now) enthusiasts can't just commandeer a suitable drive or estate road and tear-off in to the distance against a stop-watch, particularly should the organiser or any competitor be a member of a club registered with the Motor Sports Association (MSA) who control the majority of motor competitions in the United Kingdom. A host of permissions would have to be obtained and at considerable cost. Obviously, the answer was to use host clubs who had 'ready-made' events on tap and who in many cases were looking for additions to their entry lists.

Ironically neither of the two 'gentlemen' bending my ears that night have to this date ever participated in what became, in 1995, The Bert Hadley Memorial Championship (BHMC). Comprising a mix of sprints and hill climbs the first season started off with a modest 8-round programme, though a similar number of non-championship invitations were also listed. All we needed now were more drivers!

From the very start, the series aimed at welcoming both seasoned competitors and complete novices alike with the cars divided into 'Road' and 'Track' categories. The object was the 'most fun with least hassle' and with this in mind the Regulations were as fair and as simple as possible whilst keeping the MSA happy. One or two of the larger clubs were a bit 'sniffy' at the thought that some 'quaint little Austins' might add variety to their lists, but that is all history now and their presence also presents The Pre-War Austin Seven Club to a wider audience.

With the inception of the BHMC, the Trials continued under the informal banner of the Grasshopper Challenge, with its own Trophy. The club was promoting at least three trials each season normally with good

entries. However, around the Millennium, the turn-out quite suddenly dropped by a quarter. Some regulars just disappeared whilst others, having served their 'apprenticeship' with The Pre-War Austin Seven Club went on to compete in stiffer, multi-venue events. Fair enough, but it made it difficult or worse to break-even financially and additionally, suitable venues either were too costly, or just not available. All is not lost however, the 'Grasshopper Challenge' has survived thanks to the co-operation of other clubs and the PWA7C promotes the one event at Ashover in Derbyshire which seems to have found a niche in the sporting calendar, the gap between Christmas and the New Year. Previously 'The Winter Trial' it is now called 'The Dave Wilcox Memorial Trial' after the good friend who was helping the author with the 'technical stuff' prior to the completion of this narrative. Amongst others, members of the Vintage Sports Car Club (VSCC) are invited to this event and whilst the majority of the competing cars are Austin Sevens, a selective class for 'light cars' adds variety to the proceedings. As always, the weather plays its part, but most people go home happy – and rather muddy. All we need now is for the VSCC drivers to remember to sign-on *before* Scrutineering – after all, this is a *PWA7C* event!

(Author)
CLH tries Bob Sterling's 'Ulsteroid' for size at a Curborough (Staffs) round of the BHMC.

Clive Hadley took this picture at one of the BHMC's regular visits to Loton Park Hill Climb. John Skeavington waits on the start line for the 'green light'. Hagley & District LCC were short of marshals so the author was co-opted to operate the 'hockey stick' which steadies the car.

Whenever possible Clive would visit the boys (and girls) at play and enjoyed talking to what he referred to as 'real people' and appreciated the hard work and expertise put into the cars. Over the years we met him at Curborough and Loton Park and after his move to Devon, at Gurston Down and Wiscombe Park. Meanwhile CLH continued to work for Maersk Air at Elmdon until 1999 when he experienced a medical problem which affected his ability to do his job properly. This was later diagnosed as Scleroderma, a muscle-wasting disease and for a time he was on extended sick leave. Matters came to a head when, at the age of 60, he was retired on medical grounds in 2001. Not wanting to sit around and mope all day, he drove a van for a pal who had a wholesale tile business. Lifting and off-loading wasn't a problem as this was carried out by others and whilst it lasted, Clive found the new life very interesting and remarkably stress-free.

In 2002, Jean Wheeler, Clive's partner of many years, retired from the travel business and having seen a suitable property they decided to sell up and retire to South Devon. Their new home was in the village of Holcombe, situated mid-way between Dawlish and Teignmouth, with a fine view overlooking Teignmouth Bay and beyond. Being a railway enthusiast, Clive was delighted to discover there were steam-hauled charters passing through on the famous Exeter-Plymouth Brunel line. In addition there were preserved vintage aircraft based at Exeter Airport plus the annual spectacular Dawlish Air Show. Busy little coasters scuttled in and out of Teignmouth Harbour on most days, all of which could be observed from their lounge windows. Clive also located a very acceptable watering hole down the road, namely 'The Bay Hotel'. So bit by bit, Clive and Jean settled down for a relaxing retirement.

(Author)

2002. Jean and Clive Hadley admire the views from their Holcombe balcony.

By this time, the Championship had become a regular 12-round series, one of the high-spots being our visit to Wiscombe Park Hill Climb at the end of July. Situated in a picturesque valley about 6 miles south of Honiton, the event was usually held over two days and one of its features is the appearance of contenders for the British Hill Climb Championship, the 'Formula One' end of the sport. The cars are amazingly rapid – and expensive - pieces of kit, but it could be argued that our Austins provide better value per £1 spent, with the bonus that you can take in the Devon scenery en-route to the 'Sawbench' – or so I'm told!

The Hadleys kindly invited me to stay with them over the Wiscombe week-end, which meant missing the Saturday practice, but it was very agreeable to sleep in a comfortable bed after a day's sight seeing in pleasant company. The venue is about 30 miles from Holcombe but it didn't take long in Clive's Saab 9000. Impressed by the handling and performance of his father's final car, the ex-Emmott 900 Turbo Clive eventually treated himself to a 'Carlsson' version named after Saab's famously successful rally driver. Seriously up-rated in all departments, only a handful of RHD cars came to the UK. Unfortunately, this one didn't last long as it was stolen, never to be seen again. After an extended search, an identical replacement was sourced and Clive found it an exciting drive, even more so when, without prior warning, the brake pedal snapped! Clive couldn't believe it – and neither could Saab - suggesting he'd been braking too hard! Eventually they agreed to fix it, without charge, despite being out of warranty. He decided to move it on, changing over to a 9000 2.3 Turbo, which was much more relaxing to drive and of course much cheaper to insure. Although he'd never driven competitively, I could tell Clive had inherited a lot of his father's driving skills and whilst he could be rather intolerant of 'mimsers', I always felt safe in Clive's hands. Having known both of his parents I believe CLH was quite a shy person, as was his mother Rose, but he also had an impatient streak undoubtedly inherited from Bert and Grandma Lydia. Clive could be said to be at his best relaxing with friends and with a pint in his hand, often 'people watching', an occasional pastime also enjoyed by the author.

I stayed at Holcombe a couple of times when the Austins were at Wiscombe and it was shortly after my visit in 2004, that Clive was diagnosed with lung cancer. For some time he'd been bothered by an irritating cough, the sort that 'won't go away' and after pressure from Jean, Clive eventually went for extensive tests at Torbay Hospital. Like many others, including Bert, he'd been a smoker, though in later years his father would chide him for it. From thereon, Clive would undergo various treatment sessions. The radiography he could cope with but it was the chemotherapy which Clive uncompromisingly referred to as *'shit'* that really got him down. Not the best of patients anyway, it made things difficult for Clive and Jean at times. However, the treatment did appear to be successful and Clive was certainly looking better.

(Jerry Sturman)

2004. Wiscombe Park Hill Climb.
CLH and the author *(centre rear)* watch Adam Fleetwood about to smash the
13 year old course record.

About the same time as the move to Devon, Keith Taylor (KT), after a career in the electricity generating industry, had become involved in some serious engineering projects involving old vehicles and was visiting Tom Wheatcroft over at Donington Park. Keith had carried out work for TW including the creation of the 'new' Bugatti 'Royale' some years previously. Keith's wife Anne and their son Julian had also done trimming work for Kevin Wheatcroft who has a large collection of military vehicles. Amongst the multitude of 'goodies' in TW's store was the partially dismantled Bert Hadley Twin-cam. Showing a casual interest in the Austin, KT remarked he wouldn't mind having a go at something like that, whereupon Wheatcroft growled *'you'd better tek the bugger an' gerron wi'it'* or words to that effect!

So began a 4,000 hour reconstruction of the car which had last run in August 1939. As he picked his way meticulously through the constituent parts of Murray Jamieson's design Keith began to appreciate TMJ's original thinking in various aspects of the vehicle, particularly the engine and its ancillaries. There was evidence of the previous work on the engine. A modern crankshaft had been fitted and this had to be carefully re-balanced to be compatible with a new set of connecting rods with modern shell big-end bearings. Everything that was useable was, as a whole, retained in the car. This included the ingenious

(Clive Hadley)
2003. Bert's Twin-cam in a semi-dismantled state prior to Keith Taylor's 4,000 hour resurrection.

pressurised fuel delivery system which had been discarded as 'unreliable' on the Goodacre/Dodson car by the 'anti-Jamieson' brigade and replaced with an antique hand pump. The pipe-work caused quite a problem for Keith – if only HLH had been there to explain it all...

During the rebuild process, John Skeavington and I joined up with Clive at Keith Taylor's farmhouse home in East Yorkshire. After being splendidly fed by Anne, we then went through the garden to the adjoining workshops. Inside, the chassis was partially built-up and the engine was awaiting final assembly, allowing us a rare opportunity to wonder at 'Jamie's' masterpiece at close quarters. Keith had received most of the original parts, though some components had been robbed to keep the Goodacre/Dodson car mobile, which by now was not in a running state.

(Clive Hadley)   *(Clive Hadley)*
2003. *(Left)* Bert's Twin-cam during re-assembly in Selby. *(Right)* Twin-cam engine bits including the new 'Arrow' crankshaft and the gearbox assembly which was based on a 4-speed production unit.

210

Eventually, after a 2 years plus period the No.1 car was successfully tested at nearby Breighton Airfield (where Hawker Hurricanes are being reconstructed) and later on, it briefly ran at a Wheatcroft Test Day at Donington. On both of these occasions the car seemed to run lean of fuel so a final shake-down was arranged prior to the Shelsley Walsh Centenary Meeting, where the Twin-cam was due to run in public for the first time in 66 years.

(Leicester Mercury)
2004 'elf & safety' refuelling demonstration by Keith Taylor whilst nominated driver David Fairley literally 'lends a hand!'.

On a perfect summer's morning, John Skeavington got his 'Ulster' out and together we motored over to Donington to meet up with Keith Taylor and No.1.

The Melbourne Hairpin was a feature of the final incarnation of the pre-war race circuit and today is part of a separate test facility adjacent to the Sunday Market area. We felt very honoured to be amongst those present on this occasion and the session soon got under way.

Keith had made up a neat set-up whereby the engine could be started on petrol and after a warming-up period changed over to a methanol mixture, approximating to the Shell 'brew' used in 1939. Later the petrol start would be dispensed with altogether.

The Austin was push-started without any problems (always an encouraging sign!) with a healthy rasp not unlike an ERA but, surprisingly, with a deeper note. With Keith's friend David Fairley at the wheel No.1 did a couple of cautious laps but it was obvious the engine was reluctant to 'rev' pointing to a weak mixture which, if ignored, could burn a piston crown. Dave Dye was all set to dash home and turn up a richer needle for the big S U carburettor when Keith, rummaging around in a 'box of bits' which was amongst the gear he'd collected from Tom Wheatcroft, found a slimmer needle which he fitted 'just in case'.

David went out again and this time, there was a great improvement with the engine opening up, crisp and clear, a splendid sound! However, after further laps, the driver, having had a little spin (out of our sight) decided he'd prefer normal single wheels on the rear, so the replicated inset twins that Keith had spent so much time on weren't used (the originals, like so many other items, went 'missing' from Longbridge, just after the war). The session was declared a success and we all looked forward to the Shelsley meeting with great anticipation.

PWA7C committee member the late Keith Nelson worked for Rolls Royce until his retirement. During a spell at the Company's Ansty site near Coventry, he became acquainted with a colleague with a surname which struck a chord. *'Are you by any chance related to a Thomas Murray Jamieson who was a pre-war racing car designer?'* *'Indeed I am'* replied Joseph Murray Jamieson and confirmed his father was David, TMJ's infant son, just five weeks old at the time of his father's tragic death. All the family were living in the Coventry area. The author wrote to Joseph on behalf of the PWA7C and was able to provide some details and pictures of his illustrious grandfather, particularly of his time at Longbridge. Joseph, who knew some of the family history, was delighted to have more information. Joseph was certainly carrying on in TMJ's engineering tradition, moving on to Landrover's technical base at Gaydon before he went to Alstom working on renewable energy systems.

After TMJ had succumbed to the injuries sustained at Brooklands, his widow Sybil left Stamford to return to her parents' in North Harrow with her infant son. Subsequently she was to re-marry to Harry Chatwin (HC) and they later had a daughter. Bert had met Chatwin on a number of occasions during the course of his Ministerial visits to the Armstrong-Siddeley works at Parkside, Coventry, where HC was the Chief Draughtsman in the Jig and Tool Department. In 1949, the Hadleys, over from Ashbourne, spend a day visiting various relatives in Birmingham and later met up with the Chatwins and their daughter (but not David) at Ryton Pool (now Ryton Pools Country Park) near Coventry.

Over the years HLH made numerous efforts to trace the whereabouts of David Murray Jamieson – he dearly wanted to tell the young man what a remarkable and talented person his father had been and how he'd become a great mentor and friend to Bert. HLH had heard a rumour that David had gone into the Church and this proved to be the case, but ironically they never met despite the fact he was living in Coventry throughout.

The weekend of the 19th-21st of August 2005 was blessed with perfect sunny weather for the Shelsley Walsh Centenary Hill Climb. Representing 100 years of competition were all sorts of cars, ancient and modern, either competing or being 'demonstrated'. It has to be said, some were more genuine than others but nevertheless it was an impressive assembly and thousands of fans packed the viewing areas under the trees and the paddock was so crowded with humanity, it was quite a problem to safely get the cars started up and out of the iconic 'garages' before making their way to the start area. Amongst those around the Hadley Twin-cam was owner Tom Wheatcroft, who had several other cars from The Donington Collection present including a V-16 BRM, the Taylor family, driver David Fairley and his wife and also David Murray Jamieson (DMJ) who appeared somewhat bemused by all the attention his father's masterpiece was generating. David was accompanied by most of his family including son Joseph and grandson Aaron. Clive Hadley, though not feeling at his best, was determined not to miss the occasion and having motored up from Holcombe, came with his friend Richard Burton for support.

(Author)

19th/21st August 2005. Shelsley Walsh Centenary Hill Climb.
Clive Hadley steps into his father's 'office' encouraged
by Julian and Anne Taylor.

There were many 'stars' on show or actually running but for my money, the gem of the display was the Austin – after all, it *was* the genuine article and of course *appropriate to Shelsley* and had not been publicly seen or heard in action since 26th August 1939, almost sixty-six years previously. What an occasion – with David Fairley prudently conducting the Austin, which sounded superb all day, up the hill about 2 seconds shy of a Hadley run. It truly was a momentous occasion and all recorded on hundreds of cameras and videos.

(Author)

2005. Shelsley Walsh Centenary.
Arthur Bodily's remarkable scale model Twin-cam alongside the real thing.

(Hannah Jamieson Vickery)
David Murray Jamieson experiences his father's masterpiece for the first time in the company of Keith and Julian Taylor, David Fairley and Clive Hadley.

Meeting David Murray Jamieson for the first time was most interesting and I was struck by the physical resemblance to his father and with a similar disposition as described by Bert. Soon after the event, David wrote to me saying how he enjoyed the day and enclosed a variety of copied documents and press cuttings relating to the MJ family and other items. He wrote:

'As you might expect, Sunday was a bit of an eye-opener for me. I did not realise how highly my father was thought of. Being only five weeks old when he was killed means I have no memory of him. Added to the fact that my mother would never talk about it and was determined I never get near a race track. So you can see why I know so little.

It was certainly a day to remember and I would like to pass on my appreciation to all concerned for a well organised event. To meet the son of one of those who worked with my father was quite unusual and I am therefore glad that (my daughter) Hannah was able to photograph us standing around the car.'

Having got this book underway, I wrote to DMJ in 2011 for some further information. A reply soon arrived but it was not from David. It was from his wife Pauline who explained that her husband had sadly passed away in May of the previous year. It was from cancer of the liver, a great shock as he'd always led an abstemious life. Pauline confirmed David had worked for the former Post Office Telephones since leaving school and apart from National Service, continued with them into the British Telecom era, taking voluntary retirement in 1994. He'd long held a belief that he had a calling to become a preacher (it was through the local church that David and Pauline had first met).

After retirement from BT, he ran an Anglican church within the local community centre for about a decade before starting a charity 'The Way of The Goose', a meeting place and support group for the long-term unemployed. Sadly, the charity, affected by the recession, had to be wound up by the Trustees just before David's death. In 2004, DMJ had undergone major surgery from which he had recovered comparatively well, but whilst he enjoyed his visit to Shelsley, the long day and high temperatures did present some difficulties which he bore with characteristic fortitude.

During the 2006 season, Clive met up with the BHMC crew on several occasions, including Gurston Down, Wiscombe and at Curborough in early October. He was looking better than on previous occasions but it would prove to be his last meeting with the drivers. Towards the end of the year, Clive and Jean went on a short cruise to the Mediterranean as a sort of belated honeymoon (they'd married quietly the previous year) and a birthday treat for Jean.

It was very enjoyable but towards the end Clive began to feel unwell. He managed to drive them back home to Devon but immediately went into Derriford Hospital Plymouth for further tests. Unfortunately, these showed the cancer had spread and little could be done. Various friends came to visit, including Clive's pal of many years, Mike Spencer. The author was also invited to stay overnight. Clive was pleased to have visitors, but it was clear to see he was not in good shape and requiring daily nursing. Ironically, after I left, the next visitor would be Jane Hadley, who, after years of estrangement, would be at her father's bedside at the end.

I'd been over at Gamston Airfield, North Nottinghamshire on Sunday 21st January 2007, enjoying the 'unveiling party' for Stuart Ulph's newly re-built ex-Ironside Cambridge Special, which had been resting for a number of years. On return, there was a message from Jean saying that her Clive had passed away early that morning. He was only 65.

Clive's funeral took place 10 days later at Torquay Crematorium. For late January, it was a remarkably sunny day with a clear blue sky. As we were waiting outside, a lone black Hawker Hunter passed overhead as if in tribute – the Hunter being a favourite amongst the many iconic aircraft Clive had worked on – and most appropriate. The Crematorium Chapel was packed with family, friends and former colleagues, most of whom had travelled a considerable distance to pay their last respects. Amongst these were at least a dozen members of The Pre-War Austin Seven Club, including 'Bert Hadley' drivers, giving an indication of the high regard held for Clive.

Eventually, Jean would return to Kenilworth and the author commenced this tribute, not only to Bert Hadley but to many of those who also played a part of the overall story. I had not intended to undertake this responsibility – how that came about is another story – but I'm glad I did. It's been quite a journey and I hope the reader has found something of interest along the way.

October 2006.
Curborough.

Clive's last
meeting with
the BHMC
drivers and
supporters.

(Tony Littlebury)

215

A final word about the Longbridge single-seaters (Jamieson variety). In 2007 Keith Taylor was commissioned to resurrect the blue Side-valve car, usually resident at Donington. For many years a non-runner, it needed a comprehensive overhaul similar to that received by Bert's Twin-cam. This included a new purpose-designed crankshaft and matching rods. Several of the original magnesium castings had to be replaced. Luckily, patterns were still available!

The car is the property of the British Motor Industry Heritage Trust (BMIHT) at Gaydon, where it currently rests. KT handed the car over fully tested and ready to run. If any of the Trustees happen to read this – can we please have the opportunity to see and hear this historic vehicle on the move at an appropriate venue – and fairly soon! Incidentally it was either white or latterly dark green in period. Kay Petre never drove this car as a team member and it became 'blue' around 1960 when she was to demonstrate it in public.

Kay Petre about to demonstrate the surviving Side-valve in its final shape at the 1961 VSCC Oulton Park race meeting. The unmistakable profile of Alec Issigonis in the Lightweight Special to Kay's left. Both cars are currently displayed at the Heritage Motor Centre, Gaydon, Warwickshire.

(© The McDonald Collection)

I have to admit, I think this colour does suit the car. The Goodacre / Dodson car No.10, as rebuilt at the Wheatcroft workshops in the 1970s is also owned by the BMIHT, but is normally resident within the Donington Collection. It has not been run for many years and is probably in need of some attention. Evidence suggests that the engine is actually out of the Hadley car (and vice versa).

After all the politics and disputes which surrounded the three Austins during the 1970s it was agreed that Tom Wheatcroft had Title to the Hadley car. Following its successful appearance at the Shelsley Centenary it remained at Donington, but there were rumours of a possible overseas sale. This didn't happen but after Tom Wheatcroft's death in 2009 it was finally sold to a well-known motor-sporting family (who incidentally knew the Hadleys well) and it appears to be in safe and appreciative hands. Hopefully 'No.1' will be aired in public from time to time. A final thought - it might just be possible - one day – to see all three cars out together...

There are some Bert Hadley artefacts on display at Donington though these will eventually join the many other Hadley items within the Archives of the Austin Seven Clubs' Association (A7CA).

An impressive collection of Trophies awarded to Austin team drivers, many engraved with H.L.Hadley's name.

Index